SIDELINED

SIDELINED

*How American Sports
Challenged the
Black Freedom Struggle*

SIMON HENDERSON

UNIVERSITY PRESS OF KENTUCKY

Scholarly publisher for the Commonwealth,
serving Bellarmine University, Berea College, Centre College of Kentucky,
Eastern Kentucky University, The Filson Historical Society, Georgetown
College, Kentucky Historical Society, Kentucky State University, Morehead
State University, Murray State University, Northern Kentucky University,
Transylvania University, University of Kentucky, University of Louisville,
and Western Kentucky University.
All rights reserved.

Editorial and Sales Offices: The University Press of Kentucky
663 South Limestone Street, Lexington, Kentucky 40508-4008
www.kentuckypress.com

17 16 15 14 13   5 4 3 2 1

Library of Congress Cataloging-in-Publication Data

Henderson, Simon, 1979-
  Sidelined : how American sports challenged the Black freedom struggle /
Simon Henderson.
      pages cm
  Includes bibliographical references and index.
  ISBN 978-0-8131-4154-1 (hardcover : alk. paper) —
  ISBN 978-0-8131-4155-8 (pdf) — ISBN 978-0-8131-4156-5 (epub)
  1. Discrimination in sports—United States—History. 2. Sports—Social
aspects—United States. 3. African American athletes—Social conditions.
4. African American athletes—History. 5. African American athletes—
Biography. 6. African Americans—Civil rights—History. 7. Civil rights
movements—United States—History I. Title.
  GV706.32.H46 2013
  306.4'830973—dc23   2012047714

This book is printed on acid-free paper meeting the requirements of the American
National Standard for Permanence in Paper for Printed Library Materials.

Manufactured in the United States of America.

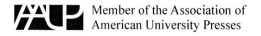 Member of the Association of
American University Presses

For Laura

Contents

Illustrations

Preface

This book originated in the PhD thesis that I completed in 2010. The project started out as an examination of the response of white athletes to the black athletic revolt of the late 1960s. This was a movement that sought to expose the prevailing ideal of racial equality in the sporting world. What emerged as this investigation unfolded was the unique part played by sport in the wider black freedom struggle. The protests that made up the black athletic revolt on the national and local stage traversed the traditional historical frameworks applied to that struggle for equality. Athletes and administrators were involved in a protest dynamic that showed the interconnectedness of the Civil Rights and Black Power Movements. Reactions to the protests of both black and white athletes provided one dimension of the white backlash of the late 1960s. This backlash helped to stifle the full potential of sport to positively affect civil rights activism and, paradoxically, reinforced the ideal that sport was an area of society that led the way in the search for racial equality.

These developments took place during a transitional phase of the black freedom struggle. The black athletic revolt straddled the conventional paradigms of the fight for black civil rights. Traditional accounts of the freedom struggle in America in the 1960s have focused on the Civil Rights and Black Power Movements. They have contrasted the tactics and strategies of these two strands of the struggle for equality. Taylor Branch, in *Parting the Waters,* refers to "America in the King years," which he designates as 1954–1963. In his concluding comments Branch argues, "Kennedy's murder marked the arrival of the freedom surge, just as King's own death four years hence marked its demise."[1] In his survey of the fight for black equality from 1890 to 2000, Adam Fairclough devotes three chapters to the "non-violent rebellion" starting in 1955 and ending with the signing of the Voting Rights Act of 1965. He then examines the rise and fall of Black Power, beginning in 1965 and ending with the first years of the Nixon administration.[2] The Civil Rights Movement has been framed as the period from the *Brown v. Board of Education* decision to the mid-1960s, when a new period of Black Power activism began. In many of these accounts Black Power was viewed, as Peniel Joseph has observed, as the "evil twin" of the Civil Rights Movement.[3]

This characterization of the black freedom struggle helps us see change but it blurs continuity and hides the true complexity of the past with a simplistic picture. Jacquelyn Dowd Hall has led those historians who argue for a different chronology, a "long Civil Rights Movement" that provides a more complex and complete picture of race relations, stretching back to the 1930s and forward into the 1970s and beyond.[4] She seeks to expand our understanding of the nuances of the struggle for equality by stretching the time frame of the Civil Rights Movement beyond the traditional parameters of study.

Identifying when that movement began is problematic. It was the constitutional amendments of the Reconstruction period that set the agenda for the Civil Rights Movement of the 1960s. These amendments enshrined civil rights as a legal fact, and liberal interpretations of those amendments by the Warren Court and Johnson administration gave birth to legislation such as the Civil Rights Act in 1964 and the Voting Rights Act a year later. So it could be argued that the Civil Rights Movement, so defined, stretched back for a hundred years. The danger with this chronological and interpretive framework is that it diminishes the distinctiveness of different phases of civil rights activism. These different phases are important. We must not allow patterns of continuity to obscure clear changes and turning points.[5] Similarly, recent scholarship on the Black Power Movement has shown both the cultural and political importance of that movement and its longer-term origins. Rather than being a frustrated response to the perceived slow change of the 1960s, it had deep roots in black radical tradition and can be traced back to the 1950s.[6]

In recognition of the issues surrounding these thematic and chronological parameters, a note on terminology is important. The terms *black freedom struggle, freedom struggle,* and *civil rights struggle* are used interchangeably throughout this study because of issues of style and to avoid too much repetition. They are used to refer to civil rights activism that stretched throughout the 1960s, originated long before that decade, and continued in its aftermath. The key reason for this is that the activism that surrounded the black athletic revolt does not fit neatly inside the conventional chronological phases of that struggle. The black athletic revolt exhibited tactics and themes that drew from the traditions of both the Civil Rights Movement and the Black Power Movement. The revolt revealed a great deal about the progress of race relations as the black freedom struggle traversed a course between these two elements of the same struggle.

A study of the black athletic revolt is a crucial element in our understanding of the civil rights struggle because sport is a vital component of the American cultural experience. For his exposition of high school football in Texas, *Friday Night Lights,* Henry Bissinger found a community that exemplified many Americans' passion for sporting competition. A blurb on the book's back cover praised *Friday Night Lights* for offering "a biting indictment of the sports craziness that grips . . . most of American society, while at the same time providing a moving evocation of its powerful allure."[7]

During the research for this project I have spoken to scores of former athletes who mention the fervor connected with this "sports craziness." Sport in America is a multibillion-dollar industry. Professional sports franchises have a massive media presence and attract thousands of fans. Crucially, high school and college sports have a huge following and provide the focal point for communities all across the United States. This is why a full understanding of the black athletic revolt needs to embrace a regional element. It is also why organized sport provides a unique and valuable arena through which to study the progress of the freedom struggle. In gymnasiums and on athletic tracks across the United States in the 1960s the racial changes dominating the political agenda were tested and adapted.

The recent emergence of fresh scholarship on both the black athletic revolt and the story of integration of American college sports is testament to the importance of these stories for an understanding of American race relations. In *Race, Culture and the Revolt of the Black Athlete,* Douglas Hartmann traces the evolution of the black athletic revolt and considers the broader cultural and racial meaning of sport. Hartmann argues that sport provides a "contested racial terrain" that has the potential to both promote and hold back racial progress.[8] Complimenting this work on the black athletic revolt is Amy Bass's *Not the Triumph but the Struggle: The 1968 Olympics and the Making of the Black Athlete.*[9] Bass focuses more directly on the black athlete as a historical figure and uses the Olympic protest movement as a focal point from which to study changes in the perception of black athletes and their own racial consciousness. Both Hartmann and Bass provide a valuable insight into the dynamics and lasting consequences of the black athletic revolt.

Contemporaneous with these developments was the slow integration of college sports, and several excellent recent studies have explored this process. Principal among them is Charles Martin's *Benching Jim Crow*, in which he argues that the construction and defense of the color line in southern college sports was complex. Martin tells the stories of the pioneers of athletic integration and those who wished to make sports the final citadel of white supremacy.[10] Focusing specifically on college football, Lane Demas has shown in *Integrating the Gridiron* how the convergence of football and race relations transcended the playing field.[11] Americans' understandings of larger civil rights struggles were often interpreted through the cultural touchstone of football.

The importance of this cultural reference point has been expertly explained by Kurt Kemper. *College Football and American Culture in the Cold War Era* focuses on controversies over postseason bowl games to show the way in which football was linked to distinctive American values and acted as a cultural barometer in the face of the Soviet Cold War challenge.[12] In the case of the white South, football provided a focus for tension between prevailing ideals of segregation and a desire to connect to a wider national culture. Where sport and racial changes intersected in communities across the United States there were significant consequences for athletes, administrators, and fans. There were complex and slowly developing stories of integration and acceptance as black and white began to compete alongside one another. In *Learning to Win: Sports, Education and Social Change in Twentieth-Century North Carolina*, Pamela Grundy tells one of the many stories that are being uncovered as historians reach further and wider into the past to understand the black freedom struggle.[13]

The recent growth of this avenue of historical enquiry has enriched our understanding of the connection between race relations and American sporting culture. It also offers a challenge to strive to further connect changes in the sporting world with the wider social changes resulting from the black freedom struggle. That is the aim of this book. Specifically, the aim is to trace the links between Tommie Smith and John Carlos's protest at the 1968 Olympics, manifestations of the black athletic revolt on campus, and the myriad consequences of the integration of college sports in an effort to assimilate these developments into historical interpretations of the black freedom struggle. The book does not pretend to incorporate all elements of the American sporting world into the wider story of the civil rights struggle. The main focus is on college athletics and the Olympic competitors who emerged from college campuses. It is on these campuses that we see grassroots activism and get a sense of how communities were affected as cherished sporting traditions were challenged by the black freedom struggle.

The methods that I utilize throughout this study provide a fresh historical dimension. As well as using extensive archival material, some of which has been untapped in previous studies of the black athletic revolt, I refer to more than fifty oral histories that I collected from international and college athletes involved in that revolt. Consulting secondary sources, contemporary newspaper coverage, archival material, and oral histories offers a triangulated approach. This allows for a rounded and deep interpretation and analysis of events. With much of the history of the freedom struggle focused on large, politically significant events and leading national characters, oral history offers a more local and individual dimension to our historical understanding.[14] Additionally, oral history can broaden the traditional chronological and thematic boundaries of civil rights studies.[15] This is a particularly important issue in light of the above discussion on different phases of the freedom struggle in the 1960s.

This is not to say that oral histories and their usage do not pose some important methodological problems for historians. The interviewer may inadvertently direct the emphasis and agenda of the dialogues. It is inevitable that the focus of the conversations that I had is in many ways shaped by the preoccupations of my own research. It is also true that individuals tend to remember dramatic and emotive events at the expense of more mundane realities. This inevitably shapes the parameters and emphasis of their recollections. Oral narratives cannot be taken at face value; they require careful scrutiny and analysis in the same way that other historical documents do.[16] This is why the interview material I have collected is cross-referenced with other sources of evidence in the triangulated approach mentioned above.

While I acknowledge these problems, the fact that the oral histories were collected some thirty-five or more years after the passage of events also allows for a more nuanced perspective to emerge. Studying athletes' feelings and actions during the 1960s in the context of their more balanced reflections with the benefit of hindsight provides insight into the continued importance of sport in the construction of race relations. The very fact that the actors involved have had thirty-five or more years to consider their actions and have in that time assimilated the influences of several decades of social and cultural change makes their views fascinating. When reflected upon many years later, opinions held during the 1960s speak to the potency of expressed beliefs and ideals, a potency that continues to reveal the importance of sporting competition to communities across the United States. The challenge these communities faced as the black freedom struggle permeated their locker rooms and playing fields is the focus of what follows.

Locating the Black Athletic Revolt in the Black Freedom Struggle

My stand was one that everybody could see I was black. I did not need to wear a banner. I did not need anything to identify me or separate me or unique me from that football team, other than to be the best ballplayer that I could be.

—Horace King, University of Georgia football player

We did a lot of kicking ass, so what I can beat you physically, but when it comes to my civil rights I can't say anything?

—Melvin Hamilton, University of Wyoming football player

In the history of the United States, 1968 was no ordinary year. It was as if a decade's worth of turmoil, of social and political upheaval, had been condensed into one tumultuous twelve-month period. Bobby Kennedy and Martin Luther King Jr. were both assassinated. The Tet Offensive seemed to condemn American hopes for victory in Vietnam. Students brought college campuses across the country to a standstill as they protested American involvement in the war. The Democrat National Convention was surrounded by running battles between demonstrators and the police, who traded volleys of tear gas and balloons filled with urine. Many of those who lived through that year felt as though the very fabric of the nation was fraying. As Todd Gitlin has observed, "Nineteen sixty-eight was no year for a catching of the breath."[1]

In the aftermath of the 1968 Olympics the president of the U.S. Olympic Committee (USOC), Douglas Roby, wrote a strongly worded letter to the Harvard rowing coach, Harry Parker; many of Harvard's oarsmen were in the U.S. Olympic team. Roby suggested that the Harvard athletes' poor showing in the Mexico City Games was partly retribution for their poor conduct during the Olympics, conduct that included support for those protesting against racial injustice. Roby asserted, "Civil rights and the promotion of social justice may have their place in various facets of society, but certainly this sort of promotion has no place in the Olympic Games."[2] The letter suggested that Harvard's reputation as an institution of academic excellence was sullied by the actions of its rowers and that Parker should be ashamed of his part in their personal and sporting development.

The immediate cause of such an extraordinary correspondence can be found in the most iconic image of the 1968 Games. When looking at the photograph of the moment when the U.S. national anthem rang out as part of the medal ceremony for the 200-meter sprint, our eyes are drawn to the raised, gloved, and clenched fists of Tommie Smith and John Carlos. Their heads were bowed as they stood in solemn defiance throughout the playing of "The Star-Spangled Banner." They did not stand alone, however. A white athlete looked straight ahead on the silver medal rostrum. Hands by his side and medal around his neck, he was wearing a button on his track suit above the Australian team badge, just as his competitors wore the same badge above the U.S. team logo. The badge carried the letters "OPHR," which stood for the Olympic Project for Human Rights. The Australian silver medalist was Peter Norman, and he was given the badge by Paul Hoffman, coxswain of the Harvard rowing crew.

Hoffman had leaned over the barriers in the stadium as the three sprinters walked out for the medal ceremony and obliged Norman's request for a badge. The Australian took it and pinned it to his track suit as an act of solidarity with Smith and Carlos. The two African Americans were part of the OPHR, an organization that had originally sought to boycott the Olympics and then resolved to make a protest during the games themselves. Theirs was a stand against racism. It was a stand for human dignity and equality made on the most visible of international stages. In that symbolic moment on an October day in 1968 sport was forever tied to the black freedom struggle. If we analyze this one moment carefully we see an encapsulation of that struggle in the late 1960s, we see the limits of sporting competition as a vehicle through which to advance civil rights, and we uncover a fascinating story of human interest.

Roby's letter to Hoffman's coach is a clear example of the backlash against the actions of Smith and Carlos. Their raised black fists captured a Black Power symbolism that dominated the racial landscape in the late 1960s. The fact that Norman stood alongside them and was helped in making his gesture of support by an Ivy League student athlete revealed the complexity of the OPHR and the wider black athletic revolt it represented. The way in which sport intersected with civil rights protest clearly displays the extent to which the lines between the Civil Rights and Black Power Movements were blurred. Black and white athletes struggled hard to negotiate the impact of wider societal changes on the sporting world. Smith, Carlos, Hoffman, and Norman were among many who tried to use sport as a forum in which racial changes could be both embraced and challenged. Theirs is a story of hope, frustration, courage, and confusion and one that illuminates our understanding of the black freedom struggle.

The Black Sportsman and the Freedom Struggle

When Hoffman passed the badge to Peter Norman he was enabling him to support Smith and Carlos's symbolic assertion that they were not immune from the racism that permeated American society. Just because they were successful sportsmen who competed on an equal footing with their white counterparts did not mean that they had transcended racial prejudice. There was, and indeed still is, a popular ideal that sport ran ahead of the rest of society in progress toward racial equality. The emergence of this idealized view can be explained by the developing place of the African American athlete in U.S. sports. Black athletes reached a position by the middle of the twentieth century that gave support to the ideal that sport acted as a positive racial force within society.

In antebellum America and before, however, the image of black athletes was largely defined by the institution of slavery. Free blacks engaged in recreational sporting pursuits but there is little evidence of their involvement in organized athletics.[3] Physical competition and sporting endeavors were crucial elements in the lives of many slaves. In the limited leisure time they were permitted they enjoyed challenging other bondsmen to horse and boat races and feats of strength and stamina. Little of this time was spent in actual combative activities, as it was believed to be anathema for one slave to inflict physical punishment on another. References to wrestling and fighting in slave narratives are examples of contests arranged by white masters.[4] This exploitation of blacks to entertain white audiences was continued in the "battle royals" and other boxing contests of the Jim Crow era.

In the late nineteenth century there was an undercurrent of fear that black athletes might be physically superior to their Caucasian counterparts. Commentators on both sides of the Mason-Dixon Line worried about the growth of the black population, fearing that African Americans' greater fecundity and physical strength would bring racial cataclysm unless the races were separated.[5] In the 1890s boxing champion John Sullivan refused to fight the black Australian fighter Peter Jackson. Described as a "human fighting animal," Jackson embodied a pugilistic spirit born of a precivilized era. Jackson was, however, also thought to be predisposed to racially defined weaknesses such as a frailty against blows to the ribs and stomach. Of course, it was argued, blacks lacked the intellect and were not capable of the same organization, leadership, and discipline as whites. There was, nevertheless, an anxiety in white America concerning the power and brutality exhibited by many African American athletes. This anxiety slowly faded in the first two decades of the twentieth century as the legal codification of Jim Crow in the South largely limited interracial contests to Olympic competition, intercollegiate sport at predominantly white northern universities, and professional boxing.[6]

The black athletes who appeared on white northern university campuses in the late nineteenth century were socially isolated and often were exploited for their athletic prowess at the expense of a quality education. Although prestigious universities like Notre Dame and many of the military academies did not allow blacks on their sports teams until the mid-twentieth century, black student athletes like George Poage, Theodore Cable, and Paul Robeson were among a small number of African Americans who competed for integrated northern universities. This was significant at a time when Jim Crow maintained a tight hold on the black experience. Nevertheless, there was considerable racial discrimination on campus, and white teammates often refused to share the same locker room or transportation. On Paul Robeson's first day of scrimmages at Rutgers his fellow players made clear their views concerning his presence on the team when he was roughed up so badly he spent the next ten days in the hospital.[7]

There was also a "gentleman's agreement" that northern colleges would not field any black players when they played against teams in the South. Private and community-run black teams similarly suffered from this application of the color bar. In the black areas of Chicago during the early twentieth century several African American basketball teams emerged with support from organizations like the YMCA and sponsorship from the black newspaper the *Chicago Defender.* When the predominantly black Phillips High School qualified for the national championship tournament to be held at Chicago University, it was not invited for fear that southern teams might boycott the event. When interracial contests did take place in the city they were increasingly loaded with the racial tension apparent in many northern cities in the 1920s. In racially charged postwar urban centers, white teams did not take kindly to being beaten by black players and there were incidents of violence on and off the court, as well as some less than objective refereeing.[8]

In the first quarter of the twentieth century interracial sporting competition was largely limited to amateur sports. Professional baseball and football adopted segregationist policies. Baseball turned professional in the late nineteenth century and the committee responsible for establishing the league outlined a policy of racial segregation. Fleetwood Walker was the last black to play in the professional leagues when his career came to an end in 1889. In the 1920s black players were gradually phased out of the National Football League (NFL), and from 1934 to 1946 no African Americans were allowed to play or try out for teams in the NFL. There was, however, less strict an apartheid in basketball. Several different leagues coexisted and allowed interracial contests before the National Basketball Association (NBA) was formed in 1949. Had the black-owned New York Renaissance team survived financially for one more season it would have been included as a part of the original NBA.[9] With the erection of barriers to competition in the major league sports, separate black leagues developed and ran alongside their white counterparts as a strong reminder of the pernicious and omnipotent nature of racial separation in the United States. As Ken Shropshire asserted, "Segregation was the route adopted by America and this included sports. Jim Crow laws were meant for all."[10]

The 1930s and 1940s saw the emergence of new protest tactics and symbolism that were increasingly exploited by African Americans. The contradictory image of Americans fighting for freedom in World War II while Jim Crow was ascendant at home was politicized by African American leaders. The New Deal and World War II heightened racial consciousness in the black community and inspired increased civil rights activism among the black working and professional classes.[11] There was a sense that African Americans were more forcefully pushing at the door to equality than ever before. The African American sportsman's role in this era was to provide a symbolic exemplification of racial pride, albeit in a relatively submissive way. Their visibility in American mainstream culture played a key role in promoting sport as an area of society with a prominent responsibility for the slow crumbling of the edifice of racial segregation.

The example of Jesse Owens in the 1936 Olympics as an all-American hero who defied the doctrine of Aryan superiority through sporting prowess played a key role in laying the foundations for the belief in sport as a color-blind institution. Indeed, Owens himself went on to preach this ideal as a sporting commentator and administrator. In the decades that followed the Berlin Olympics and the world-title-winning exploits of Joe Louis, a generation of outstanding black athletes was able to push on the doors to integrated competition. In 1947 Jackie Robinson became the first black major league baseball player of the modern era. A year earlier Kenny Washington, who had been a roommate of Jackie Robinson at the University of California at Los Angeles (UCLA), had become the first black player to feature in the NFL since the 1930s.[12] On the campus of New York University in 1940 and 1941 students protested against racial discrimination in intercollegiate competition. A significant number of the student body protested the continuance of the gentleman's agreement that saw black players dropped from the university team when playing games in the South. Seven students were suspended following the organization of a petition, and 150 of their fellows protested with a sit-in to express their objection to the university's policy. This policy, however, remained unchanged and the gentleman's agreement continued.[13]

The stimulus provided by World War II, which was then increased by the 1954 *Brown v. Board of Education* decision to desegregate public schooling, increased the pace of racial change in the United States. This change slowly had an impact on intercollegiate sport. The 1956 test case of Abner Haynes and Leon King, who became the first black players on the North Texas State College football team, showed that sport could be used to promote racial cooperation. The black players' presence improved racial understanding largely due to the fact that Haynes and King contributed to a winning team. "Since winning benefited everyone, toleration became profitable for everyone, black and white."[14] Sport was seen by many as leading the way in America's move toward desegregation. Heavyweight champion Floyd Patterson had insisted on integrated seating when he signed a contract to fight in Miami. As pressure grew on the Kennedy administration to make significant strides in the pursuit of civil rights, it is significant that it threw so much weight behind forcing the Washington Redskins to change their "lily-white" policy, as they eventually did with the signings of black players Bobby Mitchell and Leroy Jackson in 1961.[15]

These examples and many others provided momentum for the ideal

Jesse Owens memorial at the Jesse Owens museum in Alabama. Owens believed passionately in the power of sport to improve race relations and was a strong opponent of the black athletic revolt. The George F. Landegger Collection of Alabama Photographs in Carol M. Highsmith's America, Library of Congress, Prints and Photographs Division.

that sport ran ahead of the rest of society in the breaking down of racial barriers. It was in the sporting arena that African Americans could enjoy opportunities far beyond those of mainstream society. Writing in the *New York Times* in November 1967, Robert Lipsyte argued, rather critically, that the sporting establishment was fond of "patting itself on the back" concerning the opportunities it offered to black athletes. He did, however, balance his editorial with the acknowledgment that the sports world had offered the chance for some African Americans to gain an education and personal fulfillment. Sport also had the power to educate poor whites who valued a winning player and a star performer whatever the color of his skin.[16] Julius Avendorph, the founder of the first black baseball league in Chicago in the early twentieth century, cited "sports as the means to friendly relations between the races [and] as a means to college scholarships for black men."[17]

For a significant number of college athletes the integration of sporting competition allowed for a greater understanding of their black or white teammates. Indeed, white long jumper Phil Shinnick spoke of the "shattering of stereotypes" that took place during his time competing with black athletes. He learned that many of the stereotypical views about the physical abilities and physiological advantages of black athletes were incorrect.[18] Mixing together as a team of sportsmen was the most practical demonstration of racial integration experienced by many young Americans.

This positive view of the role played by the institution of sport was, however, increasingly challenged by both athletes and community leaders as the 1960s progressed. There was a growing desire to expose what Douglas Kellner later termed the "double-edged sword" of sporting integration for black athletes. Focusing specifically on Michael Jordan, Kellner argued that sport can be used as an arena from which to project a positive image of blackness while also serving to perpetuate negative racial stereotypes associated with blackness. Jordan was viewed as a positive black symbol, a role model for young people who transcended race and integration in American society. His blackness, however, also was overemphasized and was cited as a determining factor in his gambling and alleged links with organized crime.[19]

The achievements of racial heroes like Joe Louis also emphasize this "double-edged sword." Louis's victories over white opponents were significant symbols of the fight against racial oppression. His efforts were viewed by many in the black community as a direct assault on racial oppression; he very violently confronted and defeated white opponents in a way that a black man could not do in wider society. Furthermore, in his bouts with Max Schmeling of Germany he won the support of white America in a symbolic national conflict against fascism. Louis was a submissive figure outside of the ring, however. As part of a reaction against the brash and racially antagonistic behavior of the previous black heavyweight champion, Jack Johnson, he was strongly advised by his management not to challenge the prevailing racial status quo and to avoid any actions that would discredit his race.[20] White Americans could cheer Louis when he fought Schmeling, knowing that he would remain a "good," well-behaved black man. As William Van Deburg argues, they could "toast the black culture hero one day and tell 'coon' jokes the next." In this sense black sportsmen did not directly force racial change forward. Their role was symbolic. They gave hope and pride to the black community without confronting the racial problems of wider society. For white Americans, "it was far easier to praise a black champion of the arena than it was to sacrifice skin-color privilege in everyday life."[21]

The man who sought to give voice to those African Americans who wished to expose such contradictions and repudiate the prevailing idealism surrounding sport was Harry Edwards. He was the single most visible figure in the black athletic revolt that took place in the late 1960s. Edwards argued that racism persisted throughout the sporting world. Indeed, both King and Haynes were still treated predominantly as second-class citizens at North Texas when they were not on the football field.[22] Willie Brown, who was appointed as the first black member of the coaching staff at the University of Southern California in 1968, recalled that racism persisted at that time. Although the situation on campus was relatively good, he still faced racial epithets and segregated facilities when he traveled with university squads.[23] Top U.S. sprinter John Carlos complained that as a black man he could not get a beer in a bar in Austin despite being expected to perform with excellence for his school, East Texas State. He saw coaching staff berate black football players for dropping the ball, calling them "nigger" or "boy." Those who complained were told that if they did not like it they could leave.[24]

Some white athletes were also keenly aware of the continued social prejudice that their black teammates faced on campus. T. J. Gaughan, a football player at the University of Kansas in 1968, recalled the "disheartening" way that at meal times the playing squad would racially segregate itself. The black students on campus faced a significant degree of social ostracism.[25] Olympic distance walker Larry Young acknowledged the great pressure and racism that black athletes had to deal with: "When they were competing . . . they were treated as second-class citizens in terms of where they lived . . . and their social life and everything."[26] During the time he spent training in the United States, British Olympian David Hemery clearly saw the injustices black athletes encountered. He recalled the problems they faced in getting adequate off-campus accommodation.[27]

As a former athlete turned sociology professor, Harry Edwards sought to mobilize black student athletes in revolt against sporting administrators. He sought to shake black athletes out of their passive acceptance of the status quo and subscription to the color-blind ideal. The sporting arena was targeted both as an area in which racial injustice existed and as the place where protest would most likely gain attention and elicit concessions toward greater racial progress. Understanding this duality at the heart of the black athletic revolt is crucial when analyzing its successes and failures and its connection to the wider black freedom struggle. The black athletic revolt certainly grew out of a realization that black sportsmen were still the victims of racial discrimination. Indeed, educating politically submissive black performers about this reality was a major challenge for the movement. That movement, however, wanted to move beyond an educating process so that black athletes could use their position to effect racial change in wider society. In this way the black athletic revolt could connect directly with the black freedom struggle.

We can see this attempt to use sport as a power lever to bring wider racial change in Edwards's activities at San Jose State College. His principal aims were to end the situation of segregated housing that existed in the areas around the university and the discrimination black students faced in relation to course choices and fraternity membership. These were issues that affected all students and black members of the local community, not just black athletes. Edwards had experienced these problems himself when he was a student athlete at the college, and he was dismayed when he returned as a member of the sociology department to find that things had not changed. Edwards and the Black Student Union presented the administration with a list of demands and began picketing college departments on September 18, 1967. Among Edwards's demands were an end to "closed door" meetings of administrators empowered to alleviate black students' grievances, closure of all discriminatory housing near campus, an end to the discrimination shown by fraternities and sororities, and assurances that black athletes would be given the same treatment as their white counterparts in all areas—including social events.[28]

What was crucial in the approach Edwards adopted was his use of sport to force the university to take note of his demands. The college was given a week to address the problems or face significant disruption to the opening game of the football season between San Jose State and the University of Texas at El Paso.[29] This was dually significant. First, it focused the attention of the administration on a specific and traditionally important event. Kurt Kemper has highlighted the great cultural significance of college football in the postwar period as a vehicle through which wider social changes were interpreted.[30] Threatening the first college game of the season with civil rights activism had a deep impact on college administrators and San Jose State football fans. It brought the racial tensions of wider society directly into the local sporting community. Second, the potential financial implications if the game was cancelled were serious. It would likely cost the athletics department between $15,000 and $30,000.[31]

Edwards and his followers offered a direct attack against the myth that sport acted as a positive racial force. Furthermore, the emerging black athletic revolt straddled the tactical and rhetorical paradigms of the Civil Rights and Black Power Movements. The revolt that Edwards led was heavily loaded with Black Power rhetoric and posturing; however, it also utilized traditional tactics of protest that had been tried and tested in the Civil Rights Movement.

Sport and the Tactics of Civil Rights Protest

The tactical approach of Edwards and his supporters drew opposition not only from white athletes and administrators but also from black athletes. Similarly, while many commentators and historians have designated the actions of Smith and Carlos and other OPHR initiatives as part of the Black Power Movement, in reality many of their tactics and ideals were also characteristic of the Civil Rights Movement. It is therefore important to clearly place the activism of the black athletic revolt within the context of these overlapping and interconnected phases of the freedom struggle.

As activists marched through Mississippi in June 1966, Student Non-violent Coordinating Committee (SNCC) leader Stokely Carmichael repeated the slogan "Black Power" and the walking crowd echoed his words with enthusiasm. SNCC members ridiculed the ideal of nonviolence and changed the words of freedom songs. They sang as they marched, "I'm gonna bomb when the spirit say bomb . . . cut when the spirit say cut . . . shoot when the spirit say shoot."[32] Martin Luther King Jr., who had preached the doctrine of nonviolent resistance throughout his leadership of the Civil Rights Movement, was uncomfortable with the call for Black Power and with the radical and violent views of many in SNCC. King wrote in 1967, "Probably the most destructive feature of Black Power is its unconscious and often conscious call for retaliatory violence."[33] The tension between differing tactics of protest in the freedom struggle did not, however, emerge suddenly in the 1960s. The origins of Black Power predate the mid-1960s and the movement was about more than simply a violent response to oppression. As Peniel Joseph has explained, central to the Black Power Movement was a "black empowerment that was local, national, and international in scope, held political self-determination as sacrosanct, and called for a redefined black identity."[34]

A willingness to use violence to fight oppression was one facet of the Black Power Movement, however. Such was the oppression of black

Americans in the South while Jim Crow segregation was ascendant that any attempt at a mass violent revolt would have been suicidal. The race riots witnessed in many American cities in the period after the First World War took place mainly in the North. This is not to say, however, that armed self-defense was not a feature of race relations in the South. Especially following the emergence of increased black consciousness during and after World War II, some blacks were prepared to use violence to defend themselves against white oppression and mobilize for racial change. In his study of National Association for the Advancement of Colored People (NAACP) activist Robert Williams, Timothy Tyson argues that "throughout the civil rights era black southerners stood prepared to defend home and family by force. . . . The Civil Rights Movement and the Black Power Movement emerged from the same predicaments and reflected the same quest for African-American freedom."[35]

When Dr. Perry, a member of the local NAACP in Monroe, North Carolina, was threatened by the Ku Klux Klan in 1957, Williams organized a response. Sixty black men worked in shifts to protect the doctor's house and fired at the Klan from behind fortified positions. When Perry was arrested following his decision to perform an abortion for a white woman, many from the black community surrounded the police station and demanded his release; the women who joined the protest carried butcher's knives and cleavers.[36] Williams broke with the traditions of the NAACP as a middle-class organization and recruited ordinary, working-class black men and women from pool halls and street corners. These men and women had a history of grassroots, armed self-defense against racial oppression.[37] Although other scholars of the Black Power Movement argue that the roots of the movement ran deeper in the North than in the South, Tyson shows that its origins were not simply a product of the mid-1960s.

The NAACP and the Southern Christian Leadership Conference (SCLC), however, held on to the tenets of nonviolence because their model of a hierarchical organization with a strong central leader enabled them to maintain the philosophy. SCLC relied on community mobilization to organize major campaigns that demanded media attention and were therefore able to maintain disciplined nonviolence.[38] SCLC staffer Andrew Marrisett recalled that during the Birmingham campaign in 1963 people were sent away from marches and demonstrations when they arrived with guns and other weapons.[39] Well-organized, specifically civil rights demonstrations allowed SCLC to maintain a fundamentally nonviolent approach.

King recognized, however, that many in the movement were becoming disillusioned with the slow progress of change. The Kennedy administration also observed the growing frustration among African Americans and put pressure on business leaders to end segregation lest nonviolent protest give way to violent revolt.[40] The emergence of Black Power rhetoric, armed self-defense, and then violent reaction could not be successfully restrained, however. The more democratic nature of organizations like SNCC and the Congress of Racial Equality (CORE) and the extent to which they engaged with grassroots protesters meant they were more readily transformed from below than SCLC. SNCC and CORE were more fully absorbed into communities with a tradition of armed response to white oppression, and the fluid and democratic nature of their organizations precluded a repudiation of these methods by a central leadership with a rigid commitment to nonviolent protest. As a consequence these organizations were more likely to draw on armed self-defense methods at the local, grassroots level.[41]

The black athletic revolt engaged with leaders of both the Civil Rights and Black Power Movements. At a press conference to spell out the aims and demands of the OPHR, Harry Edwards was flanked by both Martin Luther King Jr. of SCLC and Floyd McKissick of CORE. King argued that perhaps a total boycott of the Olympics by all blacks was necessary, as little else in the way of nonviolent protest was available.[42] In early 1968 H. Rap Brown, the radical chairperson of SNCC, pledged his support for the OPHR. Black Panther and SNCC leader Stokely Carmichael also supported an African American boycott of the Olympics, which he referred to as that "white nonsense."[43]

In his leadership of the boycott movement Edwards adopted something of a pragmatic approach. One commentator described him as "moderate and militant; separatist and integrationist."[44] During the demonstrations that he organized to protest racial discrimination at San Jose State, Edwards used the threat of possible violence by outside agitators to pressure the administration. Simultaneously, however, he outlined the need for whites and blacks to sit down and discuss the issues constructively.[45] Prior to the boycott of an event at the New York Athletic Club in early 1968, Edwards threatened possible violent retribution for anyone who crossed the picket line.[46] When the police began to lose control of the crowd outside Madison Square Garden they gave Edwards a loudspeaker. He told the crowd that they could "rush the Garden" if they wanted but that he was heading to Harlem to be with his "black brothers." The crowd soon began to disperse and the crisis was averted. Edwards consistently

H. Rap Brown of the Student Nonviolent Coordinating Committee. Brown was among the Black Power leaders who lent their support to Harry Edwards and the Olympic Committee for Human Rights. *U.S. News & World Report* Magazine Photograph Collection, Library of Congress, Prints and Photographs Division.

argued that violence was "natural and desirable" and kept an arsenal of weapons for self-protection.[47] His approach emerged from the overlapping tactics of the Civil Rights and Black Power Movements.

The final symbolic moment of the OPHR was the clenched-fist salute of Tommie Smith and John Carlos on the winner's podium following the 200-meter final in Mexico City. This action and the supporting gesture of white Australian Peter Norman were intended as nonviolent actions. The protest was not intended to be threatening nor intimidating—although many interpreted the black fist salute as an aggressive Black Power symbol. The protest does not fit neatly into either of the conventional categories of the civil rights struggle in the 1960s.

The Olympic authorities interpreted the athletes' action as confrontational and castigated the two sprinters, who were suspended from the team and expelled from the Olympic village. Avery Brundage and the International Olympic Committee (IOC) hierarchy vehemently criticized the intrusion of politics into the sporting arena. Those who opposed the black athletic revolt continually espoused the view that blacks were achieving equality and opportunities through playing the game, both on the international stage and on high school and college fields. Throughout the 1960s the national political administration increasingly listened to and cooperated with the nonviolent protest actions of leaders like King and Roy Wilkins while criticizing the radicalism and militancy of men like Carmichael. The Johnson administration, for example, attempted to work with moderate leaders in order to exercise some form of control over the freedom struggle.[48] Black athletes who participated in boycotts or nonviolent protests were, however, largely criticized. Those who rejected such demonstrations in favor of playing the game were praised as good examples for their race. The ideals of the sports world significantly restricted the potential for athletes to dramatize the racial injustices of American society.

Yet in some areas and on some levels participating in sport could be viewed as a form of militant and, potentially, violent direct action. In contact sports, especially football, black men could use integrated sporting contests to physically fight racial injustice. In the 1960s Arthur Griffin Jr. attended Charlotte, North Carolina's, Second Ward High School, and he remembered being desperate to play against the white schools. Griffin explained, "We'd say, let's go beat the white boy's ass. We wanted to play white schools so we could beat them up and bloody them."[49] Bob Abright, a white basketball player at the University of California, Berkeley, in the late 1960s, remembered that there were fights between white and black teammates almost every day in practice.[50] University of Wyoming football player Melvin Hamilton remembered being subjected to "cheap shots" by white opponents and taking pleasure in beating those opponents and "kicking ass" on the field.[51] In professional sports black men like Johnny Sample of the Baltimore Colts and Duane Thomas of the Dallas Cowboys frightened white America with their violent and menacing displays.[52] On the field, within the confines of the rules of a sporting competition, black athletes were able to engage in a subtle form of violent direct action. They proved their manhood and asserted their equality by performing on the field and physically punishing white opponents. For some black athletes, playing the game was their way of expressing a direct and physical protest. They saw their performance on the field as evidence of their pursuit of racial equality. Nevertheless, those who chose to play the game rather than use the sporting arena to engage in protests and boycotts were often branded "Uncle Toms" by the leaders of the black athletic revolt.

It could be argued, therefore, that the direct action of those who physically engaged white opponents was not a form of protest at all. They were simply playing the white man's game. What is crucial is that the leaders of the black athletic revolt wanted the black sportsman to do more than participate in his chosen activity. Interestingly, Harry Edwards, chief among those who criticized black athletes who did not engage in the athletic revolt, acknowledged the irony of black athletes who played the game being viewed as submissive. "Black men, engaged in violent, aggressive, competitive sports actually were regarded as . . . non-violent."[53] Black athletes who physically confronted white opponents in integrated sporting contests were regarded as moderate.

The focus on male athletes and masculine responses to racial injustice further intersected with the freedom struggle. That struggle was regularly framed in a gendered way. The history of African American repression has come to be seen through the lens of challenges to black masculinity and therefore the story of liberation and struggle gives men a privileged and central position.[54] So black athletes' response to racial injustice was dominated by black male athletes. Black sprinter Wyomia Tyus, who won gold at the Mexico City Olympics, described being on the periphery of the black athletic revolt. Some black female athletes did offer their support and spoke to journalists about the situation surrounding Smith and Carlos, but they were not fully involved in the revolt.[55] Just as the Black Power rhetoric of the era had a masculine tone and spoke of a desire to reclaim African American manhood, so the black athletic revolt was heavily male dominated in both its aims and its leadership. Female athletes were in the process of pushing for greater gender equality in the world of sport and as such racial activism was relatively limited among female athletes.

The patriarchal assumptions of many Americans during the 1960s had a profound impact on the course of the black freedom struggle, and the centrality of manhood in the discourse of that struggle was significant for black and white athletes. Malcolm X continually taunted King and other leaders of the mainstream Civil Rights Movement by suggesting that their stance of nonviolence was unmanly.[56] This conception of black manhood, which was further highlighted by the Black Power Movement, intersected with mainstream sporting conceptions of manhood. Playing the game hard and fair, especially in contact sports like football, was seen as an important element of American masculinity. When Ivy League schools distanced themselves from big-time football in the late 1950s, they were criticized by many in the South and the West for being "effete" and unmanly.[57] African American leaders in the early twentieth century advocated black sporting excellence as a vehicle through which to improve their race. This "muscular assimilation" was advanced as a way to prove the black man's worth and his manhood.[58]

The leaders of the black athletic revolt, however, were not satisfied with confrontation and competition on the pitch; they wanted a more aggressive engagement with the freedom struggle off the field of play. Edwards sought to encourage black athletes to do more than simply play the game. It was this demand that antagonized many white athletes. Conrad Dobler, a white teammate of Melvin Hamilton at the University of Wyoming, argued that black athletes could prove their equality on the field of play. There was no need to take their fight for equality any further.[59] While relishing physical confrontation on the field, Hamilton was one of those black athletes who engaged with the civil rights struggle after the final whistle. He was cut from the team in 1969 when he and his black teammates attempted to protest against the racial discrimination of Brigham Young University. Hamilton argued that "kicking ass" on the field was not enough.[60]

The black civil rights activist who stood motionless as a policeman beat him for attempting to register to vote received sympathy from many in white America. His contemporary who fought against the police in response to discriminatory treatment was looked upon with more suspicion as an angry black man and a possible danger to society. The black football player who pummeled white opponents and sacked the opposing quarterback was lauded as a fine sportsman and a credit to his race. Yet if he stepped off the field and complained of the racial injustices he faced, wearing a black armband or black glove to register his nonviolent protest, he was criticized for ingratitude and for perverting the sporting ideal.

The sports world provided a unique landscape for the tactics of protest in the freedom struggle. Although the actions of Edwards, Smith, Carlos, and others have often been cited as an expression of Black Power by historians and were certainly connected to that movement by contemporaries, the reality is more complex. Furthermore, the tactics and aims of other protest incidents during the black athletic revolt reveal a nuance that simple categorization and interpretation neglects.

Black Power and White Fears

This is not to say that the major features of the Black Power Movement did not have a significant impact on the black athletic revolt. The black athlete who faced the dilemma of how to conduct himself in light of this relationship between sport and civil rights activism confronted pressure from within the black community as well as from white America. Harry Edwards explained that the black athletic revolt grew out of a wider cultural and social awakening in the black community.[61] This movement, defined as Black Power, was given voice by radical young men like Stokely Carmichael and Eldridge Cleaver. Cleaver warned white America that unless things changed, "the sins of the father [would be] visited upon the heads of the children."[62] Cleaver was one of the main spokesmen for the Black Panthers, a militant group formed in Oakland, California, in 1966. They were armed activists who demanded a radical change in the way the black community was policed and an immediate end to all forms of discrimination. With reference to the failed promise of the first Reconstruction, their party platform stated, "We believe that this racist government has robbed us and now we are demanding the overdue debt of forty acres and two mules."[63] The movement was, however, about more than demands for political and economic change; it represented a powerful cultural expression. The Black Power impulse allowed the black community to build for the future and it contributed to a rise in black self-esteem.[64] Indeed, continually frustrated by the problems of the ghetto, for many Black Power was mainly an expression of pride and dignity.[65]

The Black Power Movement had a significant effect on black athletes' response to the athletic revolt. The psychological transformation in the black community put a great deal of pressure on African American athletes. They had to maintain loyalty to their coach as members of a team and as athletic performers but were pressured to engage in the political activism of other black students, often on predominantly white campuses. The most overt symbols of this new militancy were Afro haircuts and facial hair; there were seventy-three different cases surrounding these issues in athletics departments across the country from 1967 to 1971. "The black athlete could conform to the dictates and expectations of the coach and be castigated as an 'Uncle Tom' by his black student peer group, or he could conform to the demands of the peer group and be dismissed from the team."[66]

Nevertheless, leaders of the black athletic revolt were able to combine the popularity of sports in the 1960s and 1970s with the Black Power impulse. Muhammad Ali provides the most symbolic example of a black sportsman who connected the sporting arena with a new and potent black consciousness. Ali's verbose declaration of black beauty and his boasting predictions of when his opponents would fall were part of the fusing of Black Power and the sporting arena. Ali's dispute with the white establishment reflected Edwards's conflict with the Olympic movement. As Van Deburg argues, "With remarkable speed, their dispute with the status quo spread beyond traditional sports world boundaries, promoting psychological wellness within black communities."[67] The black athletic revolt challenged black communities to reexamine their perception of the role of sport in the construction of race relations. In so doing it provoked conflicting responses among black athletes.

The revolt also confronted white America by raising fears that the Black Power Movement—particularly troubling because of its radical and confrontational calls for racial justice—was encroaching upon the sacred world of sporting competition. The movement's activities reinforced the belief among many in white America that blacks were calling for an unrealistic revolution in society. In the 1968 election Richard Nixon gained support for criticizing protesters whose revolutionary desires offered headaches and heartache for the majority of Americans.[68] A *Newsweek* special report on the "White Majority" in 1969 argued that the "President presides over a nation nervously edging rightward in a desperate try to catch its balance after years of upheaval."[69] Many white working people were uneasy about the extent of African American protest and social change during the 1960s.

This "white backlash" was not simply a response to the Black Power

Movement in the late 1960s. Its roots went much deeper and are part of the story of the rise of the New Right. What is crucial is the role played by the black athletic revolt in this backlash. Sport had for so long been seen as a site in which blacks could achieve equality and make advances ahead of developments in wider society. When black athletes—and, importantly, some prominent white athletes—challenged this notion and tried to use the sporting arena to engage in the freedom struggle, the white response was particularly critical and angry.

The black athletic revolt and the reaction to it form part of this white backlash, but we can trace its roots to well before the late 1960s. White reaction to civil rights advances was evident in postwar Detroit, for example. Public housing schemes that had been welcomed in the early New Deal were opposed from the 1940s and 1950s onward. In these decades whites throughout the city founded at least 192 neighborhood organizations with the express intent of protecting their property and resisting any move toward integrated housing. Entitlement to racially homogeneous neighborhoods became a fundamental belief of white Detroiters in the immediate postwar period.[70]

The example above serves to illustrate that the rise of conservative feeling in response to civil rights advances was not confined to a specific period of reaction to the Civil Rights Movement. George Lewis has explained that in the South "massive resistance" to desegregation programs cannot be defined as a reaction to a single event. He argues that massive resistance "must be seen as a phenomenon too sprawling and simply not sufficiently obedient to have been ushered into existence by a single landmark event." Lewis asserts that resistance by white southerners against the advances of the civil rights agenda can be categorized into three main phases. The last of these phases ended in 1965, when the passage of voting rights legislation saw the reduction of public demonstrations of white supremacy.[71]

Lewis argues that after 1965 southern leaders who opposed racial equality and possessed sufficient subtlety were able to "encode any racist appeals in such a way as to make them palatable to a broader, nonsectional audience."[72] The receptiveness of this audience grew alongside the rise of a New Right conservatism that flourished as the 1960s drew to a close. This conservatism had deep roots, and the story of its development has often been overlooked as historians have preferred to focus on the left-wing political movements that dominated the sixties. As Students for a Democratic Society and SNCC were heavily influencing the political agenda, Young Americans for Freedom, formed in 1960, was developing a new conservative leadership that would help shift the Republican Party to the right.[73] Lisa McGirr has explained how grassroots conservatism developed as the 1960s progressed and came to have a significant and lasting influence on the national political landscape as the decade ended.[74]

Proponents of the New Right ideology criticized Kennedy's New Frontier and the social and economic excesses of Johnson's Great Society. Young Americans for Freedom activist Robert Schuchman attacked the Kennedy administration in 1962 and warned that America faced a choice between "liberty and equality." He added that the rise of government power would cost Americans their liberty "in the search for a chimera of equality."[75] Although the party was defeated heavily in the 1964 presidential election, the Republicans had already in 1963 begun to plan a shift in their ideology and tactics in order to win back the White House and defeat the New Deal coalition. This effort would pull the Republican Party increasingly rightward.[76] This ideological shift was intertwined with the emerging backlash among many white Americans against the advances of the Civil Rights Movement. Economist Eliot Janeway used the term *backlash* in 1963 when he warned of potential racial conflict between white and black blue-collar workers. Black political advances in the South led many whites to vote for ultraconservatives like Lester Maddox, the Democratic candidate for governor of Georgia in 1966. By the middle of the 1960s this white backlash extended well beyond the Deep South, and Republican Party strategists attempted to tap into a rising tide of conservatism.[77]

Many less-privileged Americans felt that the drive for black advancement was being achieved at their expense.[78] In his study of the Jews and Italians of Brooklyn, Jonathan Rieder found working-class whites who felt threatened by the African American assertiveness of the sixties. The communities vehemently resisted the busing schemes of the early 1970s. The Brooklynites also criticized elements of modern culture that threatened traditional values of family and hard work. Others among them were disturbed by the very process of change itself.[79] In the late 1960s conservatives focused their efforts against government attempts to remedy the legacy of racial discrimination. These conservatives resisted plans to equalize opportunity when it affected their own schools and neighborhoods.[80]

Lewis argues that from 1965 onward, as the defeated proponents of massive resistance to desegregation in the South were absorbed into the rise of New Right conservatism, their more overt displays of white supremacist ideology became more subtle and their language more coded.

Nevertheless, in the South sport was actually used as a form of symbolic resistance against the forces of integration well into the late 1960s. The sporting arena provides for a further dimension in the study of massive resistance and white backlash. In other areas of the country white Americans, perpetuating the myth of sport as an unequivocally positive racial force, were offended by the civil rights activism of the black athletic revolt. Black people had broken the color barrier in both professional and college athletics and played on integrated teams in front of integrated audiences. Crowds cheered both white and black players; the color line was drawn by the contrasting team uniforms rather than racial difference. Some black athletes, though, still protested and complained; they boycotted games, and they stood on the winners' podium and disrespected the American flag. White athletes, sports fans, and administrators all exhibited signs of disappointment and anger toward the black—and white—athletes who challenged the essentially mythical role of sport in race relations. The anger and disappointment that were exhibited form part of our understanding of the white backlash in the late 1960s.

School Desegregation and Sport

The area of society in which white Americans were most clearly confronted by significant social change was education. The *Brown v. Board of Education* ruling that segregated schooling was unconstitutional made the classroom the front line of racial integration in the 1950s and beyond. It was in schools and universities—outside of the South before the 1960s— that young black and white athletes began to play sports with and against one another. The historical debate concerning the success or otherwise of the *Brown* decision intersects with the discussion about the nature of sport as a positive racial force. The *Brown* decision is widely regarded as a source of inspiration for civil rights activists and it holds symbolic value as the beginning of the integration of the education system—the incubator for America's future. Sport has enjoyed similar symbolic importance as an arena in which racial barriers can be broken down. The *Brown* decision and the integration of school sports did not, however, provide a simple path to racial progress.

Michael Klarman argues that there were the beginnings of a significant transformation in race relations before the *Brown* decision and that the positive impact of the decision was very limited. His "backlash" thesis maintains that the crucial role played by *Brown* was to harden southern resistance to civil rights activism and provide for a confrontation. This confrontation led to images in the media that were greeted by many Americans with revulsion and consequent support for civil rights legislation. The immediate impact on desegregation in the South provided by *Brown* was minimal. Taking the region as a whole, by 1963–1964 approximately 1.2 percent of school-age blacks were actually attending school with whites.[81] In North Carolina, for example, dual systems continued to dominate well into the 1960s.[82] An anonymous letter to the president of Mississippi State University in 1963 argued that "something more than the game [would] be lost" if the institution's basketball team broke the color barrier and competed against an integrated team.[83] The team did, however, travel out of the state to compete against their integrated opponents.

James Cobb counters Klarman's view, arguing that the revisionism of historians of *Brown* stems largely from a sense of disappointment with the achievements of the ruling and its aftermath. The decision did provide an inspiration and impetus for black civil rights activists.[84] Lewis has also asserted that the "elegant flow" of Klarman's argument is less convincing when the "intricacies and complexities" of massive resistance to desegregation are fully considered.[85] Certainly within the sporting sphere reactions to school desegregation were varied. The complexities of massive resistance to which Lewis alludes meant that there was not a uniform response to the prospect of white and black student athletes playing and training together.

Although *Brown* was aimed at elementary and secondary schools, the issue of desegregation needs also to embrace higher education institutions. Certainly in the Deep South top universities resisted the integration of sports teams even after higher education institutions as a whole had been integrated. In all areas of the nation integrated schooling could lead to increased racial understanding through playing sports. Integration also had the potential to promote tension and destroy previously successful sports programs, however.

The failings of integrated education did, nevertheless, promote a discussion that strongly affected the birth of the black athletic revolt. The successes and failures of high school and college sporting arenas were important factors in the development of the black athletic revolt. Sport did offer opportunities for black and white social intercourse beyond the parameters of wider society's racial mores. Only on the baseball field could Jackie Robinson wave a bat at a white man in relative safety. Sport provided for the breaking of certain racial barriers in the South that would have been conventionally impenetrable. Vince Dooley, University of Georgia football coach from 1964 to 1988, argued that once desegregation became widespread in the late 1960s and early 1970s, "athletics helped to integrate the South. . . . passions run so hard with sports and when they [southern people] saw white and black were playing together for a common cause then they were for that cause."[86] Pamela Grundy argues that even before the *Brown* decision of 1954 an increase in the number of integrated athletic contests opened "cracks in absolutist notions of racial separation."[87] Nevertheless, these contests were sporadic and largely comprised integrated northern teams competing against all-white southern teams.

The experience of black student athletes post-*Brown* is typical of the tensions at the heart of the relationship between race and sport. The resistance to integrated schooling in the South and the experiences of those who lived through increased integration of sports teams in schools and colleges across the country had an important impact on the specific shape of the black athletic revolt. The problems faced by black athletes even after the integration of sports became an increasing focus for that revolt. In the South the hard-line segregationist backlash against the *Brown* decision affected the integration of high school and college sports. Steve Cherry, coach at East Lincoln High School in North Carolina, was approached by a member of the booster club who warned, "There's a man that's going to blow your head off if you keep playing all them niggers on your basketball team."[88]

Highlighting a trend that will be explored further in the chapters that follow, the experiences of individuals and teams during the immediate period after integration was often shaped by the attitudes of the coaching staff. Horace King, one of the first black football players at the University of Georgia, was a senior in the late 1960s when his high school integrated. He described constant conflict on the football team and in the school system because of the attitudes of the players and their coaches. King asserted, "We should have had an outstanding football team but because of the dissension inside the team we could not compete and beat other teams like we should have." King explained how he was removed from games when he played well so that he did not break any school records. The attitude of the players on the team was a reflection of the discrimination exhibited by the coach, who treated black and white players differently. In contrast, King's experiences of integrated high school basketball was much more positive because "of the way the coaches handled things."[89]

Integrated sporting contests were visible expressions of the racial changes that the nation in general and the South in particular were experiencing in the late 1960s. White and black players working alongside one another for a common cause did help to break down barriers. This was only a partial process, however. As Grundy explains in relation to North Carolina, "Black and white students might attend school together, might work jointly on the details of offensive and defensive strategy, but after school let out they went home to different neighborhoods."[90] George Patton, a University of Georgia and Atlanta Falcons football player in the late 1960s, explained that off the field "the blacks stayed with the blacks, and the whites stayed with the whites."[91] This social separation despite athletic integration was another element of the critique outlined by Harry Edwards and the black athletic revolt he led. The revolt on college campuses emerged directly from the experiences of black and white students and athletes in the post-*Brown* education system.

What is crucial is that these racial confrontations, accommodations, and tensions were faced every day on some level by white and black athletes and coaches involved in integrated sport. It was on high school football teams and college basketball courts that blacks and whites learned to adjust to the changing racial landscape of the United States immediately after passage of the landmark civil rights legislation of the mid-sixties. The reactions to the black athletic revolt by athletes, fans, administrators, and coaches were elements of the white backlash that formed part of the rise of a new conservatism. This new conservatism saw sporting competition as a crucial component of the American national character and passionately upheld the ideal that sport provided an unequivocal example of racial integration and progress.

This powerful ideal was clearly reflected in the language that Roby used when writing to Parker in the aftermath of the 1968 Olympics. His naked anger at the Harvard crew stemmed from the perceived impertinence of an attack on the cherished notion that sport had done more than any other area of society to promote racial equality. Roby accused the Harvard men of embarking on "a rather strenuous program of civil rights and social justice with other members of our Olympic delegation to Mexico City."[92] What vexed U.S. administrators further was the convergence of tactics from the Civil Rights and Black Power Movements. Smith and Carlos could be painted as Black Power militants, angry young black men whose sporting talent had lifted them out of the ghetto but whose character remained gripped by a destructive antiwhite mindset. Paul Hoffman and his teammates wore the blazers of an elite academic institution and competed in one of the whitest sports in the games, however. They showed the potential of sport to be used as a tool to promote the black freedom struggle. Yet in many respects their stand represented the high-water mark of the black athletic revolt, as sport never fully reached its potential to positively affect civil rights activism.

The Olympic Project for Human Rights

Genesis and Response

The Olympics help to bridge the gap of misunderstanding of people in this country. There is no place in the athletics world for politics.
—Jesse Owens, quoted in the *New York Times*, November 26, 1967

He belongs to a controlled generation. . . . Does it occur to Jesse Owens that blacks are in-eligible by color-line and by endless economic obstacles to compete in some 80 percent of scheduled Olympic events?
—Harry Edwards, *The Revolt of the Black Athlete*

At the beginning of 1967, Ralph Boston was the long jump world record holder, having set the mark of eight meters, thirty-five centimeters two years previous. That was his fourth world record and he could also boast a gold medal in the 1960 Olympics and a silver medal in the Tokyo Games four years later. Boston was therefore a very likely candidate to make the U.S. team that would travel to Mexico City for the 1968 Olympics. In the year preceding these games there were calls from some within the black community to boycott the occasion as a protest against continued racial injustice in America. When asked about the possibility of this boycott, Boston gave a very clear opinion against it. "I don't see that anything at all would be accomplished by Negroes boycotting the Olympic Games," he told a reporter. "People train at least four years for this event, which is probably the greatest sporting event in the world."[1] At the age of twenty-eight Boston knew this would most likely be his final opportunity to compete in the games. As he told me some years later, "I was not in favor of the boycott. . . . I guess that was quite selfish. . . . I knew it would be my last chance and so I wanted to go [to the Olympics]."[2]

The long jumper was against the civil rights agenda impinging upon the Olympic Games to the extent that black athletes would refuse to participate. Nevertheless, he had shown seven years earlier that he was prepared to use the boycotting of events as a way of drawing attention to racial inequality. Boston had been involved in an incident in Houston, Texas, in 1961 that provides a relatively rare example of athletes using their position to protest against racial injustice in the early 1960s. He was one of thirty-eight athletes who refused to participate in a track and field event because of the provision of segregated seating for spectators. The Houston branch of the NAACP, which had organized the protest, was criticized by Jesse Owens for putting pressure on athletes to boycott the event and so restricting their individual freedoms. The NAACP responded that no pressure was put on the athletes. In a separate incident involving the picketing of Houston football games because of segregated seating, the NAACP stated that the San Diego Chargers' black players were not to be criticized if they crossed the picket line.[3] In the original incident that drew condemnation from Owens, Boston had shown that he was willing to sacrifice an athletic event to make a stand in the civil rights struggle. Clearly, though, the size of the Olympics and the prestige associated with winning medals far outweighed those of a regional tournament in Texas.

Boston was also one of those athletes who chose to boycott a New York Athletic Club (NYAC) track and field event in early 1968. Black athletes had long complained about the Jim Crow policies of the club. Boston argued that while even Soviet athletes were accommodated when visiting the venue, black athletes were treated differently. "I never once set foot inside the New York Athletic Club," said Boston.[4] He joined many black athletes in boycotting the club's meet in February 1968. This protest was organized by OPHR leader Harry Edwards. Boston was one of many black athletes who heard the rhetoric of Edwards and his supporters and had to make some life-changing decisions about how far to engage in the black freedom struggle.

For some, though, the choices were clear. In fact there were really no choices. When asked to explain what he envisaged when he stated in 1968 that the United States needed to change radically, Edwards responded, "For openers, the Federal Government, the honkies, the pigs in blue must go down South and take those crackers out of bed, the crackers who blew up those four little girls in that Birmingham church, those crackers who murdered Medgar Evers and killed the three civil-rights workers—they must pull them out of bed and kill them with axes in the middle of the street. Chop them up with dull axes. Slowly. At high noon. With every-body watching on television. Just as a gesture of good faith."[5] There was an anger and disillusionment in his words that showed he was "mad as hell at white America."[6] His was a clear expression of the Black Power ideol-ogy that loomed large over the year 1968.[7] Given the strength of feeling held by Edwards and his supporters and the racial turmoil that was tear-ing many American cities apart in the late 1960s, it was no surprise that the world of sport would be affected. Richard Hoffer has argued that "it was ridiculous to think" that the "single most aggrieved part of this soci-ety—young black men—would join in a bit of athletic pageantry without complaint or worse."[8] Nevertheless, so strong was the belief that it was in sports above all other areas of society that African Americans could excel that any challenge to this ideal was greeted with indignation and anger by the sporting establishment.

No Show in Mexico? The Origins and Initial Impact of the Boycott

A boycott of the Olympics as part of a political protest was not an entirely new idea. Egypt, Lebanon, and Iraq had refused to send teams to the 1956 Melbourne Games as a protest against the British-French-Israeli invasion of Egypt to protect the Suez Canal. Furthermore, Mel Whitfield, the Afri-can American three-time Olympic medalist, advocated that black athletes boycott the 1964 Tokyo Games because of the failure of the United States to guarantee civil rights for all of its citizens.[9] Nevertheless, the proposed black boycott of the 1968 Olympics departed from these precedents in important ways. First, the proposal in 1968 was for one part of a national team to refuse to compete; it was certainly not sponsored by the U.S. Olympic Committee. The 1956 boycott was undertaken by whole national delegations in much the same way as the Olympics would be boycotted in the early 1980s because of Cold War politics. Second, unlike the Whit-field proposal, the 1968 Olympic boycott movement was the brainchild of a serious organization with, initially, a significant number of world-class athletes making sympathetic noises in support. Certainly the aims and motivations of the OPHR were regarded by the sporting establishment as extremely alarming.

The idea of a black boycott of the Olympics had previously been considered by those sympathetic to the civil rights struggle in America but was regarded as both unlikely and problematic by Roy Wilkins, head of the NAACP. Replying to a correspondent in April 1964, Wilkins expressed doubt about the possible success of a boycott when he stated, "With opinion so divided it would be next to impossible to develop a successful campaign." More importantly, Wilkins suggested that taking part in the games and highlighting black athletic prowess would be beneficial for the civil rights cause in itself. He argued that most of the athletes themselves "feel that they achieve some positive good by participating and there is much to be said for this opinion."[10] The NAACP represented a moderate voice in the black freedom struggle and Wilkins was writing in 1964. A serious proposal to boycott the Olympics was made as part of the proceedings of a Black Power conference three years later.

There was concern among the sporting establishment about the disruption that could be caused by a boycott. In the summer of 1967 Tommie Smith, a sprinter from San Jose State College, responding to a Japanese reporter during the student games in Tokyo, stated that a black boycott of the 1968 Olympics was possible.[11] In Newark, New Jersey, in July 1967 the first National Conference of Black Power called for a boycott of the Olympics by all black athletes. It was in this way that the boycott ideal was expressed publicly. What is interesting given the wider social and political tensions of this time—indeed, Newark had experienced significant racial riots in the preceding days—was the importance attached to the sporting boycott. Attendees at the Black Power conference also responded enthusiastically to a resolution proposing the separation of the United States into white and black republics, demanded refusal of birth control policies on the basis that they sought to exterminate the black population, and called for paramilitary training for all African American youths. The headline reporting the conference in the *New York Times,* however, read "Boycott of Sports by Negroes Asked."[12] Sport provided the most visible arena in which African Americans could succeed and gain fame in the United States, and as such an attack on the institution of sport was greeted by many as extremely portentous. Amid the growing radicalism of the civil rights struggle of the late 1960s it is significant that the prospect of this radicalism having an impact on sport was given such close attention.

Edwards had shown the growing black militancy in the sporting sphere during events at San Jose State. He had support from the "Speed City" world-class sprinters at the university, Tommie Smith, John Carlos, and Lee Evans chief among them. Fresh from the victory of forcing concessions from the San Jose State administrators, Edwards and Smith contacted a number of America's top black athletes to discuss the possibility of a boycott of the Mexico City Olympics. At a meeting in October 1967 the Olympic Committee for Human Rights (OCHR) was formed and mobilization toward a black boycott of the games, termed the Olympic Project for Human Rights (OPHR), was begun. A meeting was called for November 1967 and at that meeting there was a unanimous vote to support a boycott of the Olympics.[13]

In December Edwards and Kenneth Noel met with Martin Luther King Jr., Floyd McKissick, and Louis Lomax, and at a press conference each of the civil rights leaders gave a message of support for the OCHR. After the press conference an information booklet was released that spelled out in detail the demands of the OCHR. As well as the proposed Olympic boycott, the committee called for the restoration of Muhammad Ali's world title, the removal of Avery Brundage from his position as head of the IOC (it was alleged that Brundage was antiblack and anti-Semitic), the appointment of an African American Olympic coach and Olympic committee member, and the desegregation of the NYAC. There followed a detailed explanation of the motivations and aims behind each of the stated demands.[14]

The dissemination of the OCHR's ideals prompted a great deal of attention. There was an in-depth analysis of the boycott plans in the media as various athletes and commentators aired their views. What is interesting is that the broad spectrum of response spread across racial lines. There were white athletes and administrators who were supportive of a boycott, some who were supportive of the aims but not the means of a boycott, some who were ambivalent, and some determinedly against it. Similarly, there were a number of black athletes and administrators who held contrary opinions on the matter; however, the spectrum of opinion among these African Americans was not as nuanced as that of their white counterparts.

During the black youth conference at which a boycott was discussed, former L.A. Rams player Dan Towler argued that sports had done much to help African Americans advance and that competing for one's country was a great honor.[15] This view was certainly supported later by an assistant Olympic coach, Stan Wright, and the baseball star Willie Mays, both of whom subscribed to the ideal of sport as a positive racial force that had been beneficial for African Americans.[16] High jumper Gene Johnson argued that if it were not for the opportunity to excel that sport offered, top-class African American athletes would just be anonymous black men trapped in the system of racial discrimination suffered by the rest of the black population.[17] Undoubtedly the most outspoken supporter of this view was former Olympic medalist Jesse Owens. Owens argued strongly against the boycott proposal and was later sent to counsel the black athletes against participating in such an act. He asserted that when it came to racial prejudice, the gap of misunderstanding had been bridged "more in athletics than anywhere else" and that an Olympic boycott was not the way to deal with the racial problems in the United States.[18] As Kenny Moore has argued, "Owens seemed to glory in overcoming obstacles. He preached that if a man worked hard enough, if he endured racial taunts the way Jackie Robinson and Joe Louis had, he would succeed, he would win the white man's respect and things would change."[19]

For many of the black athletes involved in the boycott plan, however, Owens represented a different generation and was dismissed as a man who was out of step with the changing contemporary racial climate. Lee Evans, who would go on to win two gold medals at the Olympics but was at the vanguard of the OPHR in its early days, argued that Owens was connected to the IOC and was "only doing Avery Brundage's bidding."[20] Tommie Smith, Evans's training partner, remarked, "Winning gold medals for a country where I don't have any freedom is irrelevant."[21] NBA star Bill Russell argued that Owens was wrong and that the boycott would not harm the black struggle for equality. Nevertheless, Russell was one of a number of black athletes who were said to be sympathetic toward the boycott but stopped short of categorically throwing their support behind it.[22]

Despite being sensitive to the racial problems that motivated the OPHR, many black athletes spoke out against the boycott. Some did this for genuine ideological reasons. Clarence Ray argued, "The U.S. should be represented by the best athletes regardless of race, creed, color or religion. I am an American first, last and always."[23] A similar note of patriotism was sounded by sprinter Charlie Greene: "It comes down to the matter if you are an American or not. I am an American and I am going to run."[24] Edwards later suggested that athletes who were enrolled in the military, like Greene, were under certain constraints and would have found it almost impossible to support the boycott for fear of retaliation by their superiors—the ultimate of which was an assignment in Vietnam.[25] Others, like Ralph Boston, were motivated by simple individual ambition for athletic success.

As publicity surrounding the potential boycott grew, the press weighed in with its own views on the subject. The majority were, predictably, highly critical of the boycott proposal. The belief that sport provided a potent force for social progress remained extremely powerful. Veteran sportswriter A. S. Young argued, "There actually is no way of telling just how important Negro athletic heroes have been to the cause of racial equality in this country. Whenever a bigot cheers for an integrated team in this country, he loses a bit . . . of his bigotry."[26] An editorial in the *New York Times* in July 1967 was more pointedly critical of the wider ramifications of the rise of black militancy, arguing that boycott calls were the acts of "black racists."[27]

Many writers felt that this was just another example of the attack on the mainstream that was gathering pace in the late 1960s. Men like Edwards and Noel were seen as angry individuals swimming against the tide and launching an assault on tentative yet significant racial progress. Many more, however, argued that the wider crime was an attack on the institution of sport itself, which had always been a positive racial force. Indeed, the Olympic Games were the very pinnacle of the ideal of equality for all.[28] Not everyone went along with this argument, however. Robert Lipsyte produced a typically intelligent and probing piece for the *New York Times*. Answering the question of what the boycott would achieve he stated, "It would, at least, give many young Negro athletes pause to reevaluate their own goals, their own identities, whether or not they finally, and painfully, decide to try to make the team. It would, at best, embarrass the country into taking more positive steps toward improving housing, education, job opportunities for black Americans."[29]

Voices in the black press also showed support and sympathy for the idea of an Olympic boycott. One example was *Chicago Defender* staff writer Lawrence Casey. He argued that simply winning gold medals did not bring racial equality. Casey wrote that many black athletes did not want to "represent a country that continues to consider them second class citizens." He went on to echo the arguments of Edwards and his supporters that athletes had to expand their role and become more involved in the wider black freedom struggle. "The struggle for decency in America is not limited to pickets outside a capitol building, campaigning for open occupancy or a sit-in at a restaurant. It may well be a refusal by young black Americans to compete in international athletic events."[30]

What seemed to be missing from this debate was any real sampling of the views of white athletes who would try to qualify for the U.S. Olympic team. After all, a black boycott could open the way for some athletes to go to Mexico City who might otherwise have failed to make the grade in the face of African American competition. Interviews with many of these athletes some thirty-five or more years after 1968 reveal a wide spectrum of opinion. Hammer thrower Hal Connolly, who was vocal in his support for the OPHR during the games, recalled that many of the white athletes were not in favor of the boycott and were fearful of any possible disruption to the Olympic team from protest activity.[31] Others were of the opinion that a boycott was a fatuous idea given how hard athletes had to work to get to the top level; to throw away the chance to compete would be to pass up a great opportunity.[32] Larry Young argued that his primary concern was "focusing on my event [and] trying to do what I could to win a medal."[33] Steeplechaser George Young claimed that he had little if any knowledge of the OPHR, such was his focus on competition. "I was mainly concerned about my conditioning program and personal training program so I really did not know [about the OPHR] and did not get into any other kind of discussions about any problems or anything like that."[34] This singular focus promoted a sense of ambivalence that characterized the response of many white athletes. Furthermore, a lot of the white athletes only very dimly understood the aims of the OPHR, possibly a consequence of the often still very racially segregated nature of sports. There was not wholesale interaction between white and black athletes and there remained, to a certain extent, a general misunderstanding of each other's views.[35] Some chose to view the OPHR, whatever its main arguments, as an example of using sport to further a political cause and argued that this was anathema to the ideals of the Olympics.[36]

Despite the dominance of negative responses to the OPHR, either because of its perceived perversion of the sporting tradition or because of sheer ambivalence, a significant minority of white athletes sympathized fully with the racial problems that were being highlighted but stopped short of supporting the boycott. These athletes took the time to try to understand the racial problems and, arguably, tried to embrace a wider interpretation of the place of sport in society. Harvard rower Cleve Livingston argued, "I thought the message of the OPHR was one which needed to be heard, it was a message of respect for human beings and the provision of equal rights in a democratic society."[37] Dick Fosbury confessed to being largely ignorant of the fine details of the OPHR program, and while he opposed the boycott he did support the black athletes who were campaigning for change, many of whom were his friends.[38] On a personal level, as has been outlined above, many white athletes could recognize the double-standard that many of their black teammates faced. They could see that sport was not the force for racial progress that many believed, but they stopped short of endorsing a plan to boycott the games. Indeed, discus thrower Al Oerter, who sympathized with the problems faced by African American athletes, argued that not competing was a strategic mistake. He asserted that if an individual had a political "axe to grind" then "there are few places on earth that command [as] much attention" as the Olympic Games.[39]

Some white athletes did initially support the black athletes' right to boycott but then changed their mind as the magnitude of such a decision emerged. White long jumper Phil Shinnick missed out on the Olympic team with a below-par performance at the U.S. trials. Shinnick was one of the original members of the OPHR but later felt that the push by Harry Edwards for athletes to boycott the Olympics was too much to expect. Shinnick was in the U.S. Air Force at the time and his superiors threatened that if he spoke out about racism he would be court-martialed. He felt that the tensions surrounding his engagement with the civil rights struggle affected his performance. He finished fourth in the trials and underperformed in relation to his previous achievements that season. With the benefit of a longer perspective on events, Shinnick argued that it is actually through involvement in competition that athletes give themselves an opportunity to make a stand on important issues.[40] Bruce Kidd, a Canadian middle-distance runner and member of the Chicago Athletic Club, took part in a debate with black opponent of the boycott, Rafer Johnson, on a local TV station. Kidd argued that for him personally a boycott was too high a price to pay but that if African American athletes chose to express their grievances in this way then he would understand their stance.[41]

There was a growing consciousness that the Olympic claim of transcending politics was disingenuous. Voicing a wider disillusionment with the sporting establishment, Hal Connolly argued that the USOC was hypocritical. To those who stated that the idea of an Olympic boycott injected politics into the games in an unacceptable way, Connolly responded that the USOC itself politicized sport. Connolly pointed to the refusal of the American delegation to dip its flag in the opening ceremony since the games of the early twentieth century. Indeed, Connolly refused to carry the flag in the Mexico City opening ceremony unless he was allowed to dip it. His request was denied.[42]

Obviously these reflections on events in 1968 have been shaped by the passage of time. Nevertheless, those who maintained their criticism of the boycott many years after the events most likely offer reliable evidence of reactions. So, while recognizing the difficulties associated with these oral histories, we can discern in these wide-ranging responses to the idea of an Olympic boycott by black athletes that there was common ground across racial lines. There was significant sympathy toward the problems faced by African American athletes, but it was the potency of the ideal of sport as a force for racial progress rather than a base racial prejudice that motivated the most negative responses to the OPHR. Those who wanted to use the sporting arena to engage in the wider racial struggle faced considerable difficulties because of the prevailing ideological framework in which race and sport were locked. Nevertheless, at this stage the boycott idea was just that. The discussions and opinions were responses to a theoretical event. The practicalities of the ideals of the boycott were to be tested in New York in early 1968.

All Not So Rosy in the Garden

Celebrating its centenary year, the NYAC held a meet at the multimillion-dollar, newly constructed Madison Square Garden in February 1968. The exclusionary policies of the New York club made it a target for the OCHR, which had criticized the NYAC in its press release of late 1967.[43] Many African American athletes were aggrieved at the treatment they received when they were competing in events held under the umbrella of the NYAC. Jackie Robinson wrote of the "disgraceful Jim Crow situation at the New York Athletic Club," in an opinion piece in the *Pittsburgh Courier.*[44] Quarter-miler Vince Matthews argued, "The New York AC policy was a contradiction: on the one hand, it was telling blacks that they weren't welcome inside their building on Fifty-seventh Street because of color and justifying this policy on the premise that it's a private club entitled to invite whomever it pleases. Yet the AC then turns around and tries to recruit or invite these same black athletes to a New York AC track meet."[45] Under the headline "Devil's Advocate," Arthur Daley wrote in the *New York Times* that the NYAC had been a cornerstone of American amateur athletics for a century and that in the previous two decades the club had invested $4 million in the sport. Daley argued that there was one particular athletics club in New York with a predominantly black membership that would have folded had it not been for continued financial assistance from the NYAC.[46]

Nevertheless, led by Edwards, the OCHR contacted Omar Ahmad, chair of the 1966 Black Power Conference; H. Rap Brown, chair of SNCC; and Jay Cooper, chair of the Columbia University Black American Law Students Association, and these men helped to organize a boycott of the NYAC meet scheduled for February 16. Support was also received from the American Jewish Congress, the Congress of Racial Equality, and the Amateur Athletic Union, and this helped to legitimize the OCHR as a genuine arm of the black freedom struggle.[47] The movement to boycott the NYAC meet gained increasing momentum, until only a handful of black athletes were intending to compete. The Grand Street Boys of New York and the Philadelphia Pioneer Club, both of which had a predominantly black team, said they would not compete. Manhattan College, New York University, St. John's, and City College said their athletes did not have to take part. Similarly, Les Wallack, the Rutgers coach, said he would not require black athletes to compete in individual events.[48] The withdrawal of the Villanova team was viewed as significant because of its traditional strength and inclusion of many standout performers.[49] Furthermore, all the Ivy League schools announced agreement with the boycott and fifty alumni of the University of Notre Dame encouraged fellow alums to withdraw from membership of the club.[50] What was significant was the biracial nature of the withdrawals, with both white and black schools refusing to send their teams. This was noted by Jackie Robinson in a *Chicago Defender* editorial. Robinson wrote, "It is heartening also to note that the black athletes are not alone in their protest. More and more, white youths from the college campuses of America are being heard."[51]

All of this was certainly a triumph for the OCHR and for its figurehead and spokesman, Harry Edwards. Indeed, after receiving a telegram from Edwards warning that the Soviet athletes who crossed the picket lines were not guaranteed safety, the Russian National Team canceled its participation in the event.[52] In a typically ebullient mood, Edwards announced on the day of the boycott that anybody who was "sincerely interested in doing something to help end racism in this society" should picket outside Madison Square Garden. He even argued that George Wallace, the infamous prosegregation southern governor, was welcome to join the pickets.[53] The organizers had to cancel their entire high school program because so many schools withdrew.[54] For those who were concerned about a black boycott of the Olympics later in the year, the support for the boycott of the NYAC meet was certainly alarming.

The club itself remained unmoved in the face of the boycott. Indeed, an indication of its defiance of the messages of the OCHR is provided by a letter written by NYAC representative James Wilson to Avery Brund-age in March 1968. Wilson offered Brundage support concerning the IOC decision to allow South Africa to compete in Mexico City. This was one of the key things that Edwards and the OCHR opposed. Wilson told Brundage, "Boycotts are not the creed of sportsmanship and I have no doubt that the 1968 Olympics will be successful regardless of threats and intimidations."[55]

For many black athletes, however, support of the NYAC boycott did not ensure commitment to a boycott of the Mexico City Olympics. Vince Matthews argued that other factors were far more important consider-ations for black athletes as the Olympics approached; particularly impor-tant, as already mentioned, was the position of the IOC in relation to South Africa.[56] Ralph Boston argued both at the time and since that there was no contradiction in his decision to support the NYAC boycott while opposing a boycott of the Olympics. For Boston, his stance represented a personal expression of protest against the racial injustices of the period, and he crit-icized those who "called him names" or "shunned" him for it.[57] As *New York Times* sports columnist Robert Lipsyte commented, "It is one thing to boycott a big track meet; it is another thing to boycott something you have been pointing your entire life at." For those athletes who felt shamed or guilty that they had not been fully involved in the black freedom struggle, this was one way for them to make a stand without risking their possible Olympic participation.[58]

What also became clear, however, was that some white and black ath-letes were very uncomfortable with the pressure and intimidation Edwards and the OCHR used to "encourage" black athletes to stay away from the NYAC meet. Edwards had warned prior to the event that "any black ath-lete who does cross the picket line could find himself in trouble, and I, nor any member of this committee, would not be personally responsible for anything that happened."[59] There was evidence that some institutions, Georgetown and Howard Universities, for example, had decided not to send a team to the events for fear of possible racial violence.[60] In all, nine black athletes did cross the picket line, the best known of whom was Bob Beamon, who would go on to win the long jump and set a new world record at Mexico City. Beamon gained entry to the arena covertly so as to avoid the protesters outside. He reported being contacted by supporters of the OCHR and facing pressure not to compete in New York. He also told reporters that he had been spoken to and unsettled by pro-boycott ath-letes during other athletic events.[61] Some of the protesters at the NYAC event were responsible for breaking sprinter James Dennis's glasses as he entered the meet. Dennis had previously received anonymous calls warning him not to compete. High jumper John Thomas had been forced to pull out of the NYAC event after also receiving threatening phone calls and being branded an "Uncle Tom" by Lee Evans, among others, in the press.[62] Those who did compete were angered that they should be threatened and pressured in such a way. Black sprinter Lennox Miller argued, "I don't like the idea of being told not to compete by somebody who does not know what track is all about or what athletics is all about."[63]

This, it would appear, was a veiled reference to Edwards and the OCHR, and certainly the reaction to the role they played goes some way toward qualifying the success of the NYAC boycott. In a theme that will be explored in greater depth below, it was the persona and tactics of the OCHR leadership that often alienated those who broadly shared their ideals. There was dislike for the influence of Black Power rhetoric and posturing alongside the strategy of a boycott that was more readily associated with the Civil Rights Movement. Even among those who aligned themselves with the movement there was unease about the leadership of Harry Edwards. Speaking of the time of the NYAC boycott, Vince Matthews describes a broad agreement with the views of the OCHR leadership but a lack of any meaningful contact with such views or in-depth understanding of the leadership's exact aims.[64] Dave Morgan, the leader of African American athletes' protest at the University of Texas at El Paso, made it very clear that he was not simply following Edwards's lead and that he had not been, nor would he be, swayed by the OCHR leader.[65]

Sympathetic white athletes were angered by the pressure put on their black teammates and the abrasive nature of the message of the OCHR and the movement surrounding it. John MacAloon saw his black teammates from the Catholic University of Washington, D.C., shaking after finishing their relay at the NYAC event; such was their fear of reprisals after competing. MacAloon argued that he and other white athletes were sympathetic to the human rights message but were dismayed by the pressure on black athletes to join the boycott and the generally uncompromising nature of the OCHR agenda.[66] Sportswriter Paul Zimmerman argued that the middle ground was becoming lost as the issues became polarized. White University of Tennessee athlete Richmond Flowers Jr. believed in racial progress and had been abused at track meets in the South because of his beliefs, but he competed at the NYAC meet because he did not agree with the political stance and methods of men like Edwards and H. Rap

Brown. Three white athletes from the University of Oregon expressed a willingness to help their black teammates' quest for human rights if they were approached in a "rational" way instead of with the scare tactics used by what they termed "black power guys."[67]

Therefore, while the boycott of the NYAC event was a publicity success for the OCHR and increased speculation about a possible Olympic boycott, the way in which it was achieved raised questions for the long-term sustainability of this form of civil rights protest through sport. Although the name of their umbrella organization carried the term "human rights," Edwards and his supporters were infusing racial protest through sport with an aggressive and uncompromising expression of black consciousness. The largely liberal ideology of the sporting world was uncomfortable with such radicalism. Sport was very clearly an institution of the American cultural mainstream, a mainstream that was increasingly under pressure as the 1960s progressed.

Edwards argued that the meet was a complete failure, that attendance was down by 50 percent and those who did attend were witness to mediocre performances. The *Chicago Defender* reported that the "boycott of the New York Athletic Club's Centennial Track meet at the new Madison Square Garden was an effective and right way of showing resentment against segregation."[68] The *New York Times* reported that the crowd may have been one thousand to two thousand fewer than the officially announced attendance that *Newsweek* termed a "near-capacity" crowd of 15,972 and that there were few good performances. This was not as unqualified an endorsement of the success of the boycott as that offered by Edwards, but it was confirmation of the significance of the OCHR efforts.[69] Edwards did praise the white athletes who supported the boycott by refusing to participate, but he qualified this with an assertion that they were only following the lead of black teammates and that many white schools took part mainly because of opposition to leaders like H. Rap Brown and himself.[70]

In many ways the NYAC boycott was the high-water mark for the OCHR. Since it had successfully used the boycott of a national sporting event to draw attention to racial discrimination, then why not a boycott of the Olympics themselves? Yet at this point there were key difficulties in extending the appeal of the movement. Even among those who supported the broad principles of the organization there was discomfort about the methods being utilized. On the "contested terrain" of race relations in sport there was a continuous realignment and repositioning in response to the pressure applied by the OCHR. Athletes and administrators, black and white, sought a position on the wider racial conflict and specifically the impact of this conflict in the sporting arena. Zimmerman argued that the middle ground was being drowned as extremes polarized the issues. Although this ground was not irreparably damaged, it was becoming increasingly difficult to inhabit as the practical realities of using sport as an arena for racial protest affected athletes and administrators.

Harry Edwards: Saint or Sinner?

Polarization arose partly because the leader of the OCHR and the proposed boycott of the Olympics was indisputedly Harry Edwards. His actions and rhetoric were heavily loaded with Black Power ideals and symbolism. For many athletes, their understanding of Edwards informed their perceptions of the movement he led. Edwards was and remains something of an enigma. One journalist described him as "moderate and militant, separatist and integrationist." President Robert Clark of San Jose State College referred to him as "both militant and responsible."[71] *New York Times* writer Robert Lipsyte described Edwards as a "moderate" in the same way that Jackie Robinson was a moderate: "Edwards thinks along constitutional avenues of protest and pressure."[72] One West Coast writer, however, described the sociology professor as a "black Hitler."[73] What is certain is that Edwards was absolutely central to the OCHR. Lipsyte argued that "without him [Edwards] nothing would have happened. . . . A powerful and polarizing figure . . . theoretically smart and tactically smart . . . he was essential."[74]

It is difficult not to concur with Lipsyte's assessment; however, we must appreciate the responses of athletes to Edwards and his ideas if we are to understand fully the progress of the OPHR in the months leading up to the Mexico City Olympics. Edwards's own experience of college sport left him extremely disillusioned with the system. He saw the sporting arena as a place in which young black men were exploited and was outraged by the double standard that persisted between life on and off the field. Edwards argued that there was no sense in playing a football game and "acting as if somehow we were representing the school. The school was exploiting us."[75] Nevertheless, he acknowledged that for many black athletes a realization of the inequalities they faced did not come easily; they needed to be educated in this respect. "The athletes did not demand a revolt; they did not foment a black athletic struggle. That was a vision that was projected, that some athletes, a minority of black athletes, subsequently identified with. It was not started by black athletes. They had to be propagandized, they had to be educated, [but] they were particularly disinclined to become involved in unconventional or controversial politics, because it could end up getting them kicked off the team, or they could lose their scholarship."[76]

It was Edwards who was the driving force behind this education process, and he won important converts to his cause at San Jose State. Teaching a class on racial minorities, Edwards had an audience of six hundred students. Tommie Smith described him as "magnetic. He challenged you. He used whatever he could to stop you in your tracks and get you to listen—black jargon, profanity, jokes, threats or a Ph.D. soliloquy on history."[77] As a former athlete himself with an imposing physical presence, Edwards won the support and following of world-class athletes like Smith, Lee Evans, and John Carlos. When he met Edwards, Martin Luther King Jr. observed, "I see why those folks are so scared of you."[78] He was one of the "few leaders of that time who was bigger than most of the athletes that he was talking to, which is great currency in the sports world."[79] Sprinter Vince Matthews found Edwards to be a persuasive figure and an imposing individual and agreed with his analysis of the place of black people in the United States.[80]

Many white athletes' views of the OPHR were shaped by their response to Edwards's message and, equally important, his manner of delivering it. Pole-vaulter Bob Seagren claimed that he was unfamiliar with the aims of the OPHR and had only a very broad understanding of what the black athletes were campaigning for. He did, however, recognize the name and rhetoric of Edwards as central to the movement before the 1968 Olympics. Seagren argued that Edwards was among the main individuals outside sports who were "trying to get the black athletes to boycott the Olympics."[81] George Young identified Edwards as the man who had started the drive for the boycott that was then kept alive by the media. Young believed this created pressure for many black athletes.[82] Hal Connolly asserted that many white athletes were "down on Harry Edwards." There was a perception that he was manipulating the athletes and there was a great concern that this could jeopardize the chances of the U.S. team at the Olympic Games.[83] Olympic swimmer Jane Swagerty believed the number of black athletes interested in some kind of boycott or protest statement to be only small and largely manipulated by Edwards and his political machine.[84] There was a perception that athletes were being influenced by outside forces. These views are consistent with a wider white unease concerning the role of militant racial forces in the late 1960s— forces, it was believed, that had a negative impact on the average African American. A 1969 *Newsweek* report found that many white "middle Americans" were increasingly uneasy and angry about the demands of black militants and the impact such demands had on the black population.[85] For many white athletes on or close to qualifying for the U.S. Olympic team, this feeling was further strengthened by a belief that sport was being sullied, that politics was intruding in an area where it was not wanted. Water polo player Bruce Bradley argued, "If there were any racial problems it was with the administration and the political situations people dragged it into. People made it more; I think Harry Edwards made it more a racial issue than it really was."[86]

Even those who gave support to the OPHR later expressed concern about the role of Edwards. Ralph Boston saw Edwards as the mouthpiece for the movement and argued, "As it turned out, it seems that Harry's whole involvement in the thing was to further the cause of Harry."[87] Phil Shinnick argued that the calls for a boycott of the Olympics that came from Edwards put too much pressure on athletes and that his demands came without a full appreciation of what a great sacrifice it was for athletes to give up an attempt at Olympic glory.[88] Hostility toward Edwards himself increased the probability that an Olympic boycott by black athletes was unlikely to materialize. Edwards's brash and abrasive character and the contentious hyperbole that flowed from him did much to promote a misunderstanding of and hostility toward the ideals of the OPHR. Even those sympathetic to the movement were not entirely comfortable with his role.

These feelings of discomfort were mutual, especially where white athletes were concerned. Edwards felt that even white supporters were not fully committed to the struggle that he was fighting. "I don't care how liberal whites were; there was a container of racism and white superiority that they could not escape." Edwards was given assurances by some athletes that they were sympathetic to the OPHR, but they expressed an opposition to the methods the movement was utilizing. "In other words, there is a price that they put on black freedom and there was no limit for us," commented Edwards. He argued that many white athletes would go only "so far up the road," and as a result the OPHR focused most of its energies on educating black athletes.[89] In this sense there was a considerable breakdown in communications at the interracial level. Edwards's hard-line position and the radical rhetoric he employed served to antagonize many white athletes, and at the same time Edwards spent little time attempting to soften the presentation of his message. In many respects, however, Edwards would have found any such softening extremely difficult. The dynamics of black militancy demanded a certain amount of machismo and radical posturing as necessary prerequisites for legitimacy in the black community. To sustain this legitimacy Edwards also had to keep up the momentum of the boycott movement.

Basketball Boycott?: An Equivocal Success

In a May 1968 profile of Harry Edwards, *New York Times* columnist Arnold Hano stated that the OPHR had achieved a great success when "twenty of the nation's finest collegiate basketball players, black and white—including Lew Alcindor, Elvin Hayes, Neal Walk, Bob Lanier, Westley Unseld, Larry Miller, and Don May—passed up the [Olympic] tryouts."[90] Douglas Hartmann refers to their nonparticipation as "another organizing success."[91] The issue was more complex than this, however. Speaking for the triumphant trio of the champion UCLA team—Alcindor, Warren, and Allen—athletic director J. D. Morgan said that their decision not to try out for the Olympics was not linked to the boycott movement. Morgan explained that the UCLA players regretfully decline their selection "due to the interruption of their academic program."[92] Alcindor argued, "School is still a big thing with me and I may have to work this summer too." All three players pointed to academic commitments and the desire to graduate as their reason for not going to the Olympics.[93] Elvin Hayes, the black Houston forward, cited the desire not to jeopardize his chances for a professional career when explaining his nonappearance at the Olympic tryouts. "I wouldn't want to do anything that would hurt my chances as a pro," he argued. "You don't just walk in there and play a game like you do in college. It's so much tougher. So I wouldn't want to report late or anything like that."[94] White basketball star Neal Walk chose not to attend the trials after consulting with his academic advisers and cited the pressures of classroom work as the reason why he would not try to make the Olympic team.[95] In a letter to the editor of the *New York Times* one reader attacked Arnold Hano's article, arguing that Westley Unseld of the University of Louisville had no part in the boycott and that he had decided not to go to the trials because he was tired. The correspondent went on to state that all at the university were proud of "big Wes," who did a lot of work in the local community and was a "true all-American." Hano replied that he

Lew Alcindor/Kareem Abdul-Jabbar. Alcindor spoke out against racism in America and boycotted the 1968 Olympic Games. *Los Angeles Times* Photographic Archive, Department of Special Collections, Charles E. Young Research Library, UCLA.

stood by his assessment pointing to the fact that the players had deliberately chosen not to go to the Olympics and argued that this was the important fact, regardless of the reasons they had given publicly.[96]

Hartmann seems broadly to support this view when he states that despite the excuses given, "most observers also recognized that many of the defections had something to do with the proposed Olympic boycott."[97] This is not, however, an entirely satisfactory conclusion. Certainly Lew Alcindor was a man who took a vocal and principled stance concerning the racial inequalities in America. He, along with Warren and Allen, to a lesser extent, had been involved in the initial OPHR proposal in November 1967, and Edwards pointed to him as an early supporter alongside Tommie Smith.[98] Indeed, Alcindor caused something of a controversy when explaining his decisions concerning the Olympics. On NBC's *Today* show in July 1968 Alcindor said that while he lived in the United States it was not really his country. A station break then interrupted the interview and Alcindor could not expand upon his statement. Alcindor gave a further interview the following week in which he clarified his comments, arguing, "We have been a racist nation with first-class citizens and my decision not to go to the Olympics is my way of getting the message across."[99] Certainly Alcindor, who later changed his name to Kareem Abdul-Jabbar after converting to Islam, was a deeply thoughtful man whose decision not to compete was born of a sharp sense of political consciousness.[100]

Nevertheless, none of the other basketball players mentioned in the Hano article went on to offer anything like the vocal support for the boycott expressed by Alcindor. To argue that by deliberately not participating they were showing support for the boycott ascribes an interpretation to their actions that is not of their own articulation. Neal Walk actually went on the record to say that he had not even contemplated the boycott; his was a truly practical decision based on the pressures of the classroom and the desire to graduate on time. "I want people to know," Walk said, "that I wanted to go to the Olympics. But I also want them to know that I was changing majors then and I knew that if I went to the trials, it would mean more delays in my school work."[101] Walk, Unseld, Hayes, and others gave no indication that they were part of a boycott, and as such it is wrong to align them with it. Indeed, Hayes told the *Chicago Defender* that he had not been contacted by any supporters of the Olympic boycott and that his main motivation for missing the games was to ensure he received an NBA contract.[102] Hano quotes Edwards as saying it is "not what they say, it is what they do."[103] On the contrary, surely given the fact that the aim of the

OPHR was to trumpet injustice and racial inequality, what athletes said and how they justified their actions was very important.

Furthermore, the USOC was less concerned about the connection between the OPHR and the withdrawal of the basketball players than it was about the actions of professional teams in poaching potential Olympic performers. In a telegram sent in March 1968, the USOC president, Douglas Roby, expressed concerns to Vice President Hubert Humphrey that NBA teams were recruiting possible members of the 1968 Olympic team. Roby asked for Humphrey's assistance in ensuring that this practice stopped so that a good-quality team could be sent to Mexico City.[104] It is certainly fair to conclude, then, in light of the evidence presented above, that the decision of several top basketball players to miss the Olympic trials was not an unqualified success for the OPHR by any means.

South Africa: The Movement Stalls

The spring of 1968 brought further ambiguous success for the OPHR, but at the same time the possibility of an Olympic boycott receded significantly. As mentioned, one of the original demands of the OCHR was that South Africa be banned from the Olympics because of its apartheid government. South Africa had been suspended from the Olympic movement in 1963 until such time as it could demonstrate an end to racial segregation in organized sport. Despite dissension by some IOC insiders, following a report that praised the advances made by the South African Non-Racial Olympic Committee in changing racial policies, a decision was made in February 1968 to reinstate the South Africans. Avery Brundage highlighted the positive force of sport and concluded that the Olympic movement had helped to improve the position of nonwhites in South Africa.[105]

President of the South African Olympic committee Frank Braun wrote to Brundage in April 1968 praising him for his stance supporting South African participation in the games to be held in Mexico. He argued that the existence of a multiracial team from South Africa would promote the cause of sports freedom. Braun wrote to Brundage in another letter, "We all feel that the Olympic movement and participation in the Games have so much to offer our non-whites that any further delays in the advancement of their opportunities in world sport will prove disastrous and bring to a stop the progress we are making in the right direction."[106] This was a classic statement of the "sport working to promote racial progress" ideal that Edwards and his supporters were so keen to expose.

Brundage was a vociferous spokesman for the belief that sport could promote social progress. He firmly believed that sport was a force for keeping "the flag of idealism flying."[107] During debate over U.S. participation at the 1936 Olympics in Berlin Brundage had stood firm against anyone who would allow politics to intrude on the sporting arena. He argued that the "Olympic Games are above all considerations of politics, race, color or creed."[108] In one of numerous letters Brundage sent to people who supported his condemnation of the actions of Smith and Carlos during the 1968 Games he outlined once again his clear philosophy. The head of the IOC explained, "We actively combat the introduction of politics into the Olympic movement and are adamant against the use of the Olympic Games as a tool or as a weapon by any organization."[109] Brundage's views concerning race, politics, and sport were somewhat one dimensional. He believed sport to be a force for social and racial progress and in this sense he endorsed its ability to influence the political realm. He firmly rejected, however, any interference by politics in the sporting world. Similarly, Brundage was a vocal opponent of any kind of racial segregation in sport; however, he was "not especially sensitive to discrimination outside of sports."[110]

For Edwards and his supporters, this one-dimensional view was characteristic of the whole sporting establishment and provided significant evidence of the need for a boycott of the Olympics. Edwards argued that the USOC displayed its racist demeanor when it supported South Africa's reinstatement and that this was symptomatic of the "intransigency of the white racist dominated Olympic movement."[111] African nations and many others in Asia threatened to boycott an Olympics that involved South Africa, and Edwards supported a proposal for an alternative African Games. The pressure on Brundage and the IOC increased as the Soviet Union threw its support behind the potential boycotters. The assassination of Martin Luther King Jr. on April 4 affected events as blacks mourned their fallen hero. African Americans across the United States grieved and raged at the death of the civil rights leader, and cities burned as race riots swept the country. Edwards pointed to the Olympic boycott as "a solemn memorial to Dr. King and his family" and increased his pressure on the Olympic authorities to expel South Africa.[112] Despite the pleading of the South African Olympic delegation that the IOC should not give in to boycotts and threats, Brundage was forced to concede to the inevitable and call a vote of the IOC members concerning South African participation. In a statement released on April 24, 1968, Brundage explained, "The International Olym-

Protesters outside the White House following the assassination of Martin Luther King Jr. in April 1968. King's death increased the pressure on African American athletes to visibly engage with the black freedom struggle. *U.S. News & World Report* Magazine Photograph Collection, Library of Congress, Prints and Photographs Division.

pic Committee is not bowing to threats or pressures of any kind from those who do not understand the true Olympic philosophy. Boycott is not a word used in sport circles." He went on to lament that the necessity of holding such a vote was "a sad commentary on the state of the world today."[113] He finally told reporters on April 28 that the South Africans were to be excluded from participation at the Mexico City Games. He remarked to a British interviewer, "We seem to live in an age when violence and turbulence are the order of the day."[114]

In his account of the Olympic boycott movement Edwards argued that, "following the example set by the OCHR and Afro-American athletes, the thirty-two nations of the Organization of African Unity declared that if South Africa were in fact allowed to participate, they would boycott the games in protest."[115] Not surprisingly, Edwards explains that it was his own organization that had taken the lead in campaigning for South African nonparticipation. Certainly, opposition to any athletic competition involving representatives of apartheid South Africa was part of the original OCHR statement of aims released in November 1967. Furthermore, when the IOC announced in February 1968 that South Africa had been invited to the Olympics, Edwards spoke out against the decision and proposed the staging of "African Games." There is also no doubt that the efforts of Edwards and the OCHR were acknowledged by the African nations that proposed a boycott of the Mexico City Games. Indeed, a letter to Edwards from the African National Congress in South Africa, dated March 5, 1968, stated, "Your views and support for our struggle against apartheid give us tremendous encouragement that all is not lost regarding public opinion in the U.S.A."[116]

The wording of this expression of gratitude is telling, however. The main role of the OCHR was to express opposition to the opinion of the USOC that South Africa should be allowed to compete in Mexico City; any impact that Edwards had was confined to the shaping of public debate in the United States. The main reasons why Brundage and the IOC had to reinstate the ban on the South Africans stemmed from the dynamics of international politics and the stance of the Mexican organizing committee, not pressure applied by Edwards and the OCHR. The potential boycott of a games including South Africa by not only African nations but also the Islamic world and the Communist bloc constituted a serious challenge to the IOC.[117] Furthermore, the Mexican Olympic hosts were determined that South Africa should not attend the games. Attempting to project the image of a defender of Third World countries and determined to cast off the perception of Mexican subservience in relation to more "developed" nations, the organizing committee intensively lobbied the IOC to ban the South African team. Indeed, Mexican president Gustavo Díaz Ordaz stated that the dignity of the nation depended on ensuring that the South Africans should not attend the games.[118] The Mexican organizing committee sent representatives to meet with the African nations that were threatening to boycott the games and assure them that they supported their aspirations and were against racial discrimination and that the decision to allow South Africa to compete was solely the choice of the IOC.[119] The Mexican authorities were aware of prevailing negative foreign interpretations of their nation—most notably from those in the developed world who supported South African participation—and the hosting of the games represented an opportunity to assemble "a coherent marketing approach that leveraged the nation's perceived strengths while simultaneously reconfiguring (and erasing) its alleged weaknesses."[120] For the Mexican organizing committee, ensuring that the South African team did not attend the games was an important element in seizing this opportunity.

In a letter to David Cecil, Lord of Exeter, Pedro Ramirez Vázquez, the chairman of the Mexican organizing committee, outlined his objections to South African participation. Vázquez spoke of his country's desire to "adhere to the lofty ideals of the Olympic Movement." He argued that the games offered an "extraordinary opportunity . . . to the Mexican people to receive the youth of the world—an opportunity now threatened by the political interests of a minority that has done nothing to provide equality of opportunity for its young athletes in its own territory."[121] There was considerable pressure from the Mexicans to stop the participation of the South Africans. They were delighted when J. W. Westerhoff, secretary general of the IOC, officially notified Vázquez of the decision to withdraw the official invitation to South Africa and asked the Mexican organizing committee to make the necessary arrangements concerning their nonparticipation.[122]

Although Brundage had clearly been in favor of the South Africans' appearance at the games, Mexican officials made clear their gratitude that he had made the decision to call a vote on the issue and then withdraw the country's invitation. Vázquez wrote to Brundage that he had conveyed the decision on South African nonparticipation to President Díaz Ordaz. He went on to assure the head of the IOC that he had "publicly declared that all your acts have been motivated by a sincere feeling of friendship towards Mexico."[123] It is notable that once the decision had been made to withdraw the invitation to the South Africans, the Mexican IOC vice president, José de Clark, was instrumental in encouraging the immediate reelection of Brundage for another four-year term as head of the IOC.[124] The main driving forces behind excluding South Africa from the games were undoubtedly to be found in the higher echelons of the IOC and its negotiations with the Mexican organizing authorities.

Therefore, the role played by Harry Edwards and the OCHR in the decision to reinstate the ban on South African participation was negligible. The main part played by Edwards and his supporters was to stimulate debate on the issue in the United States itself. What is crucial, nevertheless, is the impact of this decision on the OPHR and potential U.S. Olympians. Paul Hoffman, who was a prominent member of the group of white athletes who vocally supported the OPHR, saw an inequality in the significance of the demands made by the movement. The six main demands of the OCHR were "like an eclectic mix of big and little, or more specific and less specific," he argued. The record of the NYAC with respect to race relations was poor, but "certainly it was not a logical parallel [to draw] with apartheid South Africa."[125] Hoffman could see the greater importance of the South Africa issue alongside other demands made by the OCHR and it is fair to speculate that many athletes were able to grasp the importance of such an international issue. For some prospective competitors, the significance of the South Africa ban was accentuated by the fact that rivals for Olympic medals would not be attending Mexico City. Jane Swagerty, a teenage swimmer on the U.S. team, had the advantage of swimming her 100-meter backstroke event without competition from the world-record holder, a South African.[126]

The realization of a ban on South African participation had a major impact on the OPHR; it appeared to lessen the need for a boycott by African American athletes. Quarter-miler Vince Matthews asked his teammate and OPHR organizer Lee Evans what the direction of the movement would be after the South African decision had been made. Evans was somewhat vague in his reply: "Nobody knows where it is heading but we are going to stick together."[127] The *New York Times* reported that the decision to ban South Africa was a help to the USOC and caused members of the OPHR to have second thoughts concerning any boycott activity.[128] Certainly the IOC hoped that this would be the case. Indeed, alluding to Edwards, one member of the Olympic executive committee argued, "We did not want that chap from California coming down to Mexico City and setting off riots. We had to think of the safety of the young people involved in the Games themselves, especially the white South Africans competing. Suppose one of them should be killed in a riot?"[129] Clearly the IOC hoped that the exclusion of the South Africans was the end of the matter.

It was obvious, however, that the issue was not going to go away. With the likelihood of a boycott receding, sporting administrators became worried about alternative forms of protest that might be utilized by politically minded athletes. The USOC struggled with the problems of possible boycotts and political action to the extent that they had to take an unusually large number of athletes to altitude training and had to put off final selection of the team until much later than usual. Roby wrote to Brundage in the summer of 1968 informing him that a board of consultants had been set up to meet with athletes and counsel them against any undesirable action. Jesse Owens was made chairman of this board, which included three other African Americans. Roby also felt it necessary to mention that one of the track and field coaches, Stan Wright, and one of the medical staff, Dr. Plummer, were also black.[130] The head of the USOC seemed to be suggesting that having African Americans among the Olympic staff alone was likely to have a calming influence on politically minded black athletes.

Avery Brundage. The head of the International Olympic Committee was determined not to allow politics to interfere with sport. Avery Brundage papers, RS: 26/20/37, box 299, University of Illinois.

Part of the reason that U.S. sporting authorities were so concerned was that Edwards had been determined to keep up the pressure on the issues. The OPHR leader had argued in November 1967 that the situation in America was no different from the situation in South Africa, claiming that oppression of blacks in the United States "is as bad as that of South Africa, America has to be exposed for what it is."[131] It was this assertion that so offended many athletes and administrators. In America in the late 1960s, following passage of the major legislation of the Civil Rights Movement, the popular perception was that life for African Americans was better than it had been at any other time in the nation's history. Added to this, the powerful belief in sport as a positive racial force prohibited an appreciation of the point that Edwards and the OPHR were making. In the eyes of many, the expulsion of South Africa was seen as the final step in a quest for "justice" that had gone too far; to persist with calls for an African American boycott of the Olympics was ludicrous. It was clear, however, that even with the possibility of a boycott fast receding the ripples created by the OPHR were reaching unexpected areas of the sporting world.

A Dashiki in the Boat House: The OPHR and Harvard Crew

On August 1, 1968, the *New York Times* reported that five members of the U.S. rowing team, all Harvard men—Scott Steketee, Curtis Canning, Cleve Livingston, David Higgins, and coxswain Paul Hoffman—were expressing public support for the OPHR.[132] In a press release drafted a week earlier the rowers stated, "We—as individuals—have been concerned with the place of the black man in American society and his struggle for equal rights. As members of the United States Olympic team, each of us had come to feel a moral commitment to support our black team-mates in their efforts to dramatize the injustices and inequities which permeate our society." Expressing an expanded conception of the role of the athlete and of sport in general in the construction of race relations, the statement went on to argue, "We feel that working to correct racial injustices is the undeniable task of all athletes and all men, black and white. Surely the spirit of the Olympic Games requires us, as white participants, to explore all the means at our disposal to further the cause of brotherhood and the claims to equality of our black colleagues."[133]

The Harvard rowers were motivated by personal conviction that the racial problems in America needed to be solved by white and black communities working together. Cleve Livingston argued that the message of the OPHR was one that essentially upheld equality and democracy and, as such, was worthy of his support.[134] Having grown up in the West Indies on an island with an overwhelmingly black population, Paul Hoffman described issues of race as "totally irrelevant" to him.[135] It can be argued that the expressions of the Harvard rowers and the attention they drew marked a significant, if transitory, shift in the course of the OPHR. The general perception of the aims of Edwards and his organization was that of a radical movement intent on disrupting the sacred institution of sport and embarrassing the U.S. Olympic team and the nation. At a time of significant race riots and the predominance of a Black Power agenda, the OPHR was viewed as a threat to mainstream American values. The statement by the Harvard crew and their intended aims brought a new dimension to the Olympic protest movement, however.

The word *protest* is used intentionally here. Possibly more so than the reinstatement of a ban on South African participation in Mexico City, the involvement of the rowers signaled a move away from any real prospect of a boycott and shifted attention to what might occur at the games themselves. In their initial meetings with Edwards, Hoffman and Livingston made it clear that they were members of a team and would do nothing to jeopardize the prospects of that team. Furthermore, they stated that they were not in favor of any kind of boycott and would not waste the hard work they had put in to get to the Olympics by participating in any such activity.[136] Also, the statement released to the press hinted at an ambiguity concerning the nature of any protest. The rowers stated, "Because we do not know what specific form the black athletes' demonstration will take, we do not consider ourselves tied to any specific action. It is their criticism of society which we here support."[137]

The statement by the Harvard men that they did not know what type of protest was planned was telling. Following the renewal of the ban on South Africa and because of disquiet among some black athletes concerning the role played by Edwards and the pressure placed upon competitors to support the boycott of the NYAC, the likelihood of a boycott of the Olympics increasingly receded. Indeed, later in August it was reported that any possibility of a boycott was now dead.[138] Edwards himself later suggested that the end of any realistic attempt at a boycott came sometime in mid-August. It was decided that even if a handful of black athletes did boycott the Olympics their places would be taken by other top-class African American performers, thus rendering their gesture largely futile.[139]

The aim of the Harvard men was to stimulate discussion among fellow athletes concerning the problems facing African American athletes. As such the members of the crew produced a questionnaire that outlined their own views and invited other white athletes to engage in a discourse concerning the treatment of black athletes. Hoffman described the document as an attempt to get other white athletes "to start a dialogue with the black athletes and try and learn about what they think and what they are saying and what their experiences are and how we can make the reality a little closer to the ideal."[140]

The questionnaire, which was sent to athletes as they qualified for the Olympic team, outlined the Harvard rowers' own views on the problems facing black athletes and asked for responses to these issues from the other athletes. It reaffirmed the expanded vision of the role of sport in shaping race relations and the criticism of America's racial situation in stating, "the goal of the Games is the fostering of brotherhood, not the creation of a false image of racial harmony as a boost to our national ego." The questionnaire also made it clear that the rowers felt that they could draw attention to the plight of black athletes without having to boycott the games. It read, "we do not feel it is necessary to abandon this competition in order to demonstrate our concern for the problems of our country and to show support for our black team mates."[141] In a number of handwritten notes attached to the questionnaire and dated September 1968, members of the rowing team asked members of other sections of the Olympic squad to discuss the issues raised by the questionnaire.[142]

Scott Steketee stated, "America can only acquire greater dignity and greater hope by facing its most grievous problem openly and before the world." Edwards responded that it "was beautiful to see some white cats willing to admit they've got a problem and looking to take some action to educate their own."[143] Indeed, Edwards included the Harvard rowers among the athletes to whom he dedicated his written account of the OPHR, *The Revolt of the Black Athlete.* Certainly the symbolism of the cooperation between a group of white students from Harvard and the man who referred to the president as "Lynchin Baines Johnson" was significant. When it was announced that Edwards would be appearing at a press conference with the crew the switchboard at Harvard began flashing manically as reporters sought an explanation of the events. The sight of Edwards dressed in a dashiki, black beret, and sunglasses sitting alongside the clean-cut, collar-and-tie-wearing team captain Curtis Canning in the nineteenth-century Harvard boat house was a powerful realization of the potential of sport to bring disparate groups together to further the cause of racial equality and social justice.[144]

Possibly more significant than the press interest in the statements made by the Harvard crew were the reactions among athletics administrators. John J. Carlin, chairman of the U.S. Olympic Rowing Committee, wrote to acting executive director of the USOC Everett D. Barnes offering his suggestions for curtailing the actions of the Harvard rowers. Carlin originally considered forcing the crew to sign a "cease and desist order" or face expulsion from the team. He then considered that this could be viewed as a threat that might produce adverse publicity. Instead it was decided that the rowers should be asked to sign a statement agreeing to stop any planned demonstrations. If they did then participate in any action they could be sent home.[145] The Harvard crew had already written to the USOC a week before Carlin sent his letter to Barnes, expressing their desire to foster a dialogue among athletes on the racial problems facing wider society. The rowers argued that black athletes and those who wanted to support them were seeking to communicate to the rest of society the situation that black people faced. They asserted that this was not contrary to the spirit of the Olympics but was "in fact in accord with that spirit, for it is in the interests of brotherhood and understanding among men."[146]

Hoffman described the general attitude of athletic administrators at that time toward athletes, both black and white, as dismissive. They were given no role in the organization and governance of sport and their opinions were never sought. "All athletes were basically treated as not fully logical, thinking species that were being dressed and sent out to compete."[147] This opinion is confirmed by the fact that the response of the USOC to the rowers' reasoned explanation of their stance was a letter requesting a signature from the crew stating that they would not engage in any protest activities. When they were in training in Colorado before going on to Mexico City, the USOC attempted "outreach" toward the athletes through a liaison committee, the same committee that Roby told Brundage was going to be used to diffuse any tension and possible protest activities. The Harvard crew was lectured about the responsibilities associated with competing for their country by a USOC official. Essentially the representative of the USOC who met with them attempted to sound out their ideas and motivations and tried to ascertain the possibility of them protesting in any way.[148]

The OPHR's intended original aim was a black boycott of the 1968 Olympics. It was perceived as a radical and dangerous organization by athletics administrators and was harshly criticized. Indeed, such was the USOC's hostility to the movement that when a group of well-educated, white Harvard rowers attempted to understand the motivations of angry black athletes, to reach for the middle ground, and to open a constructive dialogue on the grievances inspired by wider American social problems, they were treated with hostility and suspicion. The threat of a boycott of the Olympics by black athletes horrified a liberal sporting establishment that had convinced itself that sport promoted racial progress. Any further intrusion into the sports world by political discussions was fiercely resisted.

Paradigm Locked: The Limits of Civil Rights Protest through Sport

The questionnaires sent out to teammates by the Harvard crew received little attention from fellow white athletes. Certainly no replies were received by the rowers—no responses to their ideas, either positive or negative. The dialogue that they tried to start was very much one-sided. It is worth noting, however, that some of the questionnaires were passed on directly to the USOC.[149] It is fair to speculate that this action can be deemed critical of the attempt to stimulate a dialogue, almost a gesture of loyalty for the line taken by the U.S. Olympic administration.

The response of white athletes and administrators to the OPHR from its inception until the eve of the games and the reaction to the stand taken by the Harvard oarsmen are characteristic of a "conditional" relationship between sport and race in the late 1960s. For many years sport was seen as a key area of American life in which blacks could achieve progress incommensurate with the advancement that could be made in the remainder of the social, cultural, economic, and political spheres. This progress came with the condition that they continue to excel within the given sporting discipline and that they play by the rules of the game. These rules extended to life off the field and out of the arena and required athletes to respect the unwritten code of veneration of the sporting ideals of fair play and equality for all. The black athlete who had achieved excellence, and with it some fame, should be grateful. Wider social and political problems were not to intrude into the sporting arena. In the late 1960s this prevailing opinion in the sporting sphere found a counterpart in the wider social world. Following the political achievements of the Civil Rights Movement, many mainstream Americans felt that the racial problem had been addressed, that black people had been given their equality and should now work to enjoy the benefits. At the same time as the OPHR and its brash spokesman, Harry Edwards, were confronting the perceived sporting ideal, so too were angry young black men challenging the prevailing political position that equality had been delivered and America was a better place.

John Roche, a former adviser to President Johnson, told *Newsweek* in October 1969 that many nonblack groups felt that the rules were being changed and that this had allowed African Americans to advance too far.[150] The view that the OPHR was breaking the rules, that it was pushing racial politics into sport, was the major reason why it received such a hostile reception. This reception displays the ideological straitjacket that restricted the sporting arena from furthering the cause of racial equality and social justice.

The attempts by the Harvard crew, and others who will be discussed in the following chapter, to inhabit the middle ground of the debate met with limited positive response. Because of prevailing racial attitudes, a commitment to the ideal of the purity of sport, a single-minded focus on a particular discipline and event, or a convergence of all three, the OPHR's attempt to produce a significant change in the attitudes of athletes and administrators failed. The events in Mexico City further highlighted the great difficulties faced by athletes who tried to engage in the civil rights struggle.

Before analyzing these events we must first turn to a closer investigation of the ways in which the black freedom struggle affected sports faculties on college campuses. Simultaneous with the development of the OPHR, there were several racially charged incidents that affected the athletics departments of universities across the United States in 1968. An exploration of these local case studies further illuminates the difficulties faced by athletes who wished to use their position as sportsmen to engage in the civil rights struggle. While some of these case studies display a genuine attempt by some individuals to transcend their position as a student-athlete and play a part in the black freedom struggle, others reveal a different dynamic.

The black athletic revolt on campus had the potential to destroy sports programs and disrupt winning teams. In a way that served only to strengthen the resolve of those who believed racial politics should not be allowed to affect the sporting arena, some young men confused discipline with discrimination. Again, by utilizing oral histories collected some thirty-five or more years after the events we can gain a wider perspective on campus unrest. The extent to which white and black athletes themselves understood each other's attitudes and motivations had a huge impact on the potential to use sport as a forum for furthering the civil rights struggle.

Not all athletes who engaged in the revolt did so with the same sense of purpose and ideological agenda as those who had supported an Olympic boycott. This created further problems for the potential of sport to significantly affect the advance of the black freedom struggle.

3

The Black Athletic Revolt on Campus

We figure it's only right. We represent our race and our school in
football, basketball, and track but still we didn't have a pom-pom girl.
                                    —Don Shanklin, University of Kansas, football

[Black athletes] were dropped into an environment that was almost
impossible for them to succeed in . . . two entirely different universes
all of a sudden converging.
                                    —Bob Wolfe, University of California, Berkeley, basketball

Far from the political activism surrounding Harry Edwards, the sprinters
of Speed City, and the Harvard rowers was the University of Kansas athletics department. The institution's teams were known as the Jayhawks—
as a reference to the violence and turmoil of the Civil War era—and were
members of the Big Eight Conference. In 1968 they would improve on
their relatively mediocre performances of the previous two years and tie
for the position of Big Eight football champions. On a Saturday in May
of that year the players gathered to participate in the varsity intrasquad
scrimmage at Memorial Stadium. Play was divided into three periods of
twenty minutes. The offense was awarded points for making first downs
or touchdowns while the defense scored when they stopped first downs,
forced fumbles, or intercepted passes. Although the defense won the first
two periods, the Jayhawk offense dominated the third period to record an
overall victory of 52–49.

Coach Pepper Rodgers declared he was pleased with the scrimmage.
He commented, "The offense beat themselves by making mistakes—
fumbles and interceptions. If you eliminate mistakes you have a chance to

win." The coach singled out a few individuals for special mention after a successful spring practice that left the team in a better position than in the previous year.[1]

Despite Rodgers's no-nonsense analysis, this scrimmage was not an entirely unremarkable event and the campus in Lawrence, Kansas, had not escaped the racial tensions that were prevalent in many other areas of the nation. Two days previous to the scrimmage that marked the end of spring practice, T. J. Gaughan, a white member of the team, entered the locker room. He began talking with other members of the team as he changed for practice. His attention was then slowly drawn to a source of amusement elsewhere in the room. One of the team was stripped and in the process of putting on his uniform when Coach Rodgers walked in. Gaughan and others began to smirk at the scene that was developing. The player inadvertently providing the levity was black. As he looked around the locker room he quickly saw that he was the only black player there. Rodgers told the young man that he had better put his clothes back on and go up to the Student Union to join the rest of the black players who were boycotting practice. Gaughan remembered, "Poor Vernon forgot about it or had taken a nap and missed it!"[2]

African American Jayhawk football players were protesting the perceived discriminatory policies of the university. They were attempting to use sport as a lever to extract concessions, just as Edwards and Noel had done at San Jose the previous year. This sort of activism took place on many campuses across the United States in 1968. In fact, Harry Edwards asserted that in the 1967–1968 academic year there were demonstrations in the athletic departments of some thirty-seven major college campuses.[3] Significant protests followed at several institutions throughout 1969. The majority of these incidents have received only brief historical attention, with just one article devoted to comparative analysis.[4] A full understanding of the course of the black athletic revolt requires that these protests be given closer scrutiny. They reveal a further dimension to the relationship between the black athletic revolt and the black freedom movement. Teams were disrupted, racial tensions heightened, and the civil rights struggle became intertwined with concerns over racial identity and team discipline. White and black athletes found it difficult to maintain a team ethos when faced with issues of racial politics. Furthermore, some black athletes, facing pressure to reconcile their role as student athletes with an increasing black militancy, confused issues of racial prejudice with team discipline. This further hardened the stance of sports administrators against any intrusion by the civil rights struggle into the sports world.

The case studies that follow have been chosen because they highlight different elements of the intersection between sport and civil rights activism on the campus. At the University of California, Berkeley, we can see the way in which an athletics department was affected by black players' search for identity as the Black Power Movement encouraged a rising race consciousness. The Berkeley case study also highlights the extent to which Edwards's calls for black athletes to engage with a more radical racial agenda could lead to confusion between discrimination and discipline. At Marquette and Kansas Universities leading college athletes used their position as leverage in order to gain concessions from the administrators of their institutions. In these cases, athletes engaged in protest activity that supported the demands of wider campus civil rights causes.

Racial Unrest Rocks Berkeley

In January 1968 racial problems engulfed the athletics department at the University of California, Berkeley. The racial situation on campuses in California, and at Berkeley in particular, created an environment that was especially susceptible to manifestations of the black athletic revolt. By the late 1960s West Coast university teams were filled with white and black athletes. Indeed, in the early 1960s students at UCLA successfully linked football to the civil rights struggle when protesting about segregated southern teams. A threatened boycott if an all-white University of Alabama squad were invited to the 1961 Rose Bowl shows the extent to which sporting integration was increasingly accepted by West Coast institutions.[5]

Furthermore, student activism at Berkeley itself was something of a tradition. The San Francisco Bay Area was one of the most left-leaning and liberal regions in the United States and this was reflected on the Berkeley campus. It was the only university in the country to sustain a faculty revolt against anticommunist policies in 1949 and 1950. A year before the Berkeley revolt of 1965, students from the campus were heavily involved in a series of successful sit-in campaigns that were designed to secure jobs for blacks with local business firms.[6] Therefore, the Berkeley campus provides a clear example of an environment that can be characterized as post–Civil Rights Movement. Support for the principles of racial integration and equality was long established on campus. The manifestation of the black athletic revolt at Berkeley revolved less around issues of racial segregation and was more focused on team discipline and racial identity.

Unlike the events at San Jose the previous year, when Edwards had used the threat to a sporting contest as leverage to force some change to university policy, at Berkeley the black athletic revolt emerged from a specific incident involving confrontation between a player and a coach. That coach was head basketball coach Rene Herrerias and the player was black star center Bob Presley. Events were not interpreted racially in the first instance, however. Indeed, as black player Waddell Blackwell remembered, "It turned racial quickly but I don't remember it being racial starting out."[7]

Herrerias suspended Presley after a breach of team discipline—he had missed a practice session. After serving two days of that suspension Presley was reinstated. The coach explained, "The matter is personal in that it is a coach-player situation and I feel that the violation involved and the penalty imposed are comparable." Herrerias expressed hopes that the matter was now closed.[8] Nevertheless, it became apparent that the matter was far from closed and in fact provided the spark to ignite racial tensions that lay beneath the surface of the athletics department. The white players on the team announced that they believed pressure had been put on the coach to reinstate Presley simply because he was black. They argued that they would refuse to play any further games until the constraints placed on Herrerias had been lifted. The white players were soon talked around by their coach but the following day twenty-five of the school's black athletes, including Presley and football star Bobby Smith, presented a list of grievances and demands.[9] The actions of the white players provoked the response of their black teammates and showed the depth of racial tension in the athletics department. The preamble to the black athletes' document argued, "Black players are sick and tired of giving their talent without receiving appreciation and due recognition from the athletic department and the mass media."[10] Several coaches were singled out for criticism and called on to resign.

The statement went on to outline the financial problems black athletes faced, alleging that summer jobs were given out to white players first and calling for the removal of business manager Pat Farran. It was further argued that coaches showed a lack of "cultural sensitivity" and assumed black athletes were academically inferior. Black students were left to fend for themselves when it came to finding accommodation. The statement went on to issue a demand for teams to be composed of the best players regardless of race and—potentially paradoxically—called on the university to hire coaching staff from a "minority background."[11] Quoted anonymously, one black athlete alleged, "There is no fraternal feeling on the athletics teams among the players, and the coaches have been unable to cope with the problem." Another stated, "This was the straw that broke the camel's back. The basketball team, as well as other school teams including football, will only allow one star and that star is always white."[12]

There had been tension between white and black players on the basketball and football teams before the Presley incident. Indeed, the swift way that incident was dealt with was expressly designed not to be provocative. Rather than sport being used as the arena to dramatize issues of wider racial conflict and injustice, at Berkeley the revolt emerged from within the athletics department and was focused specifically on the dynamic among players, coaches, and administrators. It was the complaints of the white players that their coach had been pressured to reinstate Presley that evoked the list of demands from their black teammates. They felt that the university was being too sensitive toward the black players and that fear of being accused of discrimination was compromising discipline. There were obviously racial tensions simmering under the surface in the athletics department; however, using the short-lived suspension of Presley as the trigger for a protest ensured a flawed strategy. The complaints of the black athletes expressed a clear desire for equality and a color-blind team ethic. Nevertheless, the focus on Presley and the expression of a particularly strong black identity militated against any sense of understanding from the white players on the team. More importantly, this racial identity and the public manifestations of it were perceived as excuses for indiscipline—indiscipline for which white players would be punished and for which they had no ready-made racial excuse.

The black athletic revolt at Berkeley developed a shape different from that at San Jose, but that is not to say that Edwards did not have some influence on events. He writes in *The Revolt of the Black Athlete* that his Olympic Committee for Human Rights lent its support to the "indigenous revolt" of the black students of the University of California.[13] In a fine article that covers events at Berkeley, David Wiggins states that he can find no independent written confirmation of the claim that Edwards gave support to the black athletes at Berkeley in any tangible, practical way.[14] While there appear to be no contemporary sources that corroborate Edwards's claim, basketball player Robert Abright explained that he saw Edwards on the campus "all the time."[15] Furthermore, Blackwell recalled phone calls between the San Jose professor and some black players on the team.[16] With the incident at San Jose, the demands of the OCHR, and the move to boycott the NYAC, events were not happening in isolation. It is therefore sensible to conclude that Edwards did have an influence on the events at Berkeley, even if the incident was "indigenous" in the first instance. Nevertheless, the primary focus on team unity and discipline provided far greater obstacles to the success of the revolt at Berkeley and raises questions about how that success should be defined. The dynamic of this protest was different from the OCHR's boycott against the NYAC and was certainly far removed from the kind of engagement with the civil rights struggle seen in the NAACP campaign against segregated spectators in the early 1960s. Focus on the breaking of team rules by black players provoked an extremely volatile situation.

The white players' perceptions of Presley shaped their responses to the black athletic revolt. Bob Wolfe remembered, "Presley had just been such an incredibly bad teammate all year. . . . He had been given every possible second, third, fourth, fifth, sixth, and seventh chance."[17] Tom Henderson described Presley as "a real problem."[18] Robert Tannenbaum, a spokesman for the white players, argued that Presley had constantly violated team discipline. He argued that Coach Herrerias, far from being racist or incompetent, as some black athletes had alleged, had in fact shown great restraint in putting up with Presley's attitude and consistent transgressions.[19] Essentially what the white players saw in the black players' behavior, and specifically the behavior of Presley, was the use of the race card and the targeting of their coach as a scapegoat.

The disharmony between white and black players emanated from a distinctive dynamic revolving around the relationship between the white coaches and their white and black players. It was reported that "black athletes and white athletes have taken polar stands, partly in response to one another, partly in response to their coaching staffs."[20] We see at Berkeley a significant element of the black athletic revolt on the campus and one directly addressed neither by Edwards at San Jose nor in the Olympic boycott movement; namely, the issue of team discipline. Racial explanations and justifications for conflict with coaching staff created considerable disharmony and damaged the aims of the black athletic revolt because they allowed white athletes to focus on a double standard that worked to their detriment rather than appreciating a real racial inequality that could be protested against by black athletes.

Nevertheless, the responses of the athletic administrators at Berkeley seemed to signal success for the black athletes in relation to their initial, specific demands. Basketball coach Herrerias and athletic director Pete Newell resigned in a move that Edwards described as a "victory for the rebelling Afro-Americans."[21] Herrerias was replaced as head coach by his former aide, Jim Padgett. Padgett was well liked by the black players, many of whom he had personally recruited from the Deep South. The black coach and former Cal basketball and baseball star Earl Robinson was appointed as Padgett's assistant and a black coach was also added to the football squad.[22] Further recommendations were made by the chancellor's fact-finding committee, including the establishment of a more wide-ranging black studies program and plans to bring more black students to the Berkeley campus.[23] The university responded in order to defuse the tension and ensure that the basketball team continued to function.

The changes made by the university were in some respects superficial, and while the tension on the team was reduced, the progress toward racial understanding would appear limited. In his account of events at Berkeley, David Wiggins concludes that the black athletes had a lot of respect for Padgett and recommendations were followed in order to improve relations with black students. He paints a picture of generally improved conditions on the basketball team and the campus as a whole. Herrerias was used as something of a scapegoat by the black athletes, and once they had drawn attention to the wider problems of discrimination and seen the university make changes, things improved with Padgett and Robinson in charge.[24] Indeed, Blackwell argued that Earl Robinson was a "unifying" force on the team and that things were more "harmonious" under Padgett's leadership.[25]

This harmony was only surface deep, however. The dissipation of tension on the team was perceived by some white athletes as a result of Padgett's more relaxed attitude toward discipline. Robert Abright explained that the new coach "put up with . . . Presley's actions because of his desire to win."[26] Many white players felt that a clash of ideas between Padgett and Herrerias provided part of the explanation for the roots of the tension on the team.[27] The feeling that black protests had pushed university administrators to change coaching staff and to be more lenient on the black players meant that a truly unified interracial team was compromised. The white players on the team had protested originally that their coach had been pressured into reinstating Presley just because he was black.

The events at Berkeley represent an element of the black athletic revolt very different from the stand by Smith and Carlos on the Olympic victory podium, the principled decision of Lew Alcindor, or the attempt to engage in dialogue pursued by the Harvard rowers. At Berkeley, black basketball and football players were attempting to assert their racial identity to express the double-consciousness of being both black and American. In this way they were engaging with the racial changes taking place in wider society. Theirs was not, however, an idealistic stand. It lacked the dignity and integrity of other attempts to use the sporting arena to further the cause of civil rights. Oral histories reveal a dynamic to the events at Berkeley that had roots in a power struggle indirectly influenced by racial matters. These recollections also reveal the extent to which young men struggled to shape their own identity in new and difficult surroundings.

The initial friction on the team appears to have emanated from something of a power struggle between Herrerias and Padgett. This was intimately intertwined with the disciplinary problems surrounding Presley and provided for the initial team disunity that then became a racial incident. Herrerias favored the use of a small man up front who could move the ball around and execute set plays. Assistant Coach Padgett and the black players were pushing for a different offensive tactic that utilized Presley's height and looked for fast, incisive breaks.[28] The white players felt that this clash of ideas was undermining Herrerias's position as the head coach.[29]

Tom Henderson argued that Herrerias was stabbed in the back by his assistant, Jim Padgett, who became the new head coach.[30] Abright described Padgett as "in the ear of a lot of the black players."[31] Wolfe argued that the tension on the team "amplified right from square one with Padgett's arrival as assistant coach." In Wolfe's opinion, "the sense of all the white players was that he [Padgett] just wanted all of his guys in there and he was constantly working at Herrerias to get his guys in there."[32] Padgett knew how to relate to the black players better than Herrerias, but this was perceived by the white players as detrimental to the team. The dissipation of the tension on the team with Padgett in charge was somewhat superficial. The lack of tension came from the fact that Padgett did not demand as much from the black players. He was willing to allow Presley to opt out of certain practice drills and other training routines.[33]

Active recruiting of more black students and athletes to the campus was a response to the civil rights activism of the mid- to late 1960s. In many respects the university was adopting policies that supported the ideal of sport as a positive racial force. The athletics department saw a way to improve the quality of its teams and show the racial progress that sport could bring. Nevertheless, to a large extent the university authorities had brought the Presley incident on themselves by recruiting a significant number of black athletes to the athletics department but leaving them largely isolated on a campus with very few other black students.[34] Wolfe described the black athletes being "dropped into an environment that was almost impossible for them to succeed in, . . . two entirely different universes all of a sudden converging."[35] Blackwell argued, "It was a difficult transition. . . . a lot of the guys . . . were switching worlds, they were switching languages."[36] In this environment and with the increasing pressure to play some part in the racial protest movement, black athletes could point to incidents of discrimination and lodge protests, convincing themselves that they were making a stand for racial justice without compromising their role as an athlete on a team.[37]

Many of the white players saw the protests by their black teammates as a rejection of the traditional sporting ideals of team and discipline. The anger and disillusionment of some white team members still resonates today. The dominant opinion is that Presley broke team discipline and then provoked a racial confrontation. From a very early point in the events at Berkeley there was a widening of the racial divide as white and black players took stands that made it difficult to inhabit a middle ground. With the benefit of hindsight there is a recognition that many of the problems that arose stemmed from a cultural misunderstanding. Wolfe recalled, "We were insensitive to issues that might have led to maybe cutting him [Presley] more slack."[38] At Berkeley we see less of an attempt to promote civil rights protests through sport and more of the clashing racial cultures of young white and black men thrown together on a basketball team. Events reveal an important facet of the black athletic revolt without offering an unequivocal example of sport being used to promote the black freedom struggle.

Trouble Off the Basketball Court at Marquette

In the spring of 1968 racial unrest came to the Marquette University campus in Wisconsin. The student protest group Respond issued a number of ultimatums to university officials concerning the institution's policy toward equal opportunities. In response to equivocation by the officials, several black students threatened to withdraw from Marquette. Among their number were basketball stars Frank Edwards, Dean Memminger, Joe Thomas, George Thompson, Blanton Simmons, and Pat Smith. The

George Thompson, one of the black basketball stars who temporarily left the Marquette team to protest against racial practices of the university. Intercollegiate Athletic Hall of Fame Collection, Raynor Memorial Libraries, University of Marquette Archives.

response of the coach and the white players on the team and the focus on wider university policy rather than on team discipline reveal important differences between the impact of the black athletic revolt at Marquette and its impact at Berkeley.

The incident at Marquette was not linked to the broader OPHR movement in the same way that events at San Jose and Berkeley were. Certainly, Harry Edwards was not an influential actor in the events in Wisconsin. Black player Joe Thomas explained, "We at Marquette were rather isolated in terms of what was going on in wider areas and other campuses. . . . We were not aware that there was a wider attempt through athletics at other college universities or through other civil rights movements to have a wider and greater effect."[39] Indeed, the incident at Marquette did not emanate from inside the athletic department in the way it did in California. Student protest leaders focused their attention on the racial policies of the university as a whole, and the involvement of the basketball players followed. This fact helped to ensure that the protest followed a different path than the one taken at Berkeley. The protest at Marquette revealed the extent to which a boycott could be used as leverage to elicit change. Nevertheless, the role of sport and the importance of having a winning team compromised the extent of this change and its wider significance. In many respects events at Marquette were closely in tune with the ideology of the OPHR. Students sought to use their position as sports stars to draw attention to wider civil rights struggles.

Civil rights activism at Marquette was organized by Students United for Racial Equality (SURE). The organization was founded in 1965 and was initially engaged in civil rights marches, specifically targeting the slow pace of school integration in Milwaukee. SURE members engaged in a boycott of the public school system and organized a petition to express dissatisfaction with the school board's policy, which they argued maintained de facto segregation. Conscious of their participation at a Catholic university, SURE leaders emphasized their responsibilities as both citizens and Christians.[40]

In early 1968 black and white members of SURE began to put pressure on the university to focus on those of its policies that helped to perpetuate racial inequalities. Some of the students organized a fast and several were arrested after a sit-in.[41] Leaders of the movement stated, "The black man in this country does not trust the white man, not even the white liberal," and called on the university to tackle racism within its own institutions.[42] Following slow responses from university authorities, six demands were

presented on May 8, 1968. These demands reflected the increasing dominance of black leadership among the protesters, now organized under the
name Respond. Calls for the establishment of one hundred black scholarships, the adoption of black history courses, the sacking of the head of
campus security, and the hiring of black administrators reflected similar
demands on other campuses.[43] Respond spokesmen warned that if the university did not meet its demands there would be significant consequences.
Jack Cummins, president of the graduate students' association, argued,
"There will not be violence but I promise you this—we will embarrass
this university."[44]

The black basketball players became involved in the protest movement because they shared the ideals of the demonstrators. Joe Thomas
explained that in his view Marquette had a responsibility to reach out to
the parts of the surrounding community that were poorly served by the university. The ghetto area five or six blocks down from the campus needed
an equal opportunities program to assist with the education of black youth
in the city.[45] An open letter from protesting students to university officials
argued, "Our identity as a Christian University is at stake. If we do not
involve ourselves actively and immediately in response to the racial crisis
which faces us, to the urgent needs of the poor and oppressed of our city
. . . we will simply cease to be credibly Christian."[46] Interviewed during a
rally organized by Respond, Blanton Simmons argued, "Dr. King said it
is cruel to tell a bootless people to pick themselves up by their bootstraps.
Let's join together to get those people some boots!"[47] George Thompson,
the star player of the basketball team, expressed his thanks to all those
who came to the rally and supported the demands of Respond.[48] The black
players were aware of their profile on campus and the extent to which they
especially could draw attention to the issues at hand.

University officials were concerned with the practicality of meeting
the demands of Respond and appeared to the demonstrators to be moving
too slowly. Marquette vice president Father McAuley told the protesters
that the university would try to meet Respond's demands but where more
scholarships for blacks were concerned there were funding limitations and
the university could not spend money it did not have. Respond leader Don
Wallace described McAuley's statements as meaningless.[49] As a consequence, the protest leaders issued an ultimatum that the university had to
make a commitment to hire a full-time black staff recruiter and scholarship
coordinator by May 16 or they would take serious direct action.[50]

When the deadline passed, twenty black students withdrew from the university, including the six basketball stars. This was particularly threat-ening to the basketball program because, as Thomas explained, without himself, Memminger, Thompson, and the others there would not have been much of a team.[51] Father Cooke of the Theology Department called for a forty-eight-hour truce period and gave assurances that the university would act within that time.[52] The university officials were true to their word and the six basketball players returned to the team. A small piece in the *New York Times* on May 18, 1968, reported under a small heading ("6 Negro Marquette Athletes Reverse a Decision to Quit") that the disruption to the basketball squad was over.[53] A statement released by the returning students outlined how they were encouraged by the decision to recruit a black coordinator for a scholarship program. As Thomas explained, "Once that agreement had been made the basketball players decided we [had] accomplished our goal and so we decided to come back to school."[54]

The manifestation of the black athletic revolt at Marquette reveals important differences from that at Berkeley. It was a breach of discipline by Presley that sparked the initial problems at Berkeley and led to wider protests concerning racial injustice. At Marquette, however, the protest was in no way focused on the basketball team. As white player Mike Fons explained, "There was never any kind of racial problem. . . . It was just a very normal team and that was both before and after [the protest]."[55] His teammate, James Langenkamp, concurred: "We [white players] did not feel any animosity towards them."[56] Indeed, Joe Thomas explained, "The protest was not so much against the team but against the university as a whole."[57]

The black players aligned themselves with a protest movement that emerged from outside of the athletics department and had nothing to do with actual team dynamics. Unlike the issues of discipline and tensions with the coach at Berkeley, the players at Marquette were unified by their coach, Al McGuire. It was McGuire who was instrumental in persuading the players to come back onto the squad. The college paper, the *Marquette Tribune,* praised McGuire for his success in retaining the unity of a suc-cessful and talented team. He was reported to have been involved in a "real shouting match" with student protest leader Gus Moye. Furthermore, the coach had previously told his black players that before they began speak-ing out about black power and racism they should remember that they had yet to make their mark in the world.[58] Mike Fons described his coach as the kind of individual "who would start talking to you and instantly it was like you knew him forever, he was a fabulous personality."[59]

Marquette basketball coach Al McGuire was instrumental in persuading protesting black players on the team to call off their boycott of the university. Intercollegiate Athletic Hall of Fame Collection, Raynor Memorial Libraries, University of Marquette Archives.

McGuire met with four of the six protesting players in the early hours of May 17. When the players asked if they could phone some of the protest leaders before talking to him, McGuire indicated that he would rather speak to these leaders and the players himself. He then conducted a meeting with the players, Gus Moye, and other protest leaders in a local hotel room, at the end of which the players prepared a statement announcing that they would return to the university.[60] George Thompson stated, "At this time we feel that as basketball players we can best work in support of this group [Respond] by remaining in school and working through the proper university channels."[61]

The role of McGuire would appear crucial in the events at Marquette and he did not encounter the same type of problems that Herrerias did at Berkeley. McGuire had a two-season winning record behind him and enjoyed the great respect of his players, both white and black. The "shouting match" report and the other comments attributed to McGuire suggest the coach put great pressure on the players to return. Joe Thomas revealed that McGuire had been instrumental in the black players' decision to return in a more subtle way, however. The coach used his position to encourage university officials to communicate clearly to the players that they would make efforts to meet the demands of the black protesters. Father McAuley was present at part of the meeting, during which McGuire and the players discussed the withdrawal of the basketball stars from the university. Furthermore, McGuire inspired considerable loyalty among his players and impressed Thomas and the other black team members with his wholly unprejudiced views. "As far as the racism and prejudice among the players on the team, there was not any because we knew that the coach was going to put the best players on the floor," Thomas said.[62]

Indeed, a measure of the difference between the team dynamic at Marquette and that at Berkeley can be seen in an incident that occurred several months after the six black players had temporarily left the team. In October 1968 black player Pat Smith was indefinitely suspended by McGuire after failing to make a plane connection to ensure he arrived in time for practice after a weekend at home in New York. There was no sense that this issue could be exploited to raise issues of racism and prejudice— remember, the initial problems at Berkeley had involved Presley being late for, or missing, training. Smith was quoted saying, "I've come to respect the coach's decision. I have no bad feelings towards him because he did it only to keep the team under control."[63] Smith accepted his punishment in the same way that white player James Langenkamp had done in a previous season under McGuire.[64] The black athletic revolt on the campus at Marquette saw black basketball players using their position as visible African American students to highlight the wider racial injustices inherent in university policy. They did not, however, perceive team discipline or team rules to be a source of racial tension in the same way that athletes at Berkeley did. Despite the fact that they were less closely influenced by the OPHR and the figure of Harry Edwards than those on the West Coast, the black ballplayers at Marquette adopted methods similar to those utilized by Edwards at San Jose. The issues highlighted for protest were external to the athletic department, which was eventually drawn into the wider racial struggle on campus.

Similarities on all three campuses can be seen in the tensions that faced the black athletes who were surrounded by a rising tide of civil rights activism. They had a responsibility to both their team and their race. This was no different at Marquette. When the six basketball players returned to the university and their team, other members of the Respond protest group did not. The leading spokesman for these "radicals" was Gus Moye. He argued that the university had not gone far enough in its concessions and that those who returned to the university had settled for a "very inadequate response."[65] Thomas explained that there was some tension between those who wanted to continue the protest and the basketball players who returned to the team. Indeed, Blanton Simmons and Keith Edwards, the two players missing from the meeting with McGuire, expressed disappointment that they had not been contacted about the reversal of the decision to withdraw from the university. Simmons heard Thompson's statement on the radio but had not been consulted beforehand. Simmons and Edwards both agreed to abide by the decision, however, as the black players had made a previous agreement to act as a unified group, and the majority decision to return to the university was therefore the action that would be followed.[66] Protest leaders outside of the athletics department realized that the profile that the basketball stars gave to their cause was important and that when this had gone, so had some of the potency of their message.[67]

At Marquette the strength of the team ethic and the influence of Coach McGuire helped to ensure the black players' acceptance of the concessions made by university officials. This allowed the black stars to reconcile the competing demands of team and race. The players' involvement in the protest appears as something that was essentially symbolic. The players were sincere in their support for Respond, and Joe Thomas argued that they were prepared to leave the university permanently if it did not change its policy.[68] In a letter to alumni in June 1968, however, university president John Raynor asserted that the institution would not be "governed by coercion." Furthermore, he explained that many of the general proposals made by Respond leaders were already being planned before the May demonstrations and others were subject to budget constraints. Raynor concluded, "Under no circumstances will students be allowed to dictate policy to the faculty or administration."[69] McGuire's persuasion of the players that they could further the cause of the protest movement by staying on the team was aided by the stance of university officials that they would make concessions but would not be pushed too far. The players could therefore make a symbolic stand to show they supported the movement for racial justice, but leaving the team permanently was unlikely to improve conditions on campus or their own position. They were talented enough to pick up a scholarship elsewhere in the country but in doing so they would be leaving a successful team.

At Marquette, therefore, there were limits to the extent to which a boycott—withdrawing from participation on the team—could be used to further racial progress. The role of McGuire and the unity on the team that he inspired ensured that the incident was handled more swiftly and decisively than at Berkeley. The issue of discipline and racial tensions between coach and players were not a problem. The importance of maintaining a winning team influenced the university's decision to implement some of the policies the student protesters were calling for and McGuire played a significant role in this. Nevertheless, the university was clear that there were limits to the effectiveness of this tool of protest; university administrators were not prepared to be coerced into change. Had the players made a stand with the more radical demonstrators like Moye, it is fair to speculate that their scholarships may have been terminated. The desire to maintain a winning team was a motivation in their decision to return, just as it was in the university's willingness to institute some changes to racial policy.

Kansas Football Players in Revolt

Contemporaneously with the events at Marquette, football players at Kansas boycotted spring practice in order to highlight racial injustice and inequality at the university. The black players missed only a day of practice in order to make their point and win concessions from the university. As at Marquette, the general relationship between white and black players was good and the focus of protest was outside the locker room. What is interesting, though, in this manifestation of the black athletic revolt is the conditional nature of white acceptance of their black teammates' stand. The quick diffusion of the tension ensured that no games were missed and team unity was not severely ruptured. The black players were also keen that their commitment to the team should not be significantly compromised; they were not consciously using sport as an arena for political protest. In this sense the shape of the revolt deviated in a different way from Edwards's San Jose model.

The black players supported the Black Student Union in their call for a black cheerleader, a black history course, and more African American representation at the coaching and faculty levels. Spokesman for the black Jayhawks Don Shanklin stated, "We figure it's only right. We represent our race and our school in football, basketball, and track but still we didn't have a pom-pom girl."[70] The black players boycotted practice for one day before the final scrimmage of spring practice. Black player Willie Amison explained, "It was a cause we truly believed in. . . . There had to be some kind of statement made by the team players."[71] Despite divided loyalties between his position as a member of a team and his status as a black player, Bill Green asserted, "We felt that it was something we had to do, we felt strong enough to stand behind our black players."[72]

As with other instances of black protest in campus athletics departments, black players faced a dilemma because of this dual status as representatives of their race and players on a team. What we see at Kansas is the reluctance of some team members to boycott and the very lack of political consciousness among some black athletes that Edwards and his supporters were so determined to address through the black athletic revolt. Amison explained that there were some black athletes who did not want to boycott but were persuaded by older players and "community leaders" that it was necessary to make a stand against the injustices on campus and in wider society.[73] Not all the black players felt passionately about the issues at stake, and indeed, one of their number appeared to forget about the boycott altogether.

The protest only lasted a day, and once concessions had been won the players returned to the team. The university announced that a black girl would be chosen to fill a vacancy on the cheerleader squad. There seemed to be a general acceptance among the white members of the squad that including a black member was only fair. Cheerleading rules were such that if a girl left the squad then her place would be filled by one of four reserves. When one of the team resigned because of her impending mar-

1968 University of Kansas football team. The team had a successful season in 1968 despite the impact of the black athletic revolt on campus. University archives, Spencer Research Library, University of Kansas Libraries.

riage—married women were not allowed on the squad—the four reserves relinquished their right to take her place so that a black girl could do so. A spokeswoman for the pom-pom girls said they had made the decision "in recognition of the tensions in our country today on the civil rights issue."[74] Furthermore, the university announced that a course in black history was to be offered the following academic year. The issue of black coaching staff would be addressed at a later date.[75] The black players were accepted back for the intrasquad scrimmage after a meeting with Coach Rodgers, and the team went back to preparing for the coming season.[76] Although the coaches were not happy that the players had missed practice, there was a feeling that the issue was closed and "everybody was just happy to get on and do what they were supposed to do."[77] Once the boycott had ended the coaching staff made no reference to the issue; they wanted, as T. J. Gaughan explained, for the issue "to go away and swept it under the rug."[78]

What is apparent is that the concept of the team was paramount and having a winning football program was the main focus of both white and black players. The brief period of the boycott allowed the impact of the protest on the team to be largely neutralized. Amison explained, "The problem was not our interactions with our fellow players, the problem was the injustices that were evident in the everyday lives of all of us."[79] This is not to say there was not a little tension or resentment when the black players returned from the boycott. White player Bill Bell remembered the relationships with black players on the team to be very good but was also surprised when he heard about a possible boycott and was a "little bit peeved that they got away with it." There was also some disquiet among the white players who had to play out of position to cover for their absent black teammates.[80] Although Amison explained that many of the black players felt they had to address the larger issue of racial inequality even if this meant that the team was compromised, he did not accept that they were using sport for political purposes. "We just went out to the union. . . . We were not using sports whatsoever. We were not using sport, it was just a way of using the system to get what you want."[81] It is difficult, however, not to conclude that they were using sport to an extent to dramatize the issues at stake. Also, by choosing to use a boycott of training as their form of protest they were jeopardizing the team unity that existed.

The brief period of the boycott and the swift concessions from university officials did not fully test the conflicting loyalties of the black athletes to their team and to their racial identity. It does not seem that the black athletic revolt at Kansas was as significant as those at Berkeley, San Jose, or even Marquette. There was an acceptance on both sides of the racial divide, though, that the team would have been adversely affected, and possibly irreparably so, had the black players missed some games. The white players were not prepared to allow the civil rights activism of their black teammates to interfere with the success of the team. Indeed, the ideal of team unity and equality among players was crucial to that success. Even T. J. Gaughan, who was sympathetic to the plight of the black players on campus and enjoyed many close relationships with black teammates, asserted that things would have been very different had the boycott extended to any missed games. This eventuality would have "drawn the line and some guys would have put themselves above the team and that stuff should stay out of the locker room. We are a team and we fight and bleed together and we go through some tough stuff to get close."[82]

White and black players were seen as equal in the locker room and on the field, but this sense of togetherness extended only to the sporting context. This situation was central to Edwards and his supporters' argument.

The concept of the team was conditional and as such the idea of sport as a truly positive racial force was a myth, since it disguised an inequality that still existed. What is interesting about the response of the administrators at Kansas, and to an extent at Marquette, is the motivation for the concessions to the black students. By using sport as a mechanism to gain leverage black students were successful; however, the extent to which administrators were motivated by a desire to improve situations in which they recognized persistent inequality is questionable. It seems in the case of Coach Rodgers and the Kansas university authorities and Coach McGuire at Marquette that the primary motivation was to defuse tensions on successful sports teams. Edwards correctly identified the importance of college athletics and the way this could be exploited to make civil rights gains. It was successful sporting competition that remained paramount, though, and black athletes were thrown token gestures to appease them and reduce the tension they felt as team members and black representatives on campus. The result was limited change but continued black sporting participation—participation that was vital to the success of many college teams. Indeed, Amison remembered that race relations on campus at Kansas were "not at all" better in any practical terms after the boycott. The important thing was to take a symbolic stand.[83] Once this stand had been made and the university had been seen to respond, then focus could return to winning games.

The local struggles on the campuses at Kansas, Berkeley, and Marquette were part of a wider movement of black student protest in the late 1960s. The Civil Rights Movement had exposed both black and white students to protest experiences and had given them a sense of responsibility to affect social change. Furthermore, university campuses provided the best venues for young people to engage with important societal issues. Following the desegregation of higher education institutions across the United States, black students on predominantly white campuses were able to mobilize in sufficient numbers to make their voices heard.[84] At Marquette, Kansas, and Berkeley we can see different levels of interaction between black student protest leaders and black athletes. Black athletes at Berkeley took a greater lead in their struggle against athletic administrators as they sought to expose perceived racism within the athletics department. At Kansas and Marquette black athletes added their voices to grievances generated by the Black Student Union on campus.

The actions of black student protest organizations saw a convergence of protest activity associated with the Civil Rights Movement and a more militant and racially self-conscious movement of black students in the late 1960s. The course of events at Berkeley was influenced by the wider black student mobilization across California in the 1967–1968 academic year. Over half of campuses under the jurisdiction of the California college system experienced significant black student protests in that year.[85] The militant nature of black student protest in California during this period was a contributing factor to the shape of the black athletic revolt at Berkeley. Radicalized by the black student movement, athletes were more sensitive to perceived prejudice and discrimination and so the Presley incident became a catalyst for racially motivated protests.

Stefan Bradley's study of black student protest at Columbia University in the late 1960s shows how racially integrated student movements could be altered by the influence of Black Power rhetoric and ideology. By separating themselves from white protesters, black students could bring attention to their demands as separate issues. Students wanted their universities to act to try to correct the problems of society.[86] We can see elements of this at Marquette, where SURE gave way to Respond, a more radicalized and black-dominated protest movement. Furthermore, black student protesters were able to win concessions from university officials because they did not want to be labeled as racist. When these considerations were placed alongside the desire of administrators to maintain successful sports programs, the ability of student protesters to extract short-term changes from university policy makers was enhanced.

Response to a Growing Revolt

Protests characterized by withdrawing from the university or boycotting practice sessions were useful tools for forcing concessions from university administrators; however, they represented a dangerous tactic that threatened team unity and racial understanding. At Marquette and Kansas the short-lived nature of the demonstration ensured that a strong team ethic was maintained. Also, the fact that the focus of the grievances was outside of the athletic department meant that administrators could make important symbolic gestures to amend policy and therefore give black players a sense of vindication for their stand. In these episodes the players were given a way to balance the competing demands of team and racial identity. The desire to maintain a winning team often motivated both university officials and black players, and so in many respects sport precluded more radical protest.

The role of sport in promoting a team ethic also ensured that any protest that threatened to damage the group provoked tension. This was certainly the case at Berkeley, where events were exacerbated by the fact that the root of the protest emanated from inside the athletics department. The focus of the protest was the coach himself and this opened up black players to the charge that they were not dramatizing racial injustice but seeking to excuse their own indiscipline. Although closest to events at San Jose, both geographically and in the connection to Edwards's leadership, the protest at Berkeley strayed somewhat from the original spirit of the black athletic revolt. At San Jose and through the OPHR, activists sought to use sport as an arena in which to dramatize racial inequality. The students at Marquette and Kansas, however subconsciously, were using the same methods of protest that had been utilized in the call to boycott the NYAC meet and the Olympics. This use of the sporting arena to highlight wider racial inequality was an expression of a different form of connection with the black freedom struggle than that at Berkeley. Black students at Berkeley may have intended to do the same as students at Marquette and Kansas, but by choosing the Presley-Herrerias clash as their initial focus they seriously weakened the legitimacy of their demonstration.

Scenarios similar to the case studies explored above were being played out on many campuses across the country in the spring and summer of 1968. Media interest increased because of the contemporaneous debate over the potential black boycott of the Olympics. A number of the problems on other campuses were highlighted in a series of articles for *Sports Illustrated* by Jack Olsen titled "The Black Athlete: A Shameful Story."[87] The series revealed a number of complaints by black athletes at both college and professional levels and exposed some institutions for their alleged racist practices. The National Collegiate Athletic Association (NCAA) archives file on "racial matters" is dominated by internal responses to Olsen's article. There is little evidence of discussion of the wider national debate; instead the focus was on managing the organization's public image, which, it was felt, was being damaged by Olsen's work. The crucial issue here, then, is the extent to which the NCAA attempted to combat the charges published in *Sports Illustrated.* The institution was threatened by the attack on the myth of sport as a positive racial force. In its attempts to neutralize this threat we see similarities with the approach adopted by the USOC in response to discussions of protests leading up to the Olympics.

President of the NCAA Marcus Plant wrote to public relations director Thomas Hansen in early August 1968 asking for a list of inaccuracies that were alleged to be in the Olsen articles. Plant explained he wanted to be "armed with all the ammunition I can get."[88] Hansen replied a week later with a number of rebuttals to the allegations made by Olsen in his articles. While he argued that it was unrealistic for the NCAA to refute outright allegations of racism in college sports since the organization would be speaking for over six hundred institutions, Hansen did seek to expose Olsen as someone who had used questionable evidence. The letter is exceptionally detailed. It runs to seven pages that pick out any perceived faults in Olsen's articles, and Hansen himself described the letter as a "lengthy epistle." He concluded with a hope that he had been able "to win a few rounds . . . for the people in intercollegiate athletics."[89] (The people to whom he was referring were the administrators and coaches who he felt had been unfairly represented by Olsen.) It is telling that the investigation he conducted was aimed at discrediting the claims made in the *Sports Illustrated* articles rather than looking into what could be done to improve the position of black athletes.

The NCAA was obviously sensitive to the charges of racial discrimination in college sports and was hurt by the allegation that sport exhibited as much racism as wider society. Hansen corresponded with many of the institutions mentioned in the Olsen series and sent further information to Plant later in August 1968. In a letter of thanks to University of Washington athletic director James Owens, Hansen wrote, "It's most helpful to have specific cases to show that many of the printed complaints by Negroes are simply not factually true." He further mentioned that the NCAA Council had discussed the "black athlete situation" and would do so again in the future.[90] The official minutes of the council meetings for 1968 reveal nothing of these conversations, and as such it is not clear exactly how lengthy or serious they were.[91]

The issue clearly bothered NCAA president Plant, however, and his anger concerning the *Sports Illustrated* series can be seen in his letter to Hansen. Plant wrote, "This is very valuable information and I shall use it effectively, I hope. I am seeking a good opportunity to make a public appearance and devote my remarks toward outlining the deficiencies in this article and holding it up as a horrible example of irresponsible journalism. Maybe this is an unsound idea, but the whole project bothered me so much that I am having trouble forgetting it."[92] There is no documentary evidence that Plant did devote himself to making such a statement. Nevertheless, it is clear that he was particularly "bothered" by the Olsen article.

There were signs, though, that the NCAA was aware that some action was needed to improve the racial problems that had been increasingly affecting college athletics since the original black athletic revolt at San Jose State. U.S. vice president Hubert Humphrey was troubled by the problems of African American athletes and the impact that this had on America's global image. He was concerned about the threatened boycott of the Olympics and was central to the government's attempts to open up recreational facilities to inner-city youth.[93] The minutes of the NCAA executive committee meeting on August 15, 1968, record the federal government's plan, which involved the establishment of sports facilities in the nation's fifty largest cities. The project was to be called the Summer Youth Project, and although there was an obvious racial element to inner-city programs, the committee outlined that the initiative would not be "limited to disadvantaged youth."[94] The project was to run the following year and would eventually take place in thirty-five urban areas that the federal government identified as poverty stricken. It was anticipated that thirty to thirty-five thousand young people would be involved, and the participating institutions were enthusiastic about the program.[95]

Certainly the Summer Youth Project was a step in the direction of addressing some of the concerns of African American athletes in the sense that the NCAA and the institutions it represented were trying to bring sport to inner-city young people. In this respect they were responding on a national level to some of the problems identified by the protesters at, for example, Marquette. The Marquette students had urged the university to reach out to impoverished communities in the ghettos only a few blocks away from the campus; however, the overriding attitude of the NCAA was still one of caution. They displayed anger and disappointment that the institution of college sports was being accused of racist practices rather than a desire to investigate the substance of the allegations and the problems of black athletes. A common problem faced by black athletes on predominantly white campuses was the lack of female company of the same race. This led, on occasion, to black athletes dating white girls, a practice that was consistently frowned upon. Olsen highlighted this problem in his series. Hansen countered the allegations of unfair treatment of black athletes who transgressed this racial barrier in his letter to Plant. Referencing the views of a doctor he had spoken to, Hansen ignored the racism inherent in prohibition of mixed-race relationships and suggested that black athletes "might have hit the books instead of worrying about inter-racial dating and instead of playing cards and spending hours in student hangouts."[96]

As mentioned above, Hansen did concede that it was impossible to defend the NCAA against charges of racism because of the sheer number of people who worked for its member institutions. There was not, however, a concession that the NCAA itself perpetuated racial inequality, and a primary aim of efforts to pick apart Olsen's articles seemed to be to defend the organization against such charges. By highlighting the inaccuracies in Olsen's evidence Hansen was attempting to show that racism was limited to a small number of individuals and specific incidents. Olsen's series made the same arguments that Edwards had been making since 1967 and to a varying extent highlighted problems the like of which were experienced at Berkeley, Marquette, and Kansas and on many other campuses. Douglas Hartmann correctly judges that Olsen "got the story of African-American discontent in sport right."[97] He is not correct, though, in asserting that Hansen came to a similar conclusion. To support his view, Hartmann points to a comment by Hansen that "SI [*Sports Illustrated*] isn't totally wrong, just incredibly sloppy." He argues that this comment supports Hansen's concession that the NCAA could not be defended against claims of racism. First, however, the NCAA public relations director was only conceding that all of society had racism in it and that his establishment could not be held to account for all the people under its organization. He did not concede institutional racism—the charge that Edwards continually made. Second, Hartmann takes the Hansen quote out of context. The actual sentence in the letter read "*here* SI isn't totally wrong, just incredibly sloppy." The word *here* is important because it draws attention to the specific subject of the previous paragraph, which deals with a mix-up over a photograph and a byline concerning the record-breaking UCLA relay team.[98] Hansen was commenting on this mix-up and not making a general point about Olsen's charges of racial prejudice.

By the summer of 1968 the NCAA was fully aware of the issues being highlighted by the black athletic revolt. Campus disputes of varying severity and the journalistic endeavor of Olsen in particular were publicizing the grievances of African American athletes. The response of athletic administrators at the campus level was to make concessions to the protesters in order to facilitate a swift end to the racial impasse. Often this took the form of symbolic gestures or cosmetic policy changes that seemed to be aimed at allowing black athletes to show their own community that they were successfully engaging in civil rights activism while, importantly, protecting winning sports programs. At the national level the NCAA made only limited attempts to meet the demands of the black athletic revolt. The dominant response of the organization was to continue to portray sport as a positive force for racial equality.

The correspondence of Plant and Hansen, key members of the NCAA Executive Committee, shows the anger felt toward those who wished to show that sport, too, was permeated by institutional racism. It is worth reiterating that the NCAA was limited in its ability to institute coordinated action. Still, the major focus was on defending the image of sport rather than seriously assessing the veracity of black athletes' claims of discrimination and prejudice. Focusing solely on these issues of racism in sport itself was in some respects a distraction from the use of sport to dramatize the racial problems in wider society. Dramatization of this wider discrimination and prejudice was to be most symbolic and potent in Mexico City. The actions of Tommie Smith and John Carlos on the winners' podium remain the dominant image of the 1968 Olympic Games. It is to these events that we now turn in our efforts to further dissect the relationship between the black freedom struggle and the sports world in the late 1960s.

4

Black Gloves and Gold Medals

Protests, Meanings, and Reactions at the 1968 Mexico City Olympics

We have made our way here, it is a forum from which we can launch something, so why not just go ahead and do whatever it is we can do?
—Ralph Boston, long jump bronze medalist, 1968

I think it was a disgrace. In my opinion an act like that in the medal ceremony defiles the American flag.
—Barry Weisenberg, U.S. Olympic water polo team

Ralph Boston arrived at his third Olympics with the hope that he could add to the gold and silver medals he already possessed. The favorite to win gold in the long jump was Bob Beamon. He was one of a group of athletes who had been suspended from the University of Texas at El Paso earlier in the season for taking part in a protest against the racist practices of Brigham Young University. Racial tensions at El Paso had featured in Olsen's *Sports Illustrated* series, and Beamon's actions suggested that he shared Boston's sympathy for the cause of the OPHR. Nevertheless, even though they had both rejected a boycott of the Mexico City Games, Beamon had jumped at the meet in Madison Square Garden that Boston and many other black athletes had boycotted to protest the prejudice in the policies of the NYAC. A veteran of the U.S. track and field team, Boston saw Beamon as a supremely talented yet slightly puzzling character. Indeed, he helped Beamon through his struggles in the qualifying jumps for the final in Mexico City by suggesting he move his run-up back so that he would eliminate the problem of overstepping. The advice from his veteran teammate helped Beamon qualify for the final.

In that final Beamon produced the most remarkable jump of his generation. He sailed into the sandpit, hanging in the air as though momentarily defying gravity. Once his jump had been measured it was clear that he had advanced the world record by nearly two feet. Astounded by this superhuman feat, he collapsed on the ground and had to be helped to his feet by Boston. For his part, the three-time Olympian recorded a jump that was good enough for third place. Boston therefore completed a full set of Olympic medals, adding a bronze to his gold and silver. Just as in the 200 meters, the U.S. team had won gold and bronze and the winner had set a world record in the process. The medal ceremony would be the first opportunity for any American medalists to respond to the suspension of their sprinters, Tommie Smith and John Carlos.[1]

Boston had a consistent record of engagement with the civil rights struggle, even if he had spoken out against a boycott of the games themselves. Beamon's actions in response to the black freedom struggle were less transparent. When he took the winner's podium he did so with his tracksuit rolled up to reveal long black socks. Boston stepped up to receive his bronze medal in bare feet. He had reached the forum in which he could make a stand and he did so in his own way. By the time he took his place on the podium the dynamics of the relationship between the freedom struggle and sport had altered. This was not only about the message of the OPHR to combat racial injustice; it was also about the decisions taken to remove Smith and Carlos from the Olympic village and send them home in disgrace.

Boston later explained his decision to take the podium in his bare feet. "There were two protests," he said, "racial prejudice in general and the other protest was that by the time I competed, John and Tommie had been expelled from the Olympic village. . . . My stand said basically you have kicked them out of the village, you have kicked them off the team, but you have not done anything to take their medals. You kicked them out of the village, but the medals that they have won are still included in the medal count . . . and, you know, I thought that was really hypocritical."[2]

Boston was one of many athletes, both black and white, who had to make a decision about where they stood in reaction to the podium protest made by Smith and Carlos. Theirs was a stand that surely not even Harry Edwards could have envisaged when he initially founded the OPHR. Theirs was a stand that encapsulated the complex state of the black freedom struggle in 1968. When they raised their fists they provided the iconic image of the Mexico City Games. This image was, however, the subject of contested interpretation from the moment the national anthem finished. Their stand focused attention on the complexity of the relationship between sport and the civil rights struggle, a complexity that was evident in the differing engagement with that struggle of Boston and Beamon.

Viewing Smith and Carlos's podium salute through a one-dimensional lens that is dominated by a distorted understanding of the Black Power Movement ignores the nuanced symbolism of what Smith and Carlos did. The disciplined attack on the two sprinters by the USOC has, with the passage of time, given way to an appreciation of the courage and idealism of the podium salute. Nevertheless, the changing perception of their stand has in itself diluted the meaning of their actions.

Protesting without a Boycott

The realization that a black boycott of the Olympics was not feasible had emerged in the summer of 1968 and was finally conceded by Edwards in August. Those sympathetic to the OPHR in the months that directly preceded the Mexico City Games considered the options that remained for dramatizing the plight of black Americans. Indeed, the decisions concerning the form that protest by black athletes would take were ad hoc and flexible; the extent to which Edwards directly influenced these decisions is questionable. The OPHR leader suggested that athletes could fly an African National Congress flag to show solidarity with black South Africans or raise a Black Panther flag or Black Power salute.[3] When the athletes had a final discussion in Denver before leaving for Mexico City, however, there was still no firm plan. Some suggested that they should not take the victory podium or that they should wear black armbands. The idea of painting their running shoes black was rejected because of the implications for sponsorship arrangements. It was decided that individuals would make their own decision on how best to dramatize the issues.[4] As Boston later recalled, "We could not come to a consensus as to what we should do and so each person was to do whatever they wanted to."[5]

The potential for the sporting arena to be used to make a powerful and, in their opinion, embarrassing, protest gesture was not lost on the USOC. Representatives had been sent to counsel the Harvard crew against the possibility of a further statement in favor of the OPHR. Indeed, while waiting in the departure lounge of the airport in Denver preparing to fly down to Mexico, Paul Hoffman (the coxswain of the Harvard crew) was approached by USOC representative Robert Paul. Paul, pointing to the

OPHR button that Hoffman wore on his lapel, stated that athletes were required to be in uniform and could not wear such accessories. Hoffman gestured toward Wyomia Tyus, the black female sprinter, and suggested he would take his badge off if Paul managed to get Tyus to remove hers.[6] The official's approach was successfully rebuffed but this was just one example of the USOC's heightened sensitivity to any appearance of subversion or protest.

Bruce Miroff has explained how the White House attempted to work with and exert influence over moderate social movements. This influence declined with the increasing militancy of the late 1960s, and the Johnson administration became more and more agitated by the actions of militant black leaders.[7] The USOC was similarly determined to exert its influence in order to stamp out any form of protest because it perceived such actions to be part of increased militancy. The symbolic and nonviolent protest threatened by the OPHR was regarded by the USOC as part of the rising violence and black militancy of the late 1960s. A board of consultants had been set up to try to influence athletes and dissuade them from pursuing any protest activity. Furthermore, during the Olympic Trials administrators had planned elaborate victory ceremonies after each event. When they learned of a rumored plan by black athletes to boycott these ceremonies, however, the victory celebrations were cancelled for fear of the embarrassment that would accompany African American athletes refusing to have their achievements recognized.[8]

On August 5, 1968, Avery Brundage wrote to Douglas Roby at the USOC in order to register his concern at reports suggesting black athletes might engage in some method of protest during the Olympics. He attached newspaper clippings reporting various statements by black athletes that threatened some form of action. Brundage outlined how the organizing committee had been given instructions that protests and demonstrations would not be permitted and added that "any participants are to be removed forcibly if necessary and not permitted to return." Brundage went on to state that "our Mexican friends are pledged to uphold the high ideals of the Games and nothing of this kind will be tolerated."[9] In his reply three days later Roby assured Brundage that all measures were being taken to guard against any such protests. Roby explained the fate that would await any athlete who attempted to protest. The head of the USOC stated that his organization intended "to have every athlete understand that we will countenance no nonsense and that anyone that participates or that attempts to participate in any demonstration . . . will be immediately suspended as a member of our team and returned to his home at the earliest possible date."[10]

The USOC was clearly determined to head off any trouble before the U.S. team began competition in Mexico City. Acting Executive Director Everett Barnes sent a memorandum to all members of the USOC board on September 18 referring to the activities of the Harvard rowing crew. Barnes stated that Roby had expressed concern that the rowers were attempting to engage in dialogue with other athletes about possible protests. Members of the board were sent copies of the Harvard crew's letter to other athletes and were put on notice to be vigilant concerning possible repercussions.[11] The attempt by the OPHR to highlight the plight of black athletes and the role of black people in wider American society had been met with anger and defensiveness at the USOC. There was great concern that the United States could be embarrassed on the international stage and that the sporting arena would be sullied by the intrusion of racial politics.

The sense of tension surrounding the forthcoming Olympic competition was given another dimension by events in Mexico itself. The student protests that were seen across the United States and Europe in 1968 also touched Latin America. In Mexico students took the government to task over so much money being lavished on the Olympic Games while the majority of the population existed in painful poverty. Ten days before the opening ceremony students organized a mass protest in the Square of the Three Cultures. Although it is not known exactly how many were killed, hundreds of the protesting students died when they were gunned down by the Mexican military. The student protests were not to be allowed to impinge on any aspect of the Olympic experience and were ruthlessly suppressed.[12]

The general sense of turmoil and repression of protest was also felt by supporters of the OPHR. Harry Edwards claims that he did not travel to Mexico City after being warned by Louis Lomax—citing contacts in the State Department and CIA—that such a trip would be too dangerous for his own safety and instead arranged to be in Canada while the games were taking place.[13] Pete Axthelm, sports editor of *Newsweek,* who wrote many probing articles concerning the plight of black athletes during the course of 1968, was denied press credentials by Olympic officials when he arrived in Mexico City. After a day or two Axthelm was finally given access to the press section of the Olympic stadium, where he was spotted by Robert Paul, USOC press secretary, who commented, "I see you got in. I hope you have something better to write about than niggers."[14]

At the games there was definite apprehension surrounding what the black athletes might attempt to do to express the ideals of the OPHR. When African American Jimmy Hines won the gold medal in the 100 meters he was to have his medal presented by Avery Brundage. Hines was not among the black athletes who supported the initial Olympic boycott proposal, but after winning his race he made a protest of sorts by refusing to have his medal presented by the IOC president. Hines said, "We made no formal request. We asked them who was going to present the medals and they replied, Brundage. We did not say anything, neither did we smile. Apparently they got the message."[15] Lord Burghley presented the medals and Brundage was not involved in any of the other victory ceremonies of the games. The authorities remained fearful of a black athlete protest gesture, and with good cause. On the day of their 200-meter heats, Smith and Carlos walked around wearing long black socks and OPHR buttons. Smith remarked to a reporter, "I don't want Brundage presenting me any medals."[16] The head of the IOC was reviled by many of the black athletes on the American team for his perceived racist views. Ralph Boston later commented, "My meetings with Avery Brundage left me ice cold. I was almost expecting him to come out with racial slurs towards me. That was the way that I had come to realize he was."[17]

New York Times sportswriter Robert Lipsyte had been covering the activities of the OPHR in the period leading up to the Olympics and remembers feeling that something "really strong and powerful" would happen.[18] Paul Hoffman testified that there was a palpable sense of tension. The Harvard crew had found it difficult to engage in a dialogue with other athletes about the racial problems highlighted by the OPHR in the period leading up to the games. Once in Mexico City, however, they were able to spend more time with other athletes. Nevertheless, the reaction that Hoffman received from some members of the U.S. team was symptomatic of the strong feeling against any attempt to use the sporting arena to make a political statement. The small, 110-pound coxswain was pinned up against a wall in a basement mail room by one of the U.S. boxing coaches, who warned Hoffman not to talk to his boxers and to stop intimidating them. Hoffman remarked that he could not have intimidated the family cat, never mind a squad of boxers. When sitting on buses to take athletes to events, coaches would call their competitors over and warn them not to sit next to Hoffman, Livingston, or other Harvard oarsmen.[19]

The prospect of a protest against racial injustice on an international stage involving both white and black athletes was anathema to both the

IOC and the USOC. Alan Guttman has argued that Brundage's "commitment to the preservation of sports as a sacred realm apart, unsullied by commerce or politics," made him opposed to political protest on the grounds that sport should transcend the struggles of wider society.[20] Brundage argued that "the Olympic Games are not the place for demonstrations of any kind." In reference to the decision to exclude the South African team from the Olympics because of the political problems of apartheid, the IOC leader argued that the situation "was a criticism of our so-called civilization rather than of the Olympic Games, which are trying to promote international friendship and respect."[21]

USOC fears over any protest were, however, founded in an ideological framework that implicitly contradicted the rationale of Brundage's objections. For the United States, the Olympic Games were an extremely political event. "In America, sports were not games anymore, nor were they in Olympic competition. Ideologies, systems, religions, races and nation-states all turned to the Olympics for evidence that they were as powerful or as true or as inevitable as they claimed to be."[22]

The Cold War heightened the intensity of international sporting contests and added greater profundity to victory and defeat. Brundage asserted that the games were no place for any kind of political demonstration, but the main fear of the U.S. authorities was that their political agenda for the Olympics would be compromised by any protest activities.

The Olympic Games were undoubtedly loaded with political symbolism. Indeed hammer-thrower Hal Connolly had first accepted and then rejected the honor of carrying the American flag in the 1968 opening ceremony. Since 1908 it had been U.S. practice not to dip its flag when passing the reviewing stand. Connolly perceived this as arrogant and disrespectful and he informed the USOC that he would break with protocol and dip the flag. They responded with a threat that he would be arrested if he did so and Connolly subsequently rejected the flag-bearing responsibilities.[23] The raising of flags and the rendition of national anthems during victory ceremonies gave a political and nationalistic focus to the sporting competition. Individual excellence was irresistibly linked to national prestige. For twentieth-century America, sporting competition played a key role in the development of national identity. As Steven Pope has observed, "Sports tradition evoked the resilience of individualism, the work ethic, democracy, class conciliation; and, thereby, helped shape an emergent national identity."[24]

It was the U.S. Olympic authorities' desire to utilize international sport for their own political ends in the Cold War era that motivated the policy to silence dissenting voices of American athletes, both white and black. Within the geopolitical considerations of the federal government, civil rights demonstrations, southern white resistance, and race riots caused problems for the State Department, as they were seen to "lead to legitimacy-threatening world attention."[25] For the U.S. Olympic authorities, what was at stake in Mexico City was the continued projection of American exceptionalism through triumphant sporting performance. Black athletes and their white allies were warned against any attempt to use the games to voice their social and political grievances because the Olympics were not the place for such activities. In reality the games were very much the place for this activity, and what U.S. authorities feared most of all was that their own agenda would be hijacked and the divisions in American society would be exposed on the world stage.

The Defining Image of the Games

On October 16, 1968, the Olympic 200-meter final took place. Both Tommie Smith and John Carlos almost failed to make it to the starting blocks. Smith had strained an adductor muscle in his semifinal and required ice treatment while preparing for the final.[26] Carlos had stepped out of his designated lane in his heat and avoided disqualification only because officials failed to spot the error.[27] Nevertheless, they both ran in a race that became the prelude to an act that defined their lives thereafter. Smith won in a world record 19.83 seconds. Carlos, who slowed and turned to look at his teammate in the last few strides, came in third after being passed on the line by Peter Norman. Carlos later argued that he slowed to let Smith win so that he would not be alone on the podium but would have another black athlete to stand with in solidarity.[28] In his most recent account of events Carlos asserted, "As for me, I didn't care a lick if I won the gold, silver or bronze. I wasn't there for the race. I was there for the after-race."[29] Looking at the footage of the race and studying Smith's form throughout the year leading to the Olympics seems to discount Carlos's claims, however. Smith was simply faster, and the grimace on Carlos's face betrayed a man desperately trying to win.

Earlier in the Olympic track and field competition Tommie Smith and 400-meter runner Lee Evans had sat in the stands and discussed what they would do if Avery Brundage tried to shake their hands during a medal ceremony. Evans suggested that they should each wear a black glove and hide their hands under their sweatshirts, revealing the black gloves at the last moment and therefore frightening Brundage. The athletes' wives purchased the gloves, which were then added to their kit bags.[30] The exact mechanics of the events that unfolded in the holding area before the 200-meter victory ceremony are a little unclear, with each individual offering a slightly different picture of the past. It would, however, seem that Smith was the driving force behind the protest that followed. Lee Evans explains that "Carlos never even came to a meeting" of the OPHR and that it was he and Smith who were the principal athletes involved in the movement.[31] Carlos concedes that he was not one of the original members of the OPHR, but once involved, he argues, he played a crucial part in the movement.[32] It was Smith who produced the gloves that the two athletes were to wear and who told Carlos, "The national anthem is sacred to me, and this can't be sloppy. It has to be clean and abrupt."[33] Peter Norman stated that Carlos did not have any gloves with him and it was Smith who took the lead in the discussions that were held under the stadium before the medal ceremony.[34] Recalling the events in the lead up to the podium moment some thirty years later, USOC press secretary Robert Paul stated that he had been aware some gesture was going to be made. Head Coach Payton Jordan and Sprint Coach Stan Wright told Paul that they had given the two sprinters permission to wear black handkerchiefs and black socks underneath their sweat suits.[35]

Sportswriter Neil Amdur describes Smith as an "indomitable" competitor and saw Carlos's gesture as "a part of what Tommie [Smith] was in total."[36] Certainly the bend in Carlos's raised arm on the podium compared with Smith's straight, strong gesture and comprehensive explanation of the protest after the event seem to suggest a greater sense of purpose on the part of the gold medalist.[37] Carlos later explained that his arm was bent so that he could "throw down a hammer punch" to protect himself from anyone who tried to attack him on the podium.[38] Smith and Carlos outlined to Norman what they were going to do on the podium. The Australian silver medalist explained that he supported what they were doing and would show his solidarity by wearing the OPHR badge if they could find him one. As the three men walked out to receive their medals Smith and Carlos wore their gloves; the former had a black scarf wrapped around his neck and the latter a necklace of beads hanging from his. Paul Hoffman leaned over the barrier at the side of the track to wish the men all the best and Carlos asked for the OPHR badge he was wearing. Norman pinned the badge on his sweatshirt.[39] As the national anthem rang out the two black

1968 200-meter medal ceremony. The iconic image of the 1968 Games. Copyright AP/Press Association Images.

sprinters bowed their heads. Smith raised his right fist and Carlos his left in the defining moment of the 1968 Olympic Games.

The *New York Times* reported that the incident "passed without much general notice in the packed Olympic stadium."[40] Yet many observers reported booing and jeering from the crowd in response to the actions of Smith and Carlos.[41] Carlos himself describes a mixture of boos and aggressive, defiant singing of the national anthem by those who then abused the two sprinters as they left the arena.[42] Paul Hoffman described the crowd reaction as "more confused rather than angry."[43] Furthermore, steeplechaser George Young, who took the podium in his medal ceremony immediately after Smith and Carlos's salute, explained, "We had a pretty good reception. I think people were a little bit stunned and did not know how to react."[44] Clearly the profundity of the act and the strength of the reaction that was to follow were not immediately apparent. The athletes were led from the stadium by an Olympic official and were not seen again until ABC sports reporter Howard Cosell interviewed Smith the next day. Smith explained the significance and symbolism of the gesture thus: "I wore a black right-hand glove and Carlos wore the left-hand glove of the same pair. My raised right hand stood for the power in black America. Carlos's raised left hand stood for the unity of black America. Together they formed an arch of unity and power. The black scarf around my neck stood for black pride. The black socks with no shoes stood for black poverty in racist America. The totality of our effort was the regaining of black dignity."[45] Smith's explanation gave added potency to the gesture and accentuated the dignified and thoughtful nature of the protest. An impulse that had begun with Harry Edwards's call for black athletes to boycott the Olympics had seemingly ended in the symbolic gesture of two sprinters. In reality, however, things had only just begun. Smith and Carlos's actions provoked significant reaction from white administrators and athletes but also from their black teammates.

The initial response of the USOC was to censure Smith and Carlos without formally removing them from the Olympic village.[46] It should be noted that Roby had given Brundage assurances in his August 8 letter—discussing the problems posed by protests—that any athlete who was involved in such activity would be sent home.[47] Brundage was furious at the actions of Smith and Carlos; he raged that "warped mentalities and cracked personalities seem to be everywhere and impossible to eliminate."[48] It was the head of the IOC who was the driving force behind the expulsion of Smith and Carlos from the Olympic village. Brundage insisted that unless the two men were expelled from the games and all future Olympic competition, the U.S. track and field team would be barred from the rest of the days of competition.[49] Brundage told one correspondent after the games, "In order to get action we had to intimate to the USOC that if it could not control its team perhaps it should take them all home."[50] The historic irony is that Brundage's reaction to the actions of Smith and Carlos elevated their importance; by making martyrs of the sprinters, the IOC chief contributed to the immortalization of their protest. Czech gymnast Vera Caslavska turned her head away from the Soviet flag during her multiple medal ceremony appearances in protest of the suppression of political freedoms in Prague. No action was taken against her and no media storm developed as it did around Smith and Carlos.

Facing Brundage's threats, the USOC board released a statement that condemned the actions of Smith and Carlos and removed them from the Olympic team and the competitors' village. The statement of October 17, 1968, read,

> The United States Olympic Committee expresses its profound regrets to International Olympic Committee, to the Mexican Organizing Committee and to the people of Mexico for the discourtesy displayed by the two members of its team in departing from tradition during a victory ceremony at the Olympic Stadium on October 16th. The untypical exhibitionism of these athletes also violates the basic standards of good manners and sportsmanship in the United States and therefore the two men involved are suspended forthwith from the team and ordered to remove themselves from the Olympic village. This action is taken in the belief that such immature behavior is an isolated incident. However, if further investigations or subsequent events do not bear out this view, the entire matter will be re-evaluated. A repetition of such incidents by other members of the United States team can only be considered a willful disregard of Olympic principles that would warrant the imposition of the severest penalties at the disposal of the United States Olympic Committee.[51]

The wording of the USOC statement reveals the desire to neutralize the impact of Smith and Carlos's gesture. Neither man is mentioned by name nor are details given of the nature of their protest. The "untypical exhibitionism" comment presents the case that this was an isolated incident and distances the athletes involved from the rest of the team. There is no mention of the racial and political context of the action or the activities of the OPHR before the Olympic Games; sporting traditions and "good manners" are defended, but the issue of human rights is ignored. Here we again see a desire by U.S. authorities to ensure that their political agenda was not hijacked.

Brundage's belief that politics should not be part of the Olympic Games was at the forefront of his stance; however, the fact that he himself was a U.S. citizen made him particularly sensitive to the actions of Smith and Carlos. In his response to the many correspondents who expressed both criticism of and praise for his decision to send Smith and Carlos home, Brundage continually expressed that politics had no place in sport. The head of the IOC repeatedly used the phrase "good manners and sportsmanship should take precedence over athletic ability in the Olympics Games."[52] He defended the ideal of sports purity against the pernicious influence of political forces. Brundage also, however, showed that as an American he was particularly angered by the actions of Smith and Carlos. He argued that "people of that kind should not have been on the Olympic team at all."[53] In a vociferous reply to a supportive correspondent Brundage stated, "The actions of these two negroes was an insult to the Mexican hosts and a disgrace to the United States."[54]

Although evidently some members of the USOC board were not prepared to expel Smith and Carlos immediately after the podium protest, it is clear that Brundage had no hesitation in insisting that they should be sent home. Furthermore, the words of Roby in his correspondence with Brundage prior to the Olympics suggest that he was personally in favor of the decision to punish Smith and Carlos severely. The desire to stop racial politics from intruding upon sports clearly dominated the response of U.S. administrators.

Symbolism, Protest, and the Black Freedom Struggle

Opinion of the Smith and Carlos protest in the U.S. press was varied. The *Los Angeles Sentinel,* an African American publication, argued on its sports page that the protest was out of place and that the Olympics were no arena for such acts. Columnists elsewhere in the paper praised the heroic effort of Smith and Carlos. The *Los Angeles Times* referred to the podium gesture as a "Hitler-type salute." *Time* magazine changed the Olympic motto of "faster, higher, stronger" to "angrier, nastier, uglier" when describing the "public display of petulance" by Smith and Carlos.[55] The *Pittsburgh Courier* provided coverage from an African American perspective that praised the black sprinters and criticized the racism of the IOC. The *Courier* ran a cartoon of a giant black-gloved fist rising above the Olympic stadium with the caption "pride prevails."[56] In a balanced piece, *Newsweek* reported, "Judged against some of the alternatives that black militants had considered, the silent tableau seemed fairly mild."[57]

The *Chicago Defender,* another African American paper, offered positive views of the actions of Smith and Carlos. Jackie Robinson, who had supported the idea of a boycott of the Olympics, said that he "admired the pride in their blackness" shown by the two sprinters.[58] In a particularly sarcastic piece carried by the paper, the USOC and the attitude of white America was lampooned:

> The American constituency has spent five years not hearing the Negroes, who in their way, keep telling us something is wrong and I see no reason why we should start hearing it now in Mexico City. The Olympic Committee came to the rescue, however. They kicked the two boys out of Olympic City because they were rude, which is not an American trait despite what anyone says about the whites in Milwaukee who throw stones. Perhaps they can go one step further and take the record away from Tommie Smith and give it to someone more deserving, some nice white fellow.[59]

It is clear that much of the differing opinions both then and now stems from the enigmatic nature of the podium salute. As a symbolic gesture it encapsulated so many facets of the racial struggle in America in the late 1960s that it was open to a myriad of interpretations. Many such interpretations, in fact, mixed competing or contradictory messages of the civil rights agenda. For example, a piece reporting the podium salute in the *Pittsburgh Courier* focused on the black pride inherent in the raised fist, a potent symbol of "Black Power." The same article, however, asserted that "Smith's and Carlos' stand was a visual expression of the theme song 'we shall overcome.'" [60] In the same article in an African American publication, therefore, the podium protest was linked to the mainstream civil rights anthem and the more militant Black Power agenda, two different strands of the racial struggle of the 1960s. Indeed, the ideological father of the Black Power Movement, Malcolm X, had famously mocked the singing of that anthem as contradictory to a black revolution.

In his TV interview after the podium salute Smith articulated a message that conveyed the protest as solemn and dignified. He had told Carlos before the ceremony, "The national anthem is sacred to me, and this can't be sloppy."[61] Choosing to make their stand during the anthem provided an expression of the duality that many black Americans felt, a double consciousness of being both American and black. The racism of American society imposed an identity problem on black citizens. The response to this has had an effect on how African Americans express patriotism. The gesture by the two sprinters embodied an "iconoclastic patriotism," the like of which had been expressed by Paul Robeson in the early twentieth century and Martin Luther King Jr. in his opposition to the Vietnam War. Smith and Carlos rejected traditional patriotism and fundamentally challenged American racism. In so doing their stand contrasts with those of Frederick Douglass during the Civil War, W. E. B. DuBois before World War I, and Al Sharpton after 9/11, who subscribed to the belief that loyalty and devotion to American culture and ideals would eventually be rewarded with racial equality. Smith and Carlos showed devotion to the United States by fundamentally challenging American racism.[62] The expression of black pride and strong group identity simultaneously with the playing of "The Star-Spangled Banner" powerfully expressed a double consciousness.

While Smith stressed the solemn and essentially nonviolent or nonaggressive nature of the protest, in a postceremony press conference Carlos infused the podium salute with greater anger and confrontation. Carlos fumed, "If we do the job well, we get a pat on the back or some peanuts. And someone says, 'Good boy.' I've heard boy, boy, boy all through the Olympics. I'd like to tell white people in America and all over the world that if they don't care for the things black people do, then they shouldn't sit in the stands and watch them perform."[63] Carlos expressed a powerful race consciousness that provided a more aggressive expression of black power than the statement by Smith. What should not be forgotten is that there were three people on the winners' rostrum. Peter Norman, the white Australian silver medalist, wore an OPHR button. He added an interracial element to the protest that contrasted with the message of strident racial pride that is emphasized by viewing the protest through a distorted Black Power lens, a lens that views Black Power in a one-dimensional way, focusing on the black militant and violent elements of that movement while ignoring its other, more nuanced aims and developments.

The podium salute is remembered as a Black Power protest. A 2008 BBC documentary focusing on the incident was titled simply *Black Power*

Salute. The reporting of the incident at the time, and since, has placed great emphasis on the raised, gloved fist and the Black Power symbolism to which it is connected. Certainly the raising of a black fist was the most recognized symbol of the Black Power Movement and various items of merchandise could be purchased that displayed this symbol. African American publications also used the raised fist in cartoons with great regularity. It is not the contention here that Smith and Carlos were not consciously adopting the symbols and meanings of the Black Power Movement in their stand; they undoubtedly were. What is important, however, is to recognize the way their protest was misinterpreted and criticized in the same way that the Black Power Movement was. Furthermore, their stand showed the interconnected nature of the Black Power and Civil Rights Movements.

The stand by Smith and Carlos and the gold medalist's explanation of the podium salute were deeply infused with racial consciousness. Smith talks of black pride, black unity, and black dignity. The beads around Carlos's neck were a clear symbol of Black Nationalism. The reaction of the IOC and the USOC saw an attempt to isolate the sprinters as representatives of a minority opinion, a small group of angry young black men who represented a threat to the sanctity of the Olympic movement and society as a whole. The racial prejudice of the U.S. Olympic organization was barely veiled. The relative ignorance of the USOC to the cultural and racial sensitivities was revealed further when one of their representatives spoke to Smith and Carlos after the podium salute. After it had been explained to the sprinters that they were to be expelled from the village the USOC administrator dealing with the matter asked, "You boys know why you did it?" Smith snapped back that they were not "boys." Discussions of these references in the meeting of the executive committee were accompanied by laughter and jokes from those around the table.[64]

The reaction to a reference to black athletes as "boys" by the USOC representative and the angry words of Carlos expressed in the postceremony press conference reveal the issue of black manhood in the protests of the OPHR. Black male athletes were so often treated as performers and belittled as men in the process. The stand by Smith and Carlos reflected the clear desire by black male athletes to be treated as men. The desire to reclaim black manhood was a key element of the Black Power Movement and was clearly part of the message that the two sprinters expressed in their podium salute. It was also a key ingredient in the protests by many black male athletes during campus revolts.

The USOC attempted to construct a popular perception of the podium salute as the action of two angry and isolated young black men. The inter-racial support for the stand made by Smith and Carlos and the deeper significance of their actions were consciously ignored. Jesse Owens—who was part of the board set up before the games to advise athletes against engaging in any protest activity—was sent by the USOC to judge the mood of black athletes and counsel them against any further demonstrations. Owens was viewed by the Olympic community as the personification of the ideal that sport was a positive racial force, that a black man could receive whites' respect through outstanding competitive achievements. In an interview given in the lead-up to the 1968 Olympics Owens had argued, "Athletics has provided negroes with the best chance to break down the barriers of prejudice and to offer models to young people. Attacking the Olympics is like burning down the building we live in. I think it is foolish."[65]

Harry Edwards and his supporters, however, represented a new generation of black athletes who were no longer prepared to play by these rules. He argued during the campaign for the original boycott of the 1968 Games, "You can no longer count on the successors of Jesse Owens to join in a fun-and-games fete propagandized as the epitome of equal rights so long as we are refused those rights in white society."[66] There was a distinct sense that Owens was out of touch with black athletes and was simply a mouthpiece for the Olympic authorities. Vincent Matthews wrote of Owens, "He was a messenger sent by the USOC to determine the mood of the black athletes. The fact that Jesse was black gave him a calling card."[67] Lee Evans commented, "Jesse, I don't know what he was thinking, he was connected to the Olympic committee."[68] Carlos saw Owens as a man out of touch with events in 1968 and suggested he should have done more to further the cause of racial equality.[69] Pointing to Owens's outdated views, Edwards wrote in his account of the OPHR, "He belongs to a controlled generation, the inheritors of Binga Dismond running on the outside. Does it occur to Jesse Owens that blacks are ineligible by color-line and by endless economic obstacles to compete in some 80 per cent of scheduled Olympic events?"[70] Owens faced a credibility gap and his approach to the black and white athletes sympathetic to Smith and Carlos reveals much about the breakdown in relations between the U.S. Olympic authorities and a significant portion of their athletes.

The twenty-five or so teammates whom Owens was sent to address included some notable white athletes. Owens preached the liberal ideals of integration and gradual racial progress. Nevertheless, when confronting this interracial group of Smith and Carlos supporters he responded by asking the white athletes to leave. Owens said, "It's nothing against you other men personally, but these are my black brothers, and I want to talk to them. I think you can understand."[71] Owens asked why white hammer throwers Hal Connolly and Ed Burke were present. Connolly remarked, "He was upset at seeing white athletes there, especially me."[72] Owens obviously felt that it would be easier to persuade black athletes of his point of view without a white audience. He perhaps believed that this racially pure environment would help him to make the point to black athletes that they should behave as narrowly defined ambassadors for their race. Owens, as a spokesman for the USOC, was attempting to construct a view of the podium salute as an unwise expression of a black militancy that could only damage the sporting sphere.

Owens wanted to use race as the distinguishing factor when attempting to dissuade athletes from any further protest. Lee Evans and other black athletes present insisted that their white teammates stay in the meeting, wherein Owens counseled those present not to do anything they would regret. He reminded them of their patriotic duties and the importance of the Olympic Games. The black athletes were "cordial" but largely ignored a man they perceived as "out of touch" with the situation.[73] Nevertheless, his appeal was directed specifically at his "black brothers"; he wanted them to realize what he saw as the folly of conducting any further demonstrations.

The attempt to see the podium salute as simply the expression of black militants distorts its wider symbolic significance. The button that was worn by Peter Norman and other white athletes during the games represented the Olympic Project for Human Rights, not the Olympic Project of Black Power nor the Black Militant Olympic Movement. The OPHR button had a wreath as the focal point and was designed by white students at San Jose State College. That Smith and Carlos were making a stand for black people and for justice in racist America is undeniable, but there was an interracial message to the symbolism and meaning of that podium salute that has often been overlooked. The USOC's desire to paint the protest as an episode of black militancy was threatened by the vocal support offered for Smith and Carlos by white athletes like Tom Waddell, Hal Connolly, and the Harvard rowing crew. Hoffman was very nearly suspended from the rowing final simply for giving Peter Norman the button that he wore on the winners' rostrum. U.S. Olympic authorities were adamant that politics should not enter the sporting arena, but they were also worried that an interracial protest would be much harder to neutralize. It was one thing to have two angry young black men throw a Black Power salute during the national anthem, quite another to have white teammates offering support and threatening to pull out of the rest of the games. It was reported that black and white athletes might go home in protest at the treatment of Smith and Carlos.[74]

The USOC was extremely concerned about the actions of white athletes like Hoffman and the Harvard crew who supported the actions of Smith and Carlos. In a letter sent after the games to the Harvard rowing coach, Harry Parker, Douglas Roby argued that the crew had "embarked on a rather strenuous program of civil rights and social justice with other members of our Olympic delegation to Mexico City." Roby continued, "Civil rights and the promotion of social justice may have their place in various facets of society, but certainly this sort of promotion has no place in the Olympic Games, and particularly when they are held in a foreign country, which country is not particularly involved in these internal problems of ours."[75] Furthermore, decathlete Tom Waddell, one of the white athletes who had voiced support for the OPHR, was asked by a reporter if he thought Smith and Carlos had discredited the American flag. Waddell replied that he felt that Smith and Carlos, as African Americans, had been discredited by the flag more often than they had disgraced it. When questioned about whether the image of the United States had been tarnished, he argued that the nation's image was so bad already it could not get any worse.[76] Waddell, who was a medical doctor serving with the army, saw his comments widely reported in the press. He received a cable from his commanding officer ordering him to retract his remarks or face a court-martial.[77]

There was a definite interracial dynamic to the OPHR movement. Harry Edwards himself struggled to negotiate the divide between white liberals and a growing black militancy. Edwards dedicated his account of the OPHR to the white athletes who supported the cause and commended the Harvard crew for their commitment to understanding the problems in black America. Nevertheless, the brash and abrasive character of Edwards and the contentious hyperbole that flowed from him did much to promote a misunderstanding of and hostility toward the ideals of the OPHR. Even those sympathetic to the movement were not entirely comfortable with his role. Furthermore, Edwards explained sometime after the events of 1968 that he was skeptical about the extent to which whites could help the cause he was seeking to promote.[78]

The degree to which the protest by Smith and Carlos and the reaction to it represented the tensions of the wider black freedom struggle has often been overlooked. Certainly it suited the agenda of the Olympic authorities and the U.S. government—the 1968 Olympic team was not invited to the White House for the customary reception with the president—to portray the podium salute as part of the militant Black Power agenda. The wider message of interracial support for the advancement of civil rights was ignored. Images of Smith and Carlos were placed in the same symbolic context as race riots in cities across America in the spring and summer of 1968. Historical accounts of the sixties or specifically of 1968 often include the image of the podium salute alongside pictures of the slain Dr. Martin Luther King Jr., Black Panther rallies, or scenes of racial violence, usually with a generic caption about Black Power or racial turmoil. What needs to be recognized is that the Smith and Carlos protest reflected the very complex state of the black freedom struggle in the late 1960s. The presence of Norman on the podium wearing the OPHR badge and the support Smith and Carlos received from some of their white teammates showed liberal white sympathy for their cause. Their actions were not, therefore, a simple, one-dimensional expression of black militancy. It is crucial that this is recognized in full and that the subsequent meaning of the protest on the victory podium is not reduced.

It would be fascinating to learn what Martin Luther King Jr. would have said about the podium salute had he not been assassinated six months before the games. His support of the original boycott idea can be interpreted as part of his increasingly radical agenda as his career progressed. Nevertheless, he had strongly objected to the use of the slogan "Black Power" as part of the Civil Rights Movement. He would have admired the courage and dignity of Smith and Carlos, but how would he have responded to the raised black fists? The NAACP, the main moderate civil rights organization, has nothing relating to the Smith and Carlos salute in the sports files of its archives.[79] It is difficult not to conclude, however, that what Smith and Carlos did was in many respects "moderate" and not connected to the black radicalism of the late 1960s in the way it was simplistically portrayed. It was in fact very much in the spirit of nonviolent and dignified protest that both the NAACP and King had long endorsed. *New York Times* sports correspondent Robert Lipsyte later reflected that in the context of things that they could have done, the build-up to the Olympics, and the threatened boycott, the sprinters' gesture hardly seems very extraordinary.[80] A letter to the editor in the *New York Times* stated that

Tommie Smith "did not riot, or loot or burn. . . . His gesture was restrained, even dignified. What more can America conceivably ask from people who have been second-class citizens for so long?"[81]

The fact that sport had so long resisted the political intrusion of the civil rights agenda intensified the negative reaction to the podium salute, but also important was a fundamental misinterpretation of the message of Black Power. Here again the Smith and Carlos protest encapsulates a key component of the wider civil rights struggle in the late 1960s. The sprinters were cast as ghetto militants; men who shared the same ideology as those rioting and raging against the forces of law and order. Their defiance of Olympic protocol was extended as a metaphor for the defiance of white authority by the black underclass. Here were two black men in U.S. uniforms betraying their country by disrespecting the flag. Smith and Carlos, however, bowed their heads on the podium. They did so to remember the fallen heroes of the Civil Rights Movement. Theirs was a solemn and relatively nonthreatening defiance of injustice.

The negative reaction to their gesture and its association with racial disorder was and is based on a fundamental misinterpretation of the Black Power Movement. As Van Deburg asserts, "Black power was not a one-dimensional social movement sponsored by a small but vocal minority of Afro-Americans whose passion was racism and violence."[82] It was in fact an effort to raise black consciousness and facilitate African Americans' gaining of influence on the national stage. This is precisely what Smith and Carlos were aiming to do. The fact that their stand was so anathema to the sporting authorities contributed to the portrayal of the protest as a manifestation of the negative interpretation of Black Power. One correspondent to Brundage in the aftermath of the decision to send Smith and Carlos home regarded that decision as misguided precisely because it would promote the sprinters as black militants. Rather than being seen as a silent and peaceful protest, the podium salute would be viewed as a stand by "black power" heroes because of the expulsion of the two men from the Olympic village. This would in turn widen the mistrust and anger felt toward their white countrymen by many in black America.[83]

While the Smith and Carlos salute is connected to these different strands of the civil rights struggle in many clear ways, there is a sense in which the symbolism and explanation of their salute revealed a more nuanced development in this struggle. In wearing no shoes on the victory rostrum the two men were highlighting the poverty of black America, while their arms formed an arch of unity for black America. This unity was increasingly illusory, however, as the poverty of some in black America contrasted with the economic progress of a growing middle class. The violence, destruction, and looting that were linked to the Black Power Movement by the media had poverty as its root cause. Before his death King was organizing a poor people's campaign that called for a fundamental redistribution of American wealth. The civil rights legislation of the 1960s had not solved the problems of the ghetto but it had helped to promote the growth of an affluent black middle class. By making their stand Smith and Carlos sacrificed any hope of a lucrative professional sports career; they restricted their opportunity to climb out of the poverty they were protesting against.

In the aftermath of the Olympics Smith was denied a chance to pursue a career with the Los Angeles Rams, who had negotiated a possible contract with him before the games. He played on the Cincinnati Bengals' taxi squad before being cut and playing some football in Canada. Carlos too played football in Canada, having been unable to make it in the United States. Smith's marriage broke down; he received death threats and was unable to make ends meet before taking a coaching job that he was overqualified for in Santa Monica. Carlos did not complete his college degree and so had no qualifications to fall back on. He had to do odd jobs, including working as a bouncer in a bar. He later explained, "We had four children, and some nights I would have to chop up our furniture and put it in the fireplace to stay warm." His wife committed suicide in 1977 and Carlos admitted this had a lot to do with the legacy of 1968.[84]

Tarnished by the dominant negative interpretation of their stand in Mexico City, the two men were victims of the endemic racial prejudice of American society. One element of the podium salute reflected a cry on behalf of an impoverished black underclass that was largely untouched by the legislative advances of the Civil Rights Movement. In the decades that have followed an affluent black middle class has benefited from that legislation while an underclass has remained. The radical messages of the civil rights struggle have been ignored as a conservative agenda has sought to proclaim the successful emergence of a color-blind society in which individuals of any race or creed have equality before the law. Since the 1980s Smith and Carlos have been lionized as civil rights heroes and their stand offered as a touchstone for racial pride. The broader and more complex meanings of their protest have been ignored, and they have instead been cited as courageous men who made a stand for equality in sport and wider society. This popular cultural message looks past the deeper significance of the podium salute. Smith and Carlos wore no shoes to highlight black poverty. They stood as symbolic representatives of a diverging black freedom struggle that was increasingly focusing on the economic deprivation of African Americans and demanded true social justice. This aspect of their podium salute has not been fully acknowledged by popular culture representations.

The stand by Smith and Carlos is celebrated and memorialized with a superficial gloss. Robert Lipsyte described Smith and Carlos on that podium as "statues in history."[85] In many respects what they stood for and what their protest symbolized has been set in stone. The podium salute is there to be admired; it changed the Olympic landscape and provides a context for African American athletes. The image of Smith and Carlos is, therefore, used in much the same way as King's "I Have a Dream" speech. King has been placed in the safe category of civil rights hero and great orator. In the process of commemorating his achievements the more radical elements of his message have been forgotten. King has been portrayed as a "non-abrasive hero" who can be used as a resource for "rocking our memories to sleep."[86]

Similarly, the symbolism of the salute by Smith and Carlos has been diluted in an attempt to create a usable past. It provides a cultural reference within a popular narrative of the black freedom struggle that highlights a number of heroic moments that changed the racial landscape. This simplifies the reality of race relations and narrows the scope of the civil rights struggle.[87] In the short- and medium-term aftermath of the 1968 Olympics the sprinters were represented as angry young black men who disrespected the nation that gave them the opportunity to compete and succeed on the world stage. Within twenty years of their stand they were transformed into American heroes whose personal courage drew attention to the struggle for human rights and racial equality. These two extremes ignore a much more nuanced reality.

There is a tendency to see the symbol of the podium salute without exploring the crucial messages inherent in it. It is important to look closely at what Smith and Carlos's actions said about the state of the racial struggle in America in the late 1960s and what this now says about the situation forty years later. The image of Smith and Carlos was rehabilitated in the lead-up to the 1984 Olympics in Los Angeles and in the years thereafter. Both Smith and Carlos were enlisted as consultants by the Los Angeles Organizing Committee. In popular culture their stand has increasingly been seen as heroic.[88] A statue commemorating their protest was built on the San Jose State campus, and in 2008 they were presented with the Arthur Ashe Award for Courage. The statue was erected in 2005 after a campaign by students to honor the stand of the two sprinters. The statue is an example of an effort to both redress the racial transgressions Smith and Carlos faced and memorialize their stand. It is designed to allow individuals to interact with the memory it is commemorating, as the second-place spot on the podium is empty.[89] Yet in so doing the statue ignores the role of Peter Norman and represents an incomplete memorial to that iconic moment in Mexico City.

To unsophisticatedly categorize the podium gesture as a Black Power salute misses a far more nuanced reality. Simple classification of the black freedom struggle into nonviolent and violent, moderate and radical phases, and integrationist and Black Nationalist impulses perverts the complexity of the racial struggle. Smith and Carlos's podium salute encapsulated that complexity in many different ways. If the iconic image of those bowed heads and raised fists is accompanied by the simple title "Black Power salute," then the subtle ways in which the podium protest reflected the civil rights landscape in 1968 will be lost, as will some important racial challenges for the future. Over forty years hence it is important that this is not lost. If it is, if the search for meaning is diluted, then the significance of Smith and Carlos's effort is compromised.[90]

Letting the Team Down?

The reactions of those on the U.S. Olympic team, both at the time and since, reflect a contested interpretation of the memory of Smith and Carlos's stand. The way that their teammates interpreted and responded to the podium salute further highlights the important search for the meaning of their stand. The fact that even after the passage of forty years many teammates are still critical of various elements of Smith and Carlos' protest is interesting. The failure of some to embrace the now-dominant popular memory of the podium incident as an example of individual courage in support of an abstract notion of equality is illuminating. The concept of team and the traditional ideals of sporting competition have a critical influence on memories of the protest.

The initial response to the suspension of Smith and Carlos was a radicalization of leading black athletes, many of whom had made statements against the original boycott aims of the OPHR. Following the Smith and Carlos protest the black athletes who were not competing crowded into section twenty-two of the Olympic stadium and gave a clenched fist salute every time a black athlete won a medal.[91] There was now an impulse to protest not just racial injustice but the specific treatment of Smith and Carlos. Ron Freeman, a black sprinter, commented, "This is terrible. I think there will be a lot of guys going home."[92] Ahead of his long jump final Ralph Boston stated, "I don't want Brundage giving me a medal either, if I win one."[93] On the victory podium Boston and world-record breaker Bob Beamon made a symbolic protest against the treatment of their African American teammates. Incensed by the treatment received by Smith and Carlos, 400-meter runner Vincent Matthews wrote "down with Brundage" on his bedsheet and hung it from his window in the Olympic village.[94] For many, the reactions of the USOC were symptomatic of the problems of interracial sport that the OPHR was protesting. Black athletes were given conditional equality. They were expected to play whites' games by whites' rules. In protesting against racial injustice they had transgressed to the extent that they were removed from the U.S. team. The medals they had won were retained in order to improve the competitive standing of that team, however.

For the black athletes on the U.S. team who were due to compete in the days after the suspension of Smith and Carlos, there was tremendous pressure to make some sort of statement of protest. Particularly affected by this pressure was 400-meter runner Lee Evans. Evans had been one of the founding members of the OPHR and had originally favored the boycott of the games. He and Smith were the most prominent athletes to join with Harry Edwards. The events surrounding his 400-meter final show the twin pressures that threatened the success of the OPHR. These twin pressures came from the Olympic authorities on the one hand and the radicalized wing of the black athletic revolt on the other. At first Evans felt as though he could not run his race after seeing what had happened to Smith and Carlos. His Speed City coach, Bud Winter, thought otherwise, however. Winter used several relaxation techniques to calm Evans down on the afternoon of the 400-meter final.[95] Furthermore, Evans's suspended teammates reminded him of what the athletes involved in the OPHR had agreed: "You run, you win, and then you do your thing."[96] Evans had received numerous death threats before and during the Olympics and felt the weight of both expectation and condemnation around his neck. As he and his fellow competitors were warming up for the race, USOC representative Douglas Roby approached Evans, Larry James, and Ron Freeman (the two other African American finalists) and read the sprinters "the riot act." Evans remembered he was "talking about if we make it to the victory stand and if we try something, it was hard to listen to this guy, because it was ten minutes before the race, we were nervous, we [couldn't] be still, we were fidgeting and rolling our eyes."[97]

The runners went on to take all three medals, with Evans winning while setting a new world record. "God, I think I would have run even faster if I did not have that [political pressure] around my neck," Evans later reflected.[98] Attention then switched to the medalists' actions on the victory podium. Under the subheading "Not Quite the Same Thing," the *New York Times* carried a picture of the men smiling and wearing black berets, with their right fists (without gloves) held in the air. When the national anthem began the men stood perfectly still, conventionally respectful.[99] Evans explained, "It was planned some months earlier and we did not change it because of what Tommie and John did. We did it by event and our protest was to wear black berets."[100] After winning the 400-meter relay Evans and his teammates—Vince Matthews joined the three individual medal winners to make up the quintet—held their left hand under their jersey until they had received their medal and then as one they held them in the air in salute before standing motionless for the national anthem.[101]

The athletes faced questions about whether they were holding back during the individual 400-meter ceremony and whether they felt they had done enough to protest. Speaking about the second medal ceremony, Ron James said, "By then I could do without the ceremony. They could even keep the medal. It was the year and a half getting ready for this that was important. The victory ceremony? That seemed as if it were for someone else."[102] For many, the 400-meter runners, and Evans in particular, had not done enough. Evans had "disappointed his people," as Edwards described it in a stinging attack in his account of the OPHR. Edwards explained, "Torn between his desire to capitalize on his Olympic victories and his need to maintain the respect of his wife and of black people at home Evans tried to do the impossible—he attempted to stand up and be counted on both sides of the fence at once."[103] Much was made of the professional football contract that awaited Evans on his return to the United States, and certainly the fear that any actions might jeopardize their future played heavily on the minds of the young sprinters, especially in light of the treatment received by Smith and Carlos.[104] Evans remains hurt by Edwards's criticism and explained, "Without me he would never have had Carlos and Tommie, I always had to convince Tommie to come to the [OPHR] meetings."[105] Nevertheless, Evans returned to San Jose State as something of a "pariah" in the black community.[106] That this should be the case highlights the great difficulty for those involved in the OPHR in attempting to communicate their grievances and express solidarity with the actions of Smith and Carlos. Black athletes faced pressure not only from the IOC and USOC but also from radical leaders in their own community.

The USOC also displayed its great anger at the role played in events by Harvard rowing coxswain Paul Hoffman. Hoffman had given his OPHR button to Peter Norman, who then wore it on his jersey during the victory ceremony. He later explained, "I must have been seen by Bob Paul or someone. I was certainly seen hovering around there with them." The U.S. rowing team officials felt that Hoffman had participated in the political protest of Smith and Carlos and they were under instructions from the IOC and USOC to ensure that the coxswain was questioned concerning his involvement. Hoffman remembered that one of the rowing officials approached some of the crew the day before their final and said, "Listen, don't worry, we have got a ruling that if you are suspended from a team sport for a political protest we can get a substitute; even if something happens to Paul you guys will still be able to row."

Later in the day it became clear that Hoffman had been suspended from competition pending an enquiry. Hoffman was brought before a committee of between eight and twelve administrators from the USOC. "I was charged with conspiring to aid a demonstration, and I had one very simple position on that—I was not guilty because I had not done it." Hoffman was cross-examined with his coach, Harry Parker, alongside him. They probed his political beliefs and questioned his actions after the 200-meter final. Hoffman explained, "The closest it got to spiraling out of control was when they asked me didn't I think this [his part in aiding Smith and Carlos' protest] was violating the spirit of the Olympics. I thought what they [Smith and Carlos] were doing was within the Olympic spirit of brotherhood."[107] Another member of the team, Scott Steketee, had told journalists on the day after the Smith and Carlos suspension that their punishment was "unfair and tragic."[108] This was clearly not a view shared by the USOC.

Men like Lee Evans, Vince Matthews, and the Harvard rowing crew represent examples of U.S. Olympians who supported the actions of Smith and Carlos. One of the rowers, Cleve Livingston, reflected on the symbolism of those actions over thirty-five years after the games in Mexico City. He argued, "I thought it was a very forceful but affirmative message of both protest and hope. I think it was a statement of two black athletes who had been brought up in poverty . . . and who had been able to excel in track and field, it was a message saying that the United States needs to do better in both its tolerance, but more importantly, appreciation of the value of diversity. . . . It was also a statement of hope, an affirmative statement of hope that the message would be heard and through peaceful and nonviolent means."[109]

By making such a statement Livingston showed he embraced the dominant popular meaning of the podium salute that emerged from the 1980s onward. Yet oral histories show that this is not the dominant interpretation of events among many of the athletes who made up the U.S. team in 1968. This reveals the important role played by concepts of team and traditional sporting ideals in the interaction between sport and the civil rights struggle.

Athletes at the time and in their reflections some years later criticized the forum used by Smith and Carlos and the nature of their protest. Decathlete Bill Toomey argued that the Olympics was a place for competition only, and swimmer David Perkowski stated that the games was not the place for politics and that Smith and Carlos were not acting like members of a team.[110] Water polo player Bruce Bradley asserted that it was an honor to receive a medal and that, having seen Smith and Carlos behave as they did, the U.S. Olympic Committee was "well within its rights [to send them home]. It must maintain some sort of order."[111] Speaking years later, Bradley softened his stance a little, suggesting that the decision to send Smith and Carlos home was somewhat harsh. The criticism of the podium salute itself remained, however. Bradley asserted, "I don't think they should have used the forum" to make the statement that they did.[112] Pole-vaulter Bob Seagren, who had secured his own gold medal moments before Smith and Carlos took the podium, responded to their gesture with the comment, "If they don't like the United States they can always leave."[113] Seagren's criticism was noted by his black teammate Lee Evans, who recalled seeing television interviews in which Seagren "said some things which I thought were stupid."[114] Speaking with the considerable benefit of hindsight, the pole-vault champion conceded that he had been somewhat naïve in his outlook as a young athlete in 1968. Seagren argued that the timing of the protest by Smith and Carlos, taking place during the national anthem, contributed to the overreaction of many athletes and administrators.[115]

Controversy over different performers' interpretation of "The Star-Spangled Banner" and the contested imagery of the Stars and Stripes was not confined to the actions of Smith and Carlos in 1968. Days before the Olympics in Mexico City José Feliciano had received widespread criticism for his "bluesy" rendition of the national anthem during Game 5 of baseball's World Series. Furthermore, Jimi Hendrix's rendition of "The Star-Spangled Banner" at Woodstock in 1969 was largely regarded as a reflection of the loss of faith in American ideals and a call for redemption amid the turmoil of the Vietnam era. Smith and Carlos, like Hendrix and Feliciano, used the anthem as a forum for their own expression of nationalism.[116] The potent symbolic importance of the raising of the flag and performance of the anthem, coupled with the long sporting traditions of the victory ceremony, had a large impact on the response of athletes.

Indeed, it was the forum chosen for the raised fists and the interpretation of the intent and meaning of this gesture that angered many white athletes. Bruce Bradley's water polo teammate Barry Weisenberg told the press, "I think it was a disgrace. In my opinion an act like that in the medal ceremony defiles the American flag."[117] George Young sympathized with the plight of African American athletes and the wider problems of race relations in the United States, but he remembered disagreeing with the time and place selected by Smith and Carlos for their protest. "I don't think it was the right place to do it, and I think, as a matter of fact, they both lost more than they could have by winning the gold medal." Young reflected that, having gained a place in the limelight after excelling in their chosen event, they should have returned home and then pressed their agenda. "I think that showing themselves to be good athletes shows Black Power without having to stand and hold up a gloved black fist. That to me was not very impressive, their performance was impressive, but on the stand I did not really appreciate it."[118]

Young argued that he and others watching the protest gesture of Smith and Carlos had little idea of what they were actually trying to communicate. The concept of "Black Power" was particularly ambiguous. After all, here were two black athletes standing on a victory stand and representing America while simultaneously complaining about conditions in America. Young still considers this "a kind of contradiction in itself."[119] Smith and Carlos had proved that they did have opportunities in the United States by their very presence on the podium. American swimmer Jane Swagerty reflected that she saw a little cowardice in the actions of Smith and Carlos, that they did "not really embrace the moment for themselves; they were heavily influenced by Harry Edwards."[120] Smith and Carlos would contend that theirs was a personal response born of a great conviction that the issue of America's race problems needed to be highlighted. Swagerty, however, described how she and her swimming teammates were shocked by the actions of the sprinters and "actually rather embarrassed." They believed that Smith and Carlos had "disgraced America" and had chosen the wrong place and time to make the stand that they did.[121]

Many of the athletes who were competing for their country did so with a reverential respect for sporting traditions and the customs of the Olympics. As a consequence, they argued that Smith and Carlos had transgressed. The two sprinters' actions may have been courageous, but they were also seen as misguided both then and now. High jumper Dick Fosbury asserted that while using sport to make a political stand was acceptable in some ways, "I do believe they made a serious mistake by doing a demonstration on the podium. That is a ceremony and there are standards that we have as a society and as a culture as to how we should behave when we are in a ceremony and it should not be made political."[122] Fosbury argued that Smith and Carlos should have used the fame they had achieved as a result of sport to express their opinions once they had stepped outside of the stadium. Similarly, white hammer thrower Ed Burke had counseled black teammate Ralph Boston that he should go to the Olympics, achieve fame, and then use this as a springboard to highlight the problems faced by African Americans.[123] In this way sporting recognition could be harnessed as a force for a political message to be disseminated without the arena of sport being invaded by the political agenda itself.

There are a number of athletes, therefore, who saw then, and years after, something inappropriate in the actions of Smith and Carlos. There are also some whose views reflect the changing popular interpretation of the podium salute. For example, long-distance walker Larry Young explained his opinion following the podium salute: "My initial reaction was, well, is this really appropriate during the ceremony when they were accepting their medals when the U.S. flag was being raised?"[124] On reflection, though, he argued, "I really think that what they did was just fine. You have to understand what was going on in the country at that time. Tommie and John [were] treated as second-class citizens in terms of where they lived and where they stayed . . . but the Olympic team wanted their gold medals."[125]

The fact, however, that Smith and Carlos's teammates were still divided years after in their interpretation of the podium salute is revealing. The concept of team and the dominant ideals of sport continue to have a large impact on the way the protest is viewed. This also highlights the unique relationship between sport and the civil rights struggle. Furthermore, the contested understanding of what Smith and Carlos were trying to do and the conflicting interpretations of the symbolism of their efforts in the immediate aftermath of the 1968 Olympics had an indirect impact on the continued racial struggle on the nation's campuses. The following chapter will explore some of these struggles and explain the ways in which the sporting establishment hardened its attitude toward the use of sport to further the civil rights struggle. The shifting focus from using sport to protest racial injustice in wider society to a revolt against racism in sport was part of a series of complex developments that made it increasingly difficult for athletes to successfully engage in the black freedom struggle. Smith and Carlos were attempting to use the platform afforded by sporting success to highlight racial problems in America. This was something different from the protests at the University of California, Berkeley, and from the predominant manifestation of the black athletic revolt on the campus in 1969.

5

Beyond Mexico City

Sport, Race, Culture, and Politics

You're dealing with a new breed of young people today . . . kids who
[don't] have anything better to do than rebel against discipline, rebel
against the Establishment.
                    —Coach Jake Gaither, Florida A & M University, 1969

I could not grow facial hair, I did not shave until I was thirty years old.
. . . We had another guy . . . he could not grow facial hair either. He
went and got one of these eyebrow brushes that girls used to highlight
their eyebrows so that he could draw on his face to highlight that he
had a mustache, but he really could not grow one.
                    —Haskel Stanback, football player, University of Tennessee

In 1969, the University of Wyoming Cowboys were dominating the
Western Athletic Conference football standings. By the middle of October, they were unbeaten and ranked just outside the top ten college teams
in the country. Coach Lloyd Eaton ran a talented and racially integrated
team with black athletes recruited from across the United States. Eaton
demanded discipline and total commitment and coached his team in the
style of a military dictatorship. White player Alan Zerfoss later recalled,
"Everyone respected [Eaton] because he was a very good disciplinarian,
and you followed his rules. . . . What he was doing was working; we did
not lose many games."[1]

Problems emerged when some of the players wanted to challenge his
rules. The problems were exacerbated because the players who sought
change were the fourteen black players on the squad. Eaton denied their
request to wear black armbands to protest the racist actions of Brigham

Young University. Not only did he deny it, but he threw the players off the team. The Cowboys' performances deteriorated and their winning streak was replaced with a series of losses and a mediocre season. The efforts of the "black fourteen" have parallels with the podium salute of Smith and Carlos. They attempted to make a solemn and dignified protest against injustice. They tried to use their position as athletes to affect the civil rights struggle. Where Smith and Carlos sought to engage with the national community of the United States, the black Cowboys wanted to make their stand in front of the local community of Laramie, Wyoming. Their efforts were greeted with derision, confusion, and recrimination. Nevertheless, just as Smith and Carlos have been lionized and their podium salute captured in a statue, so the black fourteen have now been memorialized. With symbolic connections to the actions of Smith and Carlos, a raised black fist sculpture engraved with the names of the black players sits in the basement of the Student Union on the Wyoming campus.

In April 2004 one of those players, Melvin Hamilton, was speaking with a white friend who had been a student at Wyoming in 1969. The friend remarked, "I notice that the university acknowledged the black fourteen with a memorial to you guys in the Student Union." What followed both shocked and disappointed Hamilton. "What about a memorial to the fans?" the white friend asked, his suggestion being that the actions of the black players ruined the season and began the dismantling of a successful football program. Hamilton recalled, "He said the fans were the ones who got hurt, and he just denied, he failed to see the fact that it really was the blacks who got hurt. It was the blacks, some of who did not finish college, it was the blacks, some of them not going on to play professional football."[2] The recriminations and racial tension experienced by the local community because of the importance of their football team echo down through time. Referring to the statue in the Student Union, historian Lane Demas has observed, "The players' connection to the 'bogy of black power' is fixed in bronze."[3]

Media coverage of the actions of Smith and Carlos brought national attention to the connections between sport and the black freedom struggle. The ripples of dissent moved into communities previously untouched by major civil rights activism. Importantly, this activism was affecting the cherished institutions of local sports teams. The disciplined and traditional world of college sports was being rocked by the gusting cultural winds sweeping across the American landscape. These transformations were complicated because race intersected with changing notions of power and authority. Students protested the Vietnam War, grew their hair long, did not shave, and challenged the status quo in new and unforeseen ways. In the year after the 1968 Olympics the use of sport to advance the civil rights struggle faced considerable difficulties. Confusions between discrimination and discipline and a backlash against forces that were identified as threats to both the local and national sporting communities compromised the effectiveness of the sporting arena as a forum in which to successfully engage with the black freedom struggle.

In contrast to events at Wyoming, after 1968 the focus of the black athletic revolt increasingly shifted to racial politics within athletics departments and sports teams across the country, much more so than the use of sport to engage in political action that dramatized the racial problems of wider society. The sporting establishment showed continued sensitivity when faced with charges of racial injustice within its own ranks. It was, however, able to use the traditional ideal of sport as a positive racial force, combined with strategic concessions, to combat such challenges. As a consequence, the established ideal of sport as a force for positive racial change was reaffirmed. These developments, along with increased contention concerning issues of discipline, coach-player relations, and athletes' human rights, shifted focus away from the use of sport to dramatize the civil rights problems of wider society. As a result, by the early 1970s the black athletic revolt was ostensibly over.

College Athletics in Crisis

For many sports administrators it seemed as though the very institution of college athletics was in danger of collapsing in the twelve months after the stand by Smith and Carlos at the 1968 Olympics. Former California state superintendent of public instruction Max Rafferty argued in 1969, "There are two great national institutions which simply cannot tolerate either internal dissension or external interference: our armed forces, and our interscholastic sports programs. Both are of necessity benevolent dictatorships." He went on to state that at "a dozen . . . disgraced colleges, players have challenged their coaches, walked out on their own teams, and boycotted their own schools, all in name of some social, economic, or political grievance which the sport in question had never had anything to do with."[4] Rafferty was expressing an opinion shared by many college sports administrators who felt besieged by athletes' protests. This activism by college athletes was not confined to racial matters only.

Vice President Spiro Agnew argued that sport had promoted the traditional values of discipline and manhood that had helped shape America. He stated that a minority of young people in the United States were opposed to these values and chose actions that were not appropriate for the playing fields of the nation.[5] Players and administrators were caught in the cross fire of a tumultuous period for intercollegiate athletics, a time when the meaning of the sporting ideal was being defined and redefined. The countercultural challenge to traditional American values evoked a deep tension that touched the world of sport, and as David Zang has asserted, "Undermined [its] claims to character-building and the tenets by which organized sports were conducted: sacrificial effort, submission to authority, controlled physical dominance, victory with honor and manliness."[6]

Novels about football written in the 1960s, like Gary Cartwright's *The Hundred-Yard War* (1968) and Robert Daley's *Only a Game* (1967), for example, invariably focus on a hero who loves the game for its own sake, whose individual flair and brilliance are confronted by a manager's or coach's insistence on regimentation. There was a "shift from earlier in the century when writers of sports fiction valued athletic work to an almost unanimous insistence that what was meaningful in sport was its endangered spirit of play."[7] The impact of the counterculture in the late 1960s, which challenged authority and saw young people rebelling against the value system of their parents' generation, was felt in sport. It is important to note that while this phenomenon was linked to the black athletic revolt, the problems college athletics experienced were by no means purely racial in character. Indeed, the interconnection between racial politics and wider cultural trends contributed to the continued difficulties experienced by athletes who wished to use sport to dramatize racial injustice in society as a whole.

In the summer of 1969, many of the problems faced by college administrators were highlighted in John Underwood's three-part *Sports Illustrated* series titled "The Desperate Coach." Underwood told of many incidents that exposed the great difficulties faced by coaching staff in dealing with a new breed of student athlete. At the University of Maryland a losing football team engineered the firing of their coach, and a small Pittsburgh college dismissed its basketball coach because he would not listen to his players.[8] A track coach in Providence, Rhode Island, found a TV set in the dormitory room of four of his athletes. He argued that TV and studying did not mix and confiscated the set. The coach advised that the students could have their TV back if they decided they did not want to be in the track team. The students duly chose the TV over their place in the team. One by one other athletes began to drop out of the team in sympathy, until there was no team left. The spring schedule had to be abandoned and the coach was fired.[9]

The above examples serve to illustrate that the problems encountered by coaching staff were not solely connected to race. Coaches faced challenges to their rules and discipline in countless examples all across the country. There were several examples, however, of clashes between coaches and players that did indeed center on race. At Indiana, Coach John Pont dismissed ten black players from his football team when they missed practice. Jim Owens at Washington suspended four black players who failed to show full commitment to the football team, after which eight other African Americans refused to go to a game at the University of California, where the Washington team was humbled 57–15.[10] In Iowa Coach Ray Nagel refused to allow two of his black football players—one of them had been arrested on a bad-check charge—to take part in spring practice. The other blacks on the team asked the coach to apologize for things he had said about their two teammates. Nagel did apologize, but the other black players said he was insincere and they all boycotted spring practice.[11] Underwood reported that many black athletes were spurred on or coerced by activists from Students for a Democratic Society or the Black Student Union. Working in concert, these organizations had "rattled athletic departments up and down the West Coast, putting heat on coaches and athletic directors, forcing the cancellation of games, threatening and coercing uncommitted athletes."[12]

This issue of "uncommitted athletes" is interesting. Many coaches and administrators believed that outside influences were affecting their players. Certainly the developments in campus activism had an impact on black athletes. Younger blacks, who were often isolated on predominantly white campuses, saw continued black social and economic inferiority despite the legislative gains of the mid-1960s. Furthermore, liberal and left-wing white activists had shifted their attention from civil rights issues to opposition to the Vietnam War. This, coupled with an increased focus on gaining black control over their own communities, encouraged black activists to make a stand against any university practices they deemed to be discriminatory.[13] This impulse had an impact on the relationship between athletes and their coaches.

One sociological study of black students on white campuses detected a pattern whereby white students withdrew from leadership of interracial activism on campus. This was followed by black-white tension on campus and the formation of segregated fraternities and social organizations.[14] This sense of separation directly affected white coaches and black players. Underwood contended that "many black athletes read race into almost everything a coach says or does. Often mistaking discipline for discrimination . . . these blacks challenge rules whenever they are contrary to their emerging cultural pride, especially as they relate to hair, and demand retribution, or more."[15] Harry Edwards explained the distinct dynamic created by the black athletic revolt on the campus. "While the philosophy of the movement depicted every white person as an institutionalized racist," hence making them legitimate objects of political attack, he argued, it decreed that "every Negro is a potential black man," thus exempting them from the type of political attack suffered by white coaches.[16]

The black athletic revolt was increasingly affected by the wider racial struggles on college campuses across the country. Throughout the 1960s the national political community had sought to address racial inequalities, and black students were empowered with the belief that they deserved to be consulted on matters that concerned them. The Black Student Union demanded a voice about issues that affected the student body and the wider community.[17] This was partly because, despite the legislative achievements of the Civil Rights Movement, mainstream institutions had not been transformed to the extent that they recognized black identity. Therefore, the emphasis of the black student movement was on the reclamation of racial identity and the promotion of black culture on campus and in educational programs.[18] This wider campus movement of the late 1960s touched the black athletic revolt and was touched by it.

What is crucial is that the growing athletic activism was part of an expression of black masculinity. Young black men were influenced by the culture of the growing Black Power Movement and its emphasis on the reclaiming of black masculinity. Black male athletes were therefore under pressure from within the black community to engage with the new sense of black consciousness in the late 1960s by making a stand for their cultural identity. This identity was intertwined with black masculinity, which was often expressed by the clothes and facial hair donned by black men. This development further contributed to the fact that the black athletic revolt was almost entirely a masculine movement. The role of female athletes was minimized and the language, aims, and methods of the movement reflected a concentration on the black male athlete.

This was a response to the growing Black Power Movement and its impact on young black men in the second half of the 1960s. Activists like Stokely Carmichael embraced a vision of manhood that focused on "black men's ability to deploy authority, violence, punishment and power."[19] Music and the arts increasingly disseminated the Black Power ideology among the young black population. James Brown's 1968 anthem "Say it Loud—I'm Black and I'm Proud" expressed a confident and assertive message of black consciousness.[20] A large element of this consciousness was a focus on black masculinity and the desire by black men to reclaim the manhood that had been suppressed by the white power structure. John Carlos spoke out in the aftermath of the podium salute in Mexico City against the attitude of coaches and the society they reflected when they referred to him as a "boy." When sanitation workers in Memphis campaigned for better conditions in 1968 the slogan they adopted was "I AM A MAN." Theirs was a conscious assertion of their manhood as central to the struggle against oppression.[21]

Young black men often chose to express their manhood and loyalty to Black Power ideals through their outward appearance. Facial hair, Afro haircuts, and dashikis were all part of the Black Power Movement of the late 1960s. Such styles were part of the striving of many African Americans to reject traditional cultural parameters and "affirm their racial personhood and shape their environment. No longer would they meekly respond to white stimuli."[22] Indeed, in his 1965 autobiography Malcolm X, the father of the Black Power Movement, wrote of the shame he felt when recalling his own attempts to straighten his hair as a young man. Malcolm argued that black men should embrace their blackness and wear their hair as it was meant to be.[23] In the late 1960s the Afro became a potent stylistic symbol of Black Power.

The case of Fred Milton provides a good example of both the increased focus on protests about racism in sport itself and the strong elements of masculinity that were connected with this focus. In February 1969, racial tension engulfed the campus of Oregon State University when black football player Fred Milton, with the support of the Black Student Union, filed complaints against Coach Dee Andros and the athletics department. Milton alleged that his civil rights had been violated when he was dismissed from the team for refusing to shave off his mustache. Andros had strict rules about facial hair and contended that Milton had openly broken the rules.[24] The coach did not permit hair over the ears or collar, overly long sideburns, or any facial hair. Andros's rules applied to all of his players, with no exceptions. Milton contended that in the off-season he did not have to obey his coach's rules. During a lengthy conversation in his office, Andros countered that his rules applied at all times and that this was part of the "deal."[25] Many black students decided to boycott all classes until the Milton affair was resolved. In response to this decision, the white athletes on campus presented a petition to university president James Jensen supporting the decision of Andros to remove Milton from the team.

There were, however, two white athletes who spoke out against the coach's actions. Dick Fosbury, the 1968 Olympic high jump gold medalist, and Bill Bryant, an All-American fullback, did not concur with the stance taken by their fellow white athletes.[26] Fosbury supported Milton's right to wear whatever facial hair he wanted during the off-season, although he did believe that the coach was within his rights to insist that he not wear it during the season. Fosbury did contend that if one of the white players had grown a mustache or a goatee Andros would have reacted in the same way; for him this was not a racial issue.[27] We see here an example of black athletes focusing on the perceived insensitivity of a coach to their cultural expression. With echoes of the Bob Presley affair at Berkeley, black athletes were charging discrimination and prejudice when in reality it was a clash between team discipline and self-expression.

For many, then, this issue was less about race and more about a conservative coach trying to instill discipline in a time of cultural change. Andros argued that the issue of facial hair was just one of his ways of maintaining discipline. "I'm fighting for a principle of education—the right to run my department," he argued, adding that he could not "abandon the concepts of training, discipline, team unity and morale." As if to assert that there was no racial element to his decision, Andros noted that he did not interfere in the social lives of his players, and this included refusing to stop his black players from dating local white girls whose parents complained to him.[28] Milton, however, claimed that his coach's actions were insensitive to black culture and argued that wearing facial hair was part of his heritage and therefore he was being denied the ability to express his racial identity.[29] To Coach Andros this was just an example of indiscipline, a manifestation of the declining standards of personal grooming.

In many respects this psychological transformation in the black community put a great deal of pressure on African American athletes, specifically black male athletes. They had to maintain loyalty to their coach as a member of a team and as an athletic performer but were pressured to engage in the political activism of other black students on white campuses. The most overt symbols of this new militancy were Afros and facial hair, and there were approximately seventy-three different cases surrounding these issues in athletics departments across the country from 1967 to 1971.[30] Harry Edwards summed up the dilemma faced by black athletes on white campuses. He argued that "the black athlete could conform to the dictates and expectations of the coach and be castigated as an 'Uncle Tom' by his black student peer group, or he could conform to the demands of the peer group and be dismissed from the team."[31] In a sporting environment that was already heavily influenced by conventional constructions of masculinity, this pressure on black male athletes was very strong.

There were examples of more constructive approaches to the problems posed by the increased pressures on athletes to embrace the heightened emphasis on black masculinity. Dick Fosbury recalled that the track coaching staff at Oregon State did not take the same hard-line approach that Andros and others did. "When we had conflicts between what the black athletes wanted to wear and what the coach was assigning as a uniform we sat down as a team and discussed what we felt would be appropriate more as a team. The coach had the final say but he was more interested in listening to the athletes and encouraging a dialogue." Fosbury gave an example of black athletes wanting to wear black socks; the school colors were orange and black. "We had team meetings and we discussed it, and we agreed that all of us would wear black socks and so we did."[32] Demands by black athletes to amend uniforms in this way were an expression of a new black aesthetic that was inspired by the Black Power Movement, but they also show the influence of events at Mexico City. Bob Beamon, Tommie Smith, and John Carlos all wore black socks during their protests on the Olympic medal stand.

When black athletes did engage in militancy on campus they invariably received help from outside agencies. This was the case at Oregon State. The NAACP endorsed the black student activism at Oregon State University. The university's Commission on Human Rights and Responsibilities ruled, after two months of deliberation, that Milton's human rights had been "violated." Recommendations were made to improve the position of black athletes on campus, but no procedures were established to ensure the recommendations were heeded.[33] Milton won his point, but this remained something of a pyrrhic victory as the university balked at putting in place strong and effectively enforced procedures to allow athletes more freedom of cultural expression. Nevertheless, Milton was able to affirm his black manhood and show he was standing up for the rights of his community. In this way he could achieve a psychological win.

The Milton affair is one of countless examples of problems between white coaches and black athletes during 1969. The black athletic revolt increasingly focused on these issues of identity and self-expression and argued that sport was tainted by racial discrimination. Significantly, though, the type of protest that black athletes pursued could all too easily be branded as simply an expression of a countercultural impulse born in declining standards of discipline among young athletes. Jake Gaither, the coach at the traditionally black college Florida A&M, recognized worsening standards among his black players. Crucially, as he was himself black he did not perceive the problem to be racial in any way. Gaither argued, "You're dealing with a new breed of young people today. I began to see it three or four years ago. Kids, who did not have anything better to do than rebel against discipline, rebel against the Establishment, rebel against the status quo."[34]

One Big Eight football coach argued, "I'm tired of this crap about protesting." One of his colleagues stated, "We've always got to understand *them.* Well maybe I can't. I can't know what it's like to be a Negro. Or live in a ghetto. But that doesn't mean I don't try, and I sure think trying works two ways: they've got an obligation to understand *me.* I'm the one giving them the scholarship."[35] The problem of resolving these tensions was something that the sporting establishment could not ignore.

Athletes' Rights and Administrators' Reactions

The black athletic revolt was accompanied by a wider athletic revolt. Athletes were increasingly insistent that they should be treated with greater respect and that they should play a part in the administration of sport. This was particularly the case among white amateur athletes. Hal Connolly and Cleve Livingston were prominent supporters of the OPHR who began to voice concerns that athletes' human rights needed to be given more consideration. These included the right to train as they wished, to take part in events that they wished, to earn a living, and to participate in the administration of the sports in which they competed.[36] John Dobroth, a lesser-known track and field competitor, worked alongside Connolly, Lee Evans, and others to set up a biracial organization called United Amateur Athletes (UAA). This organization was designed to protect the rights of athletes and to press sporting authorities for a greater say in the administration of athletics. Dobroth recalled, "We thought we were taken advantage of in those days. . . . It was archaic and we knew it had to change and we knew we had to get some power."[37]

The UAA newsletter of November 1971 stated that it was "no secret that competing athletes have periodic grievances concerning the administration and promotion of United States track and field." The newsletter went on to outline the various grievances of the athletes and suggest some proposals for change. For example, the UAA was to request a significant donation from all track and field promoters in order to help finance its activities.[38] The UAA remained, in the words of Dobroth, something of a "rump organization."[39] It did not achieve any major advances in the development of athletes' rights, and although sports administrators were aware of the threat posed by actual and potential unrest, power still remained in the hands of traditional administrative bodies. Nevertheless, the organization did give athletes a voice and served as a warning that their views needed to be considered.

The defensiveness that traditional governing elites exhibited in response to criticism has already been noted in the response of the NCAA to the charges of racial discrimination in sport made in Jack Olsen's *Sports Illustrated* series. Echoes of this can be seen in the response of the Amateur Athletic Union (AAU) to the activities of the UAA. A letter written to Dobroth from the AAU's track and field administrator, Ollan Cassell, in November 1971 was very specific in addressing what Cassell believed to be factual errors in the newsletter that Dobroth had produced.[40] From 1968 through the early 1970s the AAU, the USOC, and the NCAA were all aware of the potential threat posed by a rising desire among athletes to become more involved in the administration of sport. This issue ran alongside the growing focus on alleged racial discrimination in sport. Administrators' responses to these twin challenges to the sporting community reveal a mixture of strategic concessions and an attempt to neutralize dissent.

At the executive committee meeting of the USOC in December 1968 the members started by reviewing the report on the Mexico City Olympics and the recommendations for future games. Referring to the issues surrounding the protests of Smith, Carlos, and other athletes, the report argued, "There should have been a confrontation between coaches and team personnel and these problems should have been resolved in the United States before permitting teams to leave for Mexico City." Included in a list of seemingly contradictory recommendations were calls to "enforce statements from athletes to comply with USOC and IOC rules . . . improve indoctrination of athletes prior to departure for Games" and "consider recommendations from athletes, coaches and managers for improvements."[41] So USOC leaders acknowledged that there were problems and that athletes' suggestions for improvements should be considered but in the same breath they revealed a desire to neutralize dissent by calling for improved "indoctrination" of athletes. This was hardly a statement to please those who wanted athletes to have more freedom of thought and action.

In the December meeting of the USOC executive committee the former rower John Sayre gave a presentation on behalf of a board of consultants that had been set up to liaise with athletes in the months leading up to and during the Mexico City Olympics. This was the board that had Jesse Owens as its most notable representative. Sayre presented a statement written by athletes after the games that called for their greater involvement in the decision making of the USOC. Sayre argued, "Our athletes are mature, intelligent, aware and concerned men and women. They feel deeply the problems and divisions of today's world and see sports as a major force to give new and positive purpose to the younger generation."[42] Sayre went on to recommend several initiatives that should be adopted if further unrest was to be averted. These included seats on the board of consultants for recently retired athletes and a responsibility for members of the board to eat meals with the athletes in the Olympic village so as to gain a greater appreciation of their concerns.

The realization of a need to include the voices of more athletes in the administration of U.S. Olympic sports in the long term helped to neutralize potential unrest among athletes who were concerned with issues other than race. The UAA was a loose affiliation of athletes, and boycotts or major protest action in favor of their intended aims never materialized. What is important here is that the USOC in particular recognized the potential for political issues to be brought into the sporting arena. Sayre argued that athletes felt the "problems and divisions of today's world" and the warning was that they might use sport to dramatize these issues. The USOC had been consistent in its aversion to the intrusion of politics into sport, and making concessions toward increasing athletes' rights of representation within its own organization seemed a small price to pay to head off such an intrusion.

The problems posed by the racial turmoil on college campuses had to be approached by the NCAA. The organization responded to the increasing campus unrest and the revelations of Underwood's articles in much the same way as it had to Olsen's series a year before. The major concern was to discredit the claims of those who argued that sport was infected by widespread racial prejudice and to neutralize dissent. In this case the NCAA was not as concerned as the USOC with sport being used to highlight wider political issues. The major problem facing intercollegiate athletics was a challenge to the ideal that sport provided a positive racial force. The NCAA set about a policy of neutralizing dissent and reaffirming this traditional ideal.

In November 1969 a memorandum to NCAA executive director Walter Byers presented a list of questions to be used in an investigation to ascertain the extent to which "outside interests" may have been involved in the difficulties some universities had experienced with "Negro student-athletes." Interestingly, the vast majority of the proposed questions were aimed at discovering how students protested, what the impact was on other team members and coaches, and the level of disruption to the university as a whole. Only two of the proposed thirteen questions were actually concerned with what the athletes were "demanding" and whether or not the athletics department had met with the protesters. None of the questions, which were to be used in "off the record" discussions with coaches at Wyoming, Washington, Colorado State, Oregon State, and Iowa, probed whether black protesters' grievances were in any way legitimate or whether the universities had attempted to meet these grievances with policy changes.[43]

There is evidence that a number of press clippings and editorials were collected by NCAA staff in relation to the racial problems on the campuses mentioned above. Some of this material was passed on to Senator John McClellan, who led the Subcommittee on Investigations that had produced the Student Disturbance Act earlier in 1969.[44] Many college athletes were caught up in the antiwar movement and asserted their right to break out of what Bob McLennan, white captain of the 1970 University of California track team, called the "apolitical atmosphere which has permeated the athletic community."[45] McClellan's investigations, however, did not simply focus on dissent concerning Vietnam. Indeed, in his statement introducing the 1969 act on the Senate floor he quoted Professor Nathan Glazer in identifying "radical white students [and] militant black students as the major threat to universities." The senator went on to identify the Black Panthers among several groups that incited trouble on college campuses.[46] There was a feeling among administrators that black activist groups were attempting to influence student athletes and were instrumental in instigating some of the campus demonstrations. Certainly one of the questions that the NCAA was planning to ask in their off-the-record talks with coaching staff was whether there was any evidence of outside interests exerting pressure on their athletes.[47]

The concern of national administrators was to minimize the disruption caused by protests and to deflect charges of institutional racism. Their mindset was similar to that of men like Brundage, Roby, and Owens. Sport had provided an arena where African Americans could excel, and to disrupt that arena was an act of ingratitude and immaturity on the part of protesting black athletes. The dominant focus of the NCAA was, therefore, on how best to refute the claims that sport was in any way institutionally racist. This became the principal issue because of the shifting focal point of the black athletic revolt. The major emphasis was on protest against racism in sport as opposed to using sport to protest racial injustice in the wider society. Nevertheless, the NCAA did attempt to engage with these wider problems. One clear way to combat the attack on the long-held belief that sport was a positive racial force was to reemphasize this ideal.

In concert with the federal government the NCAA embarked on an initiative aimed at bringing the benefits of involvement in sport to inner-city youth. The National Summer Youth Sports Program (NSYSP) was to involve approximately 150 colleges running activities and events for young people aged twelve to eighteen. This program had obvious racial connections because many of America's most impoverished inner-city youth were in fact black. The NCAA was, therefore, continuing to preach the ideal that sport was a positive racial force. The NSYSP program could be cited as an example of sport being used to promote racial progress and therefore reaffirmed the very ideal that the black athletic revolt sought to challenge. Clearly NCAA administrators were pleased with the progress of the program. The minutes of the organization's executive council meeting of 1969 commend Walter Byers and other members of the NCAA for their leadership of the NSYSP project. Members of the committee watched a documentary that showed the positive impact of the activities of the NSYSP. It was noted that the continuance of the project was very much desirable, as long as the appropriate funding was supplied by the incoming Nixon administration.[48]

What we can see in the response of sporting administrators to the problems of athletic unrest in the period after the 1968 Olympics is a mixture of strategic concessions and attempts to neutralize dissent. The calls for greater athlete involvement in the running of sport were taken into account by the USOC and the AAU, and processes were set in motion that led to reforms that resulted in the 1978 Amateur Sports Act. This act provided for gender equality, sports development, and athletes' rights.[49] So a framework that could deal with athletes' calls for greater involvement without fundamentally revolutionizing the administration of sport was conclusively put in place. The contemporaneous focus on racial discrimination and prejudice within sport itself was greeted with great defensiveness by the NCAA. They were more concerned with refuting allegations and neutralizing dissent than with actually helping to improve conditions for black athletes.

What was not being discussed as these issues were worked out, however, was the role of sport in dramatizing the racial problems in wider society. Certainly the Milton affair and countless others were bringing contemporary racial politics into the sports world. Crucially, though, this was a different phenomenon than athletes using their position as sports stars to call attention to racial struggles in wider society. This latter effort had been the initial impulse of the OPHR and represents a specific connection between the world of sport and the black freedom struggle. Remember, the initial aims of the OPHR boycott movement spoke to wider political issues like the suspension of apartheid South Africa and the desegregation of sporting facilities. Smith and Carlos's stand, as Smith so eloquently explained, was designed to draw attention to the problems of poverty and racial injustice that shaped American society. The protests of men like Milton and Presley were bringing the increasing black consciousness of the late 1960s into the sports world in an interconnected but subtly different way.

It is in this context that we now turn to events in Wyoming in the fall of 1969 and discuss the waning potential for sport to be used as an arena for protesting against the racial injustice of wider society. The Wyoming protest has traditionally been discussed in relation to the general racial unrest in athletics departments across the country in 1969. Indeed, the NCAA files on racial incidents refer to it alongside other disturbances concerning black players.[50] Wyoming represents a case study of the black athletic revolt in the period after the 1968 Olympics. Just as the national sporting community reacted angrily as the Black Power Movement intruded on the sporting arena, so the local community in Wyoming blamed outside agitators for the disruption of their football program. Events at Wyoming were different from other manifestations of the black athletic revolt on other campuses in 1968 and 1969. The attitudes toward the black athletes involved were informed by these other developments, however. The twin forces of countercultural challenges to traditional authority and assertions of black masculinity made it increasingly difficult for athletes to use sport to successfully advance the black freedom struggle.

The Black Fourteen and the Problems of Protesting Racial Injustice through Sport

The attempted protest at Wyoming can be traced back to the original architect of the black athletic revolt. Harry Edwards was instrumental in helping black football players at San Jose State realize their desire to wear black armbands during a game against Brigham Young University (BYU). The bands were a protest against a doctrine of the Mormon Church that stated that black people could not be members of the priesthood. With head coach Joe McMullen offering his own criticism of Mormon policies, the San Jose State authorities produced a "right of conscience" agreement that allowed players to sit out games or express their political views on the field.[51] These events embody the initial aims of the black athletic revolt: to use the sporting arena as a place to dramatize wider racial injustice.

Black students at the University of Wyoming also expressed a desire to protest against the racial views of BYU. The fourteen black players who were subsequently suspended from their football team for attempting to protest were not boycotting any games; they were not accusing their coach of being racist or culturally insensitive. Instead, they were trying to use the sporting arena to point to a racial injustice that existed in wider society, in this case the continued racial prejudice and segregation that were features of the Mormon institution. Theirs was a protest in the spirit and style of that carried out at San Jose a year earlier.

There were very few African American students at BYU. When integrated teams visited Utah they often encountered difficulties when staying in Provo because of the racial prejudice they encountered. Indeed, there was not a suitable hotel that would accommodate an integrated team of white and black players.[52] San Jose State was not the only institution to protest the policies of BYU. Their passions raised by the assassination of Martin Luther King Jr., black student athletes at the University of Texas at El Paso, including Bob Beamon, organized a boycott of a track meet with BYU. The university's response was to cut off financial aid to the black athletes and suspend them from further competition. When the university tried to hold a home track event without the black athletes, African American female students invaded the track and held a sit-down protest, whereupon they had to be removed by city and state policemen.[53] Early in 1969, black members of the New Mexico basketball team wore black ribbons on their shirts as a protest during a game with BYU. Following this incident the school's athletics department ruled that no deviation from standard uniform would be permitted in the future.[54]

Bob Beamon in action for the University of Texas at El Paso. Courtesy of University Communications, University of Texas at El Paso.

Black members of the University of Wyoming Cowboys football team had themselves experienced racial prejudice while playing against BYU. During games they were subject to racial taunts from opponents on the field and spectators in the stand. Tackles after the whistle aimed at the Cowboys' African Americans were common, and these "cheap shots" often carried not only symbolic but also physical weight. Many of the BYU players had completed their mission and come back to play football at the age of twenty-two or twenty-three; therefore they were three or four years older than some of the Cowboys. As black Wyoming player Melvin Hamilton argued, "These guys were physically men compared to us, so they could put some damage on us."[55] The fourteen football players who met with Willie Black, the chancellor of the Black Student Alliance, in October 1969 were among approximately 150 African American students on the Wyoming campus.[56] It was Black who explained the racial practices of the Mormon Church at a black student meeting prior to the game with BYU.

This example of the impact of student activism on the university and consequently on the athletics department had long been anticipated by head football coach Lloyd Eaton. Eaton made it clear to members of his team in 1968 that they were not permitted to get involved in any political activism during their time on the team. He sent his assistants to an ROTC protest to report whether any of his players were present. He warned his team not to get involved in any protests about the Vietnam War and said that they were not permitted to form any kind of faction or group within the team.[57]

The Black Student Alliance made public a letter criticizing the racial policies of the Mormons. This letter was delivered to Eaton and indicated that "the Black Students Alliance opposed on moral and human grounds contests with Brigham Young University and that the BSA would protest any such contest including the football game with BYU scheduled for 18 October, by wearing of black arm bands."[58] Eaton responded by telling black tri-captain Joe Williams that he would not allow the players to wear the armbands at practice or on the field of play. Williams informed the thirteen other black players on the team of Eaton's decision, after which they decided to seek a meeting with the coach the day before the game to see if some form of compromise could be reached. The players were trying to engage with issues of racial discrimination outside of their own athletics department. They were not threatening to boycott any games or protesting about their own coach in the way many other black athletes were across the country in 1969.

The fourteen black players went to Eaton's office well before practice was due to begin on the morning of October 17. Each player was wearing a black cloth armband. Eaton ordered the players to the field house, where he informed them that they were "through" because they had violated his rules. The coach remarked that they could "go back on Negro relief" or play for the black schools "Grambling or Morgan State."[59] Joe Williams argued that Eaton did not understand his black players. He maintained that the black Cowboys wanted to wear armbands, or black socks, or a black cross on their helmets but had decided that if Eaton said they could not then they would be willing to protest with just their black skins. Williams maintained that the coach would not listen to their requests but instead sneered and yelled.[60] "He flew off the handle and said things about us being on nigger relief and that was the kind of thing that just incensed the whole situation there and as a result of that we were kicked off the team."[61] Because the players went to Eaton well before practice was to begin they felt they were not breaking any rule by wearing their black armbands.

Eaton, however, regarded the players' actions as an affront to his leadership and was not interested in discussing a compromise or the extent of the black grievances. The coach believed that he and the university had given the players an opportunity that they were wasting. He remarked later, "What we were trying to do for these fellows was to give them that chance to really do something for their people by getting that education."[62] Eaton had suspended the players twenty-four hours before the game against BYU. In an attempt to resolve the crisis, university president William Carlson and Wyoming governor Stanley Hathaway convened a meeting with the fourteen black players that stretched long into the night. Eaton did not attend the meeting but spoke to Carlson and Hathaway after it had concluded. The black players refused to back down because of the way their coach had approached their request. Just as Edwards had used sport as a power lever to push for concessions at San Jose State in 1967, so the black players at Wyoming realized the power they had when threatening to ruin the Cowboys' football season.[63] The real power lay with Eaton, however. He had produced a winning football program and had the support of the local community. As Melvin Hamilton later recalled, "Football at that time was really more powerful than the presidency and more powerful than the governor. . . . [The players] did not have enough power to call down the man who put the University of Wyoming on the map athletically."[64] The black players were informed that Eaton's decision would stand and they were off the team.

At Berkeley and Oregon State black players threatened to or actually did withdraw from practice sessions in order to raise awareness of various racial problems. Both Presley and Milton accused their coaches of racial insensitivity, and inherent in their protest was the argument that sport itself was the home of racial prejudice. Whereas at Marquette basketball players briefly withdrew from the university in order to put pressure on administrators to improve the institution's commitment to civil rights and social justice, at Wyoming the black players were removed from the team by the coach for requesting to protest against the racist practices of another institution. The black players did not attempt to protest against the problems that they encountered on their own campus, and complaints concerning racial prejudice at Wyoming surfaced only after the dismissal of the black fourteen. Eaton's response was typical of many coaches who felt besieged by protesting athletes during 1969. Crucially, though, the circumstances at Wyoming were different. For Eaton the request to wear armbands was not distinct from the desire to grow a mustache or sideburns; they all represented a violation of his rules. Nevertheless, there was a subtle difference. While Milton and others argued that facial hair was part of their cultural identity, the black fourteen requested to wear armbands to draw attention to racial segregation and injustice.

Certainly there were racial tensions at Wyoming before the incident involving BYU but these did not produce any significant protests. Black student and Cowboys player Melvin Hamilton had experienced some of the problems facing black students on white campuses two years before the protest at Wyoming. Hamilton was playing under Coach Eaton but was also dating a white woman on campus. The couple wanted to get married and Hamilton requested the assistance of the athletics department concerning housing and finance. It was customary for the department to assist students who were married during their time on the football team. Hamilton explained that "Coach Eaton said he could not let me marry a woman of the white race or the supporters would run him out of town, so consequently he and I had a blowout."[65] As a result Hamilton refused to play football any longer. He left the school and spent some time in the army before returning to play for the Cowboys when Eaton agreed to give him his scholarship back. Hamilton was determined not to let racism get in the way of his education but was aware of the racial issues on campus. He believed that white students saw the black athletes only as football players and not as legitimate students.[66] In his book *Sports in America*, James Michener told a story about one of the black players at Wyoming who made romantic advances toward a white girl. When news of this reached some of the white Cowboys players a posse was organized to "gun down the nigger if he makes another move."[67]

The population of Wyoming in 1969 was less than 1 percent African American. The university recruited black students from around the country, and the campus of 8,419 students had about 150 African Americans.[68] Such was the scarcity of black students that they were ostracized from the social life of the campus.[69] Willie Black, chancellor of the Black Student Union, came to Wyoming from Chicago. He argued that there was "very little overlapping of the races." In fact, Black argued that "the Cowboys are separate, the foreign students are separate, the black group is separate, there are the Eastern and hippie type and a whole lot of others. On the hierarchy of hate the blacks aren't first. First come the Mexican-Americans, then the Indians. The blacks are third."[70] The relationship between black and white members of the football team, however, appeared to be positive. One of the white players recalled being asked by a sports reporter in New Orleans in 1968 about race relations on the team and he responded that no problems existed. "We never had any problems at all until that incident happened . . . before the BYU game," said Alan Zerfoss.[71] This view was held by many team members; indeed, Michael Newton remarked, "There was a [black] young man from my hometown [on the team] that I knew very well. I thought there was a good relationship between the players."[72]

Therefore, although there were some racial problems on the campus at Wyoming, the black fourteen were not protesting against their own school. In many respects the actions of the football players at Wyoming mirrored the initial impulse of the OPHR in the sense that they were trying to use sport to dramatize the racial problems of wider society—in this case the exclusive racial policies of a leading university and the tolerance of such practices. The actions of those who protested at Wyoming were linked by the press with negative connotations to the demonstration of Smith and Carlos. Both were seen as examples of outside influences meddling in sport.[73] The major point being made by those who criticized the black fourteen and Smith and Carlos was that they had brought politics into sport. The condemnation of such demonstrations, which had been increased by the predominantly negative reaction to the Smith and Carlos salute, as well as the heightened sense of tension surrounding issues of race and discipline on campuses in 1969 help to explain the treatment received by the black fourteen.

Eaton had the support of the local community and many alumni. Petitions with thirty-five hundred signatures from the Laramie population offered praise for Eaton and urged "continuance of such actions in order to maintain a consistent, stable institution regardless of angry, radical voices which, if heeded, could bring chaos and ruin our esteemed university."[74] Phil White, the editor of the school paper, resigned after the publication gave its support to the black players. One member of the state legislature warned that if the players were reinstated it would have negative implications for the university budget. University president William Carlson inadvisably asserted that football was more important than civil rights.[75]

Nevertheless, some faculty and students at Wyoming offered a voice in support of the black fourteen. A resolution of an emergency session of the executive committee of the Student Senate of October 18 argued that the black athletes had acted on a matter of conscience "with restraint, with moderation and with responsibility." The actions of Eaton and the university board of trustees were criticized and the Senate called for an open forum between the coach and the players before their reinstatement on the team. If this did not happen then further action was promised, with the aim of the "removal of theories and individuals which are responsible for the unfortunate situation."[76] On October 22 a statement was released by the joint Student-Faculty Committee that stated, "The committee [is] meeting continuously with all parties to work toward resolution of this incident. . . . [and] it feels it is making substantive progress for the benefit of all concerned." A handwritten note on the statement instructed faculty to read it out to all classes.[77] In a meeting of the Faculty Senate a week later a resolution was passed that included a "repudiation of Coach Eaton's actions in dismissing fourteen black students from the football team. . . . We disassociate ourselves from the coach's actions and call for the immediate reinstatement of fourteen black students to the football team with no penalties or recriminations."[78]

Eaton, however, argued that as football coach he had a rule that had been in place for over a year that banned any attempt at protest or demonstration on his team and that the players had violated this rule. In his testimony to the court adjudicating the lawsuit eventually brought by the black players and the NAACP, President Carlson asserted that as a coach Eaton had the right to impose such rules on his players.[79] While Eaton did agree to review the athletic scholarships with each player individually in the new year, Carlson asserted that the athletes had "openly, defiantly and premeditatedly violated the rules." Carlson added that he and the state governor had taken the black players aside and asked if they would play against BYU without wearing the armbands. "They said they would not and they would not play for Coach Eaton."[80] This is, however, at odds with the recollections of Joe Williams and Melvin Hamilton. The players' position had not been defiant in the first instance. Instead the standoff was provoked by the fact that Eaton was totally unwilling to entertain any thought of compromise.[81] Hamilton argued that the players had "the right to work within the constitution and this is what Coach Eaton denied us the opportunity to do."[82]

The issue would not go away, as various protest groups weighed in on the debate on the side of the black players. The Black Student Alliance sent a statement to other schools in the Western Athletic Conference urging support for the black fourteen and thanking those who had already protested against BYU. November 1 was designated "Black Wyoming Fourteen Day," on which students at other campuses should wear black armbands as a symbol of protest and send letters to the Western Athletic Conference commissioner, Wiles Hallock.[83] At Colorado State University black students also asked that no games be scheduled with Wyoming until the black fourteen had been reinstated.[84] When the BYU team traveled to Texas the black fourteen scored a convincing victory, however. During the game many members of the crowd wore black armbands in a show of solidarity with the Wyoming black players. Indeed, five members of that crowd were arrested after scuffling with police while taking part in a protest. The attendance was six thousand below average, which was seen by some as a consequence of the request by a black fraternity group for local residents to boycott the game.[85]

As these examples of support for the black fourteen increased, Hallock commented, "It was unfortunate. Personally, I don't feel it was necessary for Lloyd [Eaton] to go as far as he did."[86] In fact, the rule that Eaton had used to justify his decision to throw the players off the team—that no players were permitted to take part in any protest action—was rescinded by the coach immediately after the black fourteen were dismissed. As the Black Student Alliance highlighted in a newsletter, the university president had told faculty that "we are altering the rule [on demonstrations] so it applies only to players while directly participating in team activities."[87] The change indicated that officials had acknowledged that the players had been wearing their armbands outside of "team activities"—practice was not to start for another ninety minutes after the players went to meet their coach. Eaton and the university administration also apparently realized that the rule as it had stood might have impinged on the players' rights to

Protesters after suspension of the "black fourteen." University of Wyoming students campaigned against the decision of Coach Eaton to throw the "black fourteen" off the football team. Irene Schubert Collection, box 2, folder 7, American Heritage Center, University of Wyoming, image -ah10405_0122.

free speech under the First Amendment. The fact that this concession was made but the black fourteen were still not reinstated only served to further infuriate protesters.

The support that the black fourteen received from student activists and civil rights groups at other Western Athletic Conference institutions and across the country simply acted to strengthen feelings in the local Laramie community that they were under siege. Many local residents thought that the forces of Black Power had been at work in the black fourteen incident. Booster organizations praised the response of the university. Many saw Eaton's stance as the sort of strong, conservative leadership that the country as a whole needed.[88] There was also a clear belief that the black players were being manipulated by radical activists from outside the campus. Hamilton later confirmed that the players did get some support after the fact from the NAACP and the Black Panthers in Denver, Colorado, but the initial protest came entirely from the Black Student Union on campus. White students and local residents were nevertheless convinced that "busloads" of Panthers were ready to converge on Laramie.[89] White player Alan Zerfoss later argued, "The militants got to our black athletes."[90] Fellow white Cowboy Gary Fox speculated, "I assume some politically active group got hold of and talked them into this protest."[91]

The incident also had a significant impact on the fortunes of the team. The formerly successful program suffered a long-term losing streak in the seasons following 1969. The white players on the team had to deal with this reality and were left feeling confused and disappointed that their football futures had been jeopardized by the incident. Alan Zerfoss argued, "There was a lot of disappointment because we were all a family. . . . We never thought they would turn against our team and do some kind of foolish rebellion just because of the Mormons' beliefs. We thought it was ridiculous."[92] Ken Hustad described being "angry" and "disillusioned"; he "felt they [the black players] were centered on themselves and not on the team." Although he admitted that with the benefit of hindsight he was able to see the wider cause the black players were focused on and would have supported their protest, at the time the general mood of the white players was frustration and disappointment.[93] For the rest of the season and for much of the next, the Cowboys were greeted by protests whenever they played games on the road. Getting off the bus they faced lines of protesters screaming abuse; indeed, everywhere the team went there was agitation to greet them. This had a considerable impact on the morale of the team and affected their play on the field. "When we went to New Mexico there were protests, the blacks were all over. We would get off the bus to go to the hotel and they were there with their signs and this bothered us and we lost our last four games."[94]

The perception of the white players prior to the incident was that their team was united, that football was the unifying force. As Gary Fox remarked, "We were just a bunch of kids who wanted to play football; I mean, that is what we were doing there, right? From my standpoint there was no tension of any kind, they were just a bunch of young kids like we were. They were there to play football and go to school."[95] This team ethos was, however, quickly altered when the black players were cut from the team by Eaton. The white players were not privy to the meeting held with the coach and simply found out about their black teammates when they did not appear for practice. The white team members felt that the protest of the black players was not justified, and in many cases they did not fully understand what it was that their teammates were protesting against.[96] "There was no talk whatsoever [of compromise]. There was no discussion as to whether or not we were going to support them and not our coach," remembered Michael Newton.[97] A general feeling was that the black players should express themselves by excelling on the football field, a field that was no place for political activism. Ken Hustad argued, "The uniform is of the school and it belongs to the school and players certainly can't be modifying their equipment. We are out there to play a game not carry out some political cause."[98] With an echo of the traditional view of sport as a positive racial force, the field was seen as a place of equality where a man excelled on merit. Football was not the place for political activism.[99]

Again we see that the attempt to bring politics into the sporting realm, to use that realm to dramatize racial injustice in wider society, posed great problems for black players and their white teammates. Those white teammates believed the prevailing ideology that sport had delivered racial progress. For black players to then use the sporting arena to try to protest about racial injustice seemed paradoxical to many white athletes. This attitude can be linked to what George Lipsitz has called "liberal individualism." This doctrine argues that society has delivered racial justice and that African American activists are wrong to press for further change.[100]

The concept of liberal individualism interacted with the specific context of attempting racial protest through sport in 1969 during events at Wyoming. Protests at the 1968 Olympics had hardened the attitudes of athletics administrators against the intrusion of politics into the sporting arena. Furthermore, the increasing attention of supporters of the black athletic revolt to issues of racism in sport and other clashes between coaches and their players over issues of discipline all helped to shape the reactions to the actions of the black fourteen. The attempted protest by the black fourteen was more in the spirit of the original intentions of the OPHR than any of the other campus protests that have been highlighted in this study. The context provided by these protests and the countercultural assault on college athletics created a framework that was hostile to the demands of the black fourteen. Their failure further elucidates the limitations of using sport to protest civil rights injustice and points to a failure to realize the potential of sport to successfully contribute to the black freedom struggle.

In light of the events at Wyoming, the decision and words of Coach Jim McMullen at San Jose State are particularly interesting. When they played against Wyoming the San Jose Spartans wore armbands in an act of solidarity with the fourteen suspended black players.[101] Coach McMullen told one reporter, "You can't just be involved in football, you have to be involved in life." The stand taken by the white coach and his racially integrated team was fully supported by acting president of the university Hobart W. Burns. Furthermore, San Jose State resolved to cancel all future games with BYU.[102] Stanford also severed all sporting ties with BYU. University president Kenneth Pitzer stated that their policy was "not to schedule events with institutions which practice discrimination on a basis of race or national origin."[103]

The fact that the lead in protesting against BYU was taken by San Jose State is perhaps no surprise. It was at this institution that the black athletic revolt had been born. It was here that Harry Edwards and Ken Noel had used sport as a lever to gain concessions from university officials in 1967 by causing the cancellation of the opening football game of the season. In this protest, the true birth of the black athletic revolt, Edwards used sport to dramatize the problems of segregated housing in the areas around the campus and the lack of a black political voice in university policy that directly influenced black students.

When Edwards called for a black boycott of the Olympics he did so to dramatize the plight of African Americans and the continued racism of American society. The demands of the OPHR spoke to wider political issues. When Smith and Carlos stood with their raised clenched fists and shoeless feet they did so to highlight the poverty and injustice faced by black Americans. Yes, the OPHR recognized that sport was tainted by racism just as was the rest of society, but this was not its original or principal concern. It was in the period after the boycott had failed and Smith and Carlos had stood with courage and dignity that racism in sport became the main focus of the black athletic revolt. As a consequence the stand made by the black fourteen at Wyoming was more closely connected to the original ideals of the OPHR than other incidents of racial unrest on campuses in 1968 and 1969.

Coach McMullen's comment was particularly insightful. He argued that it was not enough to be "involved in football" but that one also had to be "involved in life." This was the essence of the original ideals of the OPHR; that athletes should use their position as athletes, as visible and respected members of the community—either their local college community or the wider national community—to draw attention to the continued racial problems facing the United States in the late 1960s. The prevailing ideology that sport ran ahead of the rest of society in racial affairs, that it was a leader in civil rights, constantly restricted opportunities for athletes to participate in such protest activity. Furthermore, the disciplined resistance to the intrusion of politics and the counterculture of the late 1960s into the sporting arena provided further problems. The black athletic revolt faced a twin backlash against Black Power and against indiscipline and a countercultural challenge to traditional conservative authority. The idea that sport was pure and should not be tainted by politics was in itself disingenuous. Sports administrators were consciously and subconsciously promoting their own political agenda by asserting that sport was a leader in the realm of civil rights.

We will see in the next chapter the distinctive dynamic of the relationship between sport and race in the South and the extent to which the black athletic revolt failed to significantly affect that region. Developments in Dixie perhaps did as much as anything to cement the ideal that prevails today, that sport provides a uniquely positive arena for the improvement of race relations in the United States. The fact that the actions of the black fourteen and the leadership of McMullen and his Spartans represented the last real attempts to use sport to dramatize the wider civil rights struggle of this era shows the limited success of the black athletic revolt. By this I mean the limited success of using sport as a platform from which to speak to the concerns of the civil rights struggle in the late 1960s in the original way intended by Edwards and the OPHR.

6

Dixie and the Absence of
a Black Athletic Revolt

I have said this on many occasions, that athletics probably did more for
integration in the South than any other thing.
      —Vince Dooley, football coach, University of Georgia

I let Martin Luther King be Martin Luther King. I did not want to be
Martin Luther King. I appreciate everything that he did but that was not
my intent. My intent was to play football and get a degree and go on
and play at the next level.
      —Condredge Holloway, University of Tennessee football

Eddie Brown was a young white football fan in the eighth grade when his
Tennessee school integrated. His father was a big fan of the University of
Tennessee Volunteers and took his son to his first game when he was seven
years old. Eddie fell in love with the orange and whites and made his mind
up at an early age that he wanted to play for the university team. In 1970
Eddie graduated high school and had no hesitation in accepting a place
at the Tennessee institution. When his mother and father dropped him off
on campus as a freshman they saw a young black man, Haskel Stanback.
Haskel was also recruited to the Volunteers' football squad. Eddie's parents told Haskel's mother not to worry about her son and that they would
keep an eye out for and look after him.

    Haskel Stanback and Eddie Brown became roommates when they
traveled on the road together. They both later described the football team
at the university as like a big family. During a trip to Oxford, Mississippi,
to play Ole Miss, the two experienced a community that had long resisted
the integration of its university and even longer resisted the integration of

its football team. When Haskel and other black members of the Volunteers team took the field, members of the home crowd screamed "kill that nigger." Eddie remembered the atmosphere on these trips to the Deep South as often "very ugly."[1]

Throughout the 1960s southern society and identity faced the serious challenge of racial change, a challenge that clearly affected the sporting arena of the region. Confrontations over desegregation provided a paradoxical role for sport in the development of race relations in the South. Far from being more racially progressive than wider society, the sporting arena was often used as a symbol of the maintenance of white supremacy. Southerners sought to protect many of their most prestigious sports teams from desegregation. Collegiate football's Southeastern Conference (SEC), for example, remained all white for over a decade after the *Brown v. Board of Education* decision. It did not have any black varsity players until 1967, two years after the passage of the major civil rights legislation of the decade. Schools were desegregated before many major college sports teams, which remained all white in a statement of defiance against the forces of integration. Once integration of the southern sports world quickened in the late 1960s, however, sport was hailed as a positive force for social change. It was argued that black and white southerners could come together in the sporting arena in a way that proved much more difficult in wider society.

By the early 1960s there was widespread interracial sporting competition at both the professional and college levels throughout the rest of the nation. By playing the game black athletes were, in accordance with the prevailing sporting ideology, advancing racial progress and understanding. Edwards and other leaders of the black athletic revolt sought to expose that this was not the case. Sport, they argued, provided an arena in which blacks were still treated like second-class citizens. In the South there was limited interracial competition. In the Deep South sport was strictly segregated by race. This made it very difficult for Edwards's message to take root in the South. Athletes could not use sport to promote civil rights in the same way as in the rest of the nation because black athletes could not engage in this struggle from a position of participation in integrated competition. The goal for many black athletes in the South was simply to make it onto the previously all-white playing fields of the most prestigious teams of the region. Often these black student athletes were more conservative and much less radicalized than their fellow students and less likely to openly engage with the black freedom struggle on campus.

This explains why there was no black athletic revolt in the South. In fact, it was the white southern authorities who used the sporting arena to make their own racial protest. Their athletic revolt was against the forces of integration that gradually wore away the edifice of segregation. In a more real sense than in any other region of the United States, when the integration of sporting competition did come, it helped to break down racial barriers.

Sport and Southern Identity

In many respects sport was a malleable force in the development of southern culture and identity. At various times in the late nineteenth century and throughout the twentieth century it was used to draw the region more closely into the national mainstream while also providing a vehicle through which to foster a separate regional identity. In the late 1870s a U.S. professional baseball league was established, with most of the teams confined to the industrial Midwest and Northeast. An invented tradition portrayed baseball as a distinctly American pastime and ball games helped to provide a focus for Fourth of July celebrations of patriotism.[2] In postbellum Richmond, Virginia, the baseball club was owned by men who embraced the ideology of the New South. They were part of a growing national middle class and attempted to run the club with management techniques that integrated the team into a national system. Nevertheless, the Richmond team was also a potent reminder of the sectional conflict that had recently ended in defeat for the South. Many of the men who formed the Virginia Baseball Association in the 1880s were veterans of the Civil War. Ex-Confederates used baseball in Virginia to glorify the Confederacy, and the game was clearly linked to the myth of the Lost Cause that emerged in the postbellum South. Interestingly, black spectators—segregated by social custom prior to the emergence of official Jim Crow laws—watched from a separate area of the Richmond ballpark and cheered visiting teams.[3] In this example sport was very much a contested cultural site in the search for southern identity in the immediate postbellum years.

As time passed and the sectional wounds of the Civil War were healed through a process of national reunification, so sport was increasingly used to bring the South into the American mainstream. In the late nineteenth and early twentieth centuries collegiate football spread out from the Northeast and moved into the Midwest and the South. Thanksgiving football games provided a national ritual that affirmed a sense of shared tradition and identity.[4] Southerners who had learned the game at northern universities in the 1890s brought it South. The infusion of football into southern sporting culture was an element of the New South movement. Progressive southerners sought to emulate northern practices as part of modernizing the South.[5] There was, however, a distinctly regional element to football culture in the South. In the early days of southern football, teams were relatively weak in comparison to their more experienced northern rivals. In the 1920s and 1930s the University of Alabama's Crimson Tide became an increasing source of regional pride when the team won a number of games against northern opponents. Victories in the most prestigious of postseason games, the Rose Bowl, stimulated quasi-religious fervor in the region. Alabama governor Bibb Graves reveled after the first Rose Bowl win: "The hearts of Dixie are beating with exultant pride. We are here to tell the whole world the Crimson Tide is our Tide and an Alabama troop of heroes. It upheld the honor of the Southland and came back to us undefeated."[6]

Collegiate football, encouraged by the growth of Thanksgiving Day rituals, helped to move the South closer to the national cultural mainstream. At the same time it fostered a continued sense of southern pride and of distinctiveness from the rest of the nation that was deeply rooted in the unresolved sectional tensions that were a legacy of the Civil War. Andrew Doyle has argued that the Rose Bowl wins by the Crimson Tide in 1926 and 1927 were the most crucial games in southern football history, as they highlighted this incomplete absorption into the American mainstream. Football grew to be a powerful arena in which ideals of what the South should become could be projected. Doyle astutely observed, "The cultural text of southern college football possessed a symbolic plasticity that allowed southerners to mould its interpretations to serve their disparate and often conflicting needs."[7] Participation in national bowl games allowed southerners to connect with the American mainstream. Often this connection required a certain degree of flexibility in the policies of segregationists. Playing against integrated teams, it was argued, was not inconsistent with the maintenance of racial segregation. To put segregation before the "cultural validation" that was provided by national sporting contests was regarded as "a fate worse than integration."[8]

The argument that sport promoted racial progress had a distinctive tone in the South. The football teams that garnered so much southern pride were all white. Their victories represented an expression of white southern manhood and identity. As we will see below, resistance to integrated competition on southern soil was long and fierce. Despite their exclusion from such sporting contests, many black educators, contemporaneous with the development of both a regional and national sporting culture, extolled sport as a vehicle for racial progress. Progressive reformers believed that black athletes who excelled in the Olympics or on the playing fields of prestigious northern universities would increase racial pride and slowly change the white supremacist hegemony. As white southerners rejoiced at the victories of the Crimson Tide, historically black colleges promoted sporting competition. It was believed that "athletic accomplishment could strengthen the sense of racial pride among black southerners and at the same time encourage them to identify with national pastimes."[9]

The potential for sport to have a positive impact on the wider social landscape of race relations in the South was limited, however, by the strength of white supremacy and the importance of sport as a malleable element of southern culture. That culture was heavily loaded with white desires to maintain racial segregation; when those desires were increasingly threatened by the forces of social change that quickened as a result of the Second World War, white southerners sought to defend their way of life. This also meant defending racial separation in the sporting arena. Many of the most prestigious sporting institutions in the South were prepared to play against integrated teams, but they kept their own rosters lily-white until the late 1960s. Black southerners who did excel on their own sports fields and then moved north and or went on to Olympic success could engage with the national sporting culture. They were, however, excluded from a distinctly southern sporting culture.

James Cobb has explained the extent to which black southerners were denied their regional identity. They were seen as black but not as southerners. This was a product of attitudes of both white defenders of a southern way of life that focused on racial segregation and northern liberals who sought to help black southerners. The latter found it difficult to comprehend that the black population in the South would have any great allegiance to a region that was so synonymous with racial oppression and suffering. Furthermore, the rise of Afrocentrism and the black pride movement in the late 1960s emphasized links with Africa as the spiritual and cultural touchstone for African Americans. In fact, one of the most fascinating developments of the post–civil rights era is the move by many blacks to migrate back to the South and identify themselves as southerners.[10] The rapid integration of sports in the South after the late 1960s can be viewed as part of this process of African Americans reclaiming their southernness. The use of sports like football to promote an exclusive southern identity means that increased black participation on the playing fields represented part of a redrawing of this regional identity. Within this context we can further understand why there was no black athletic revolt in the South in the way there was in other parts of the nation. Playing the game marked significant progress, progress that ran behind wider social changes. As a consequence there was not the same impulse to use the sporting arena as a platform on which to engage in civil rights activism.

Sport has provided a changeable cultural reference point in the relationship between the South and the rest of the nation. It has also provided a shifting and flexible element of southern identity. Football, for example, was used to foster regional pride and defend a certain way of life. It could tie the South to a national sporting culture without requiring the region to choose between its own values and those of the rest of the nation.[11] The traditions surrounding it were in many ways artificially created, however. Football was not part of a long-term definition of what it meant to be southern. The concept of the South and regional identity is important when understanding sport in the region; nevertheless, these concepts and this identity have been shaped to fit contemporary imperatives.[12] In this sense we can see a constant struggle over the place of sport in southern identity, a struggle that has allowed a post-1960s southern sporting culture to develop that embraces racial integration and extols the values of team before race. This redefinition of the place of sport in southern identity is one factor in allowing black southerners to embrace that new identity.

Integrating the Classroom and the Sports Field

Arguably the most important struggle of the Civil Rights Movement in the South was over the desegregation of the region's public schools. For white southerners who resisted the racial changes of the 1950s and 1960s, the thought of their sons and daughters sitting in classrooms next to black children was anathema. Some of the most infamous and symbolic moments of the civil rights struggle took place in the realm of education. In 1957 in Little Rock, Arkansas, federal troops were required to protect the first black students to attend the local high school. President John F. Kennedy was forced to intervene in the controversy over the admission of James Meredith to the University of Mississippi in 1962, and a year later Governor George Wallace stood defiantly in the doorway of the University of Alabama in an effort to resist a court order to desegregate.

The struggle to integrate collegiate sporting competition in the South was no less significant. Segregationists reasoned that racial changes would produce a domino effect whereby concessions in one area of society would lead to transformations elsewhere. The most prestigious university sports teams held out against integration years after the institutions as a whole had been integrated. Focusing particularly on the SEC we can see that sport ran behind, not ahead, of other areas of southern society where racial integration was concerned.[13] This largely explains why a black athletic revolt did not occur in the South. The delay before full integration in college sports meant that when it did come it was seen as a victory in itself. Black athletes were making tangible strides forward simply by playing the game. On the whole, therefore, they did not attempt to use the sporting arena to engage in the wider civil rights struggle.

The key starting point for a study of the desegregation of education is 1954. In that year the Supreme Court ruled in *Brown v. Board of Education* that "separate but equal" educational facilities damaged black and white students and that segregation should be dismantled. In a further ruling the following year, *Brown II,* the court ordered that the integration of schools should proceed with all deliberate speed. The battle lines were drawn in the fight over integration as White Citizens' Councils were formed all over the South in an effort to resist the school desegregation process. Historian Michael Klarman is chief among those who argue that the *Brown* decision had a limited immediate impact. Furthermore, he asserts that the forces of southern racial moderation were destroyed by the massive resistance against school desegregation. It was this backlash that then created the radical and confrontational environment that spawned scenes of racial oppression in the South shown in the homes of millions of Americans on the TV news.

Klarman outlines that *Brown* had almost no direct impact on school desegregation in the South. In Upper South states like Tennessee and North Carolina, less than 3 percent of blacks attended desegregated schools in 1963–1964. In the Deep South states of Alabama, South Carolina, and Mississippi not one black child was attending school with whites in 1963. Across the South as a whole 32 percent of black southern children attended integrated public schools in 1968. It was passage of the Elementary and Secondary Education Act of 1965 that increased federal spending on public education and accelerated desegregation. Southern schools found it financially difficult to hold out against integration.[14] This is important for two reasons. First, as we shall see later in this chapter, the high school experiences of black and white college athletes often had a significant impact on how they reacted to integrated teams on campus. Their experiences were varied and heavily shaped by the different regional trends in school integration. Second, the story of desegregation of public schools provides the context for the integration of southern universities.

In the realm of higher education there was no *Brown* moment, no defining date that began the process of desegregation. Indeed, the story of the desegregation of higher education has only recently been fully explored by historians. Key symbolic moments, like the riots that attended Autherine Lucy's brief enrollment at the University of Alabama in 1956 or the Meredith and Wallace incidents mentioned above, have dominated references to the desegregation of higher education. It is important, however, that we recognize the evolutionary process of integration on the campus. The slow but increasingly steady enrollment of black undergraduates at southern universities from the early 1950s onward sets the scene for the eventual acceptance of blacks in college sports programs. Charles Martin has shown the gradual acceptance of integrated sporting contests between southern teams and squads from outside of the region in the period between the end of World War II and the beginning of the 1960s.[15] This did not lead automatically to the integration of southern sporting programs, however. Although all major southern universities had enrolled black students by 1965, black athletes did not appear on the rosters of the majority of SEC basketball and football teams until 1970. Sport was a symbolic bastion of white supremacy long after many other racial barriers of the Jim Crow system had been dismantled. In direct contradiction of the ideal that sport ran ahead of changes in wider society, the color line remained in the locker room well into the late 1960s.

By 1950 historically white schools in the border states began admitting black students. At the University of Kentucky, for example, three black undergraduates earned degrees in 1951. Maryland and Missouri were among states that amended admission procedures to incorporate black undergraduates immediately after the *Brown* ruling. By 1955 black students had enrolled in small numbers at the University of Virginia and the University of Texas.[16] States in the Deep South held out the longest against the forces of desegregation. In 1965 Mississippi State University became the last institution of the major Deep South universities to enroll a black student when Richard Holmes arrived on campus. In 1964 the University of Mississippi enrolled Irvin Walker, who was the first black student to be admitted without the need for a court order. These universities and those in South Carolina, Georgia, and Alabama, fellow members of the SEC, had all been desegregated by the mid-1960s. It is worth noting that while they had been integrated they did not have many black students in the late 1960s. Often when one of the blacks graduated there was a period where the university student body was briefly all white again until a small number of new black students enrolled.[17]

In some respects sporting competition and rivalries drove the slow integration of southern athletic teams. Non-elite colleges and universities took the lead in integrating sports in the South as they searched for some form of competitive edge against their more illustrious and well-established competitors. Atlantic Coast Conference football was integrated in 1963 when the University of Maryland recruited Darryl Hill. Texas Western College (later the University of Texas at El Paso [UTEP]) won the 1966 NCAA basketball championship with an all-black team.[18] These provincial teams led the way in the recruitment of black athletes. Indeed, this active recruitment of black athletes created opportunities for Bob Beamon and other athletes and also explains why UTEP authorities were so upset when racial trouble rocked the campus in 1968. They felt they had given many black athletes a good education and did not deserve the criticism that was leveled at them by Jack Olsen and others. In the Southwest Conference the league's three highest-status members were the last to integrate, and it was the more-established institutions of the SEC that were slowest to integrate their rosters also. In the search for a better chance of sporting success it was the less popular teams that led the way.[19]

Given the small number of undergraduate students on campuses as a whole, it was not particularly surprising that sports teams did not integrate until years after the initial instances of desegregation. After all, the athletics departments of universities represented only a small proportion of the overall student body. Crucially, though, sports, and in particular football, resisted integration in a conscious way. The football field was used as a symbol of the maintenance of white supremacy. In this respect, sport was used in the South in a way that directly contradicted the prevailing ideal that it was an arena where racial progress could be made. Edwards and his supporters encouraged black athletes to revolt because simply being allowed to play the game with whites was not enough; sporting participation alongside whites had not brought real change. In 1967 Edwards was calling for the boycott of football games at San Jose State College and then a black boycott of the Olympics. In 1968 Smith and Carlos and other black members of the U.S. Olympic team protested against the racial injustice in the United States. At university campuses across the Northeast, Midwest, and West students were protesting against the alleged racial discrimination of coaches and in some cases using sport to highlight the wider civil rights struggle. In the South in the same period, however, black athletes were being recruited to athletics programs for the very first time. Not until the academic year 1967–1968 were there any black athletes in the SEC varsity programs.

There was, therefore, no black athletic revolt in the South in the same way as there was in the rest of the nation. Sport and the black freedom struggle in Dixie had a different relationship. It would be wrong to paint a picture of blanket racial segregation on the sports fields of the South, but certainly after the *Brown* ruling there was a sustained attempt to separate the races in sporting competition. Examples of integrated sporting competition can be found in professional sports in the South. In 1953 the Savannah Citizens of the Sally Minor Baseball League, which included teams from Alabama and Florida, recruited black player Henry Aaron. In 1954 a team in minor league baseball's Southern League, the Atlanta Crackers, signed African American Nat Peeples. Following the breaking of the color line in the major leagues by Jackie Robinson, black southerners played in the major leagues, but these brief examples of integration were the exception to the rule before the mid-1960s.[20]

The number of black football players in the NFL increased as the 1960s progressed, and there were integrated sporting contests in the South. The Atlanta Falcons provide an example of an interracial team that played games in the South while many college teams were still segregated.[21] Southern racial mores still affected professional sports teams who visited the region. Between 1961 and 1964 local civil rights activists fought a series of battles to desegregate Florida facilities used by major league baseball teams for spring training.[22] In 1961 the Houston branch of the NAACP supported a picket by black fans of the city's NFL franchise because of the segregated seating in the stadium.[23]

These selected examples serve to show that professional sporting contests were inevitably affected by the racial customs of the South in the 1950s and 1960s. There were, however, also integrated teams that played in Dixie. Furthermore, there were examples of integrated contests at the college level taking place in the South before the late 1960s, and the importance of this fact for southern culture has been highlighted above. Not only was it culturally important for southern teams to play against top-ranked national opponents, but failure to do so also brought significant loss of financial revenue. Historians of sport and race relations in the

South have asserted that such integrated contests played an important role in the erosion of absolutist notions of racial segregation. Charles Martin argues, "Integrated games began to acclimate some white southerners to black and white cooperation in one important aspect of social life."[24] Russell Henderson has written about the decision in 1963 by Mississippi State University to repeal the unwritten law prohibiting contests with integrated teams. He asserts that "the color line in athletics appeared less rigid, and white sentiment less volatile over its erasure than in voting, schools, or public accommodations."[25] Nevertheless, this reading of the relationship between sport and race is too simplistic if we are to truly understand the relationship between sport and the black freedom struggle in the South and its place in the story of the black athletic revolt.

The integrated contests that have been highlighted above were between all-white southern teams and integrated northern competitors. The playing fields of many of the major colleges of the South were successfully kept all white well into the late 1960s. The color line had been eroded in schools, voting, and public accommodations before this racial barrier was broken down. Certainly, once the barrier was broken, sport did play an important role in the development of a post–civil rights identity in the South that could incorporate both black and white southerners. Sharing a locker room and winning and losing with a teammate of another race did help break down barriers to understanding. Nevertheless, there was not a straight line between the gradual acceptance of competition against integrated teams from outside the South and meaningful racial progress through interracial sporting participation. We must recognize this greater complexity so as to comprehend why a black athletic revolt did not emerge in the South. The fact that it took so long for top black athletes to put on the team colors of the Universities of Alabama, Tennessee, or South Carolina meant they were not in a position to engage with the black freedom struggle in the way that Edwards and his supporters were doing elsewhere in the nation.

In those other areas of the nation a relatively long history of integrated sporting competition gave strength to the myth that sport provided a color-blind arena that brought racial progress ahead of many other areas of society. The heart of the black athletic revolt was an effort to expose this myth and bring sports directly into the activism of the wider black freedom struggle. In the South large-scale integrated sporting competition did not emerge until after many of the battles of the civil rights struggle had been played out in other areas of society. The belief that sport helped the progress of race relations was not strongly held in the South in the mid- to late 1960s in the way it was elsewhere in the nation. This was precisely because at this time sport was still being used by many in the white power structure to uphold white supremacy. The retrospective views of many black and white athletes of the time are that sport helped the progress of race relations. There is a large element of romanticism in these views, which should be acknowledged. The crucial point is, however, that these beliefs were formed in the late 1960s and early 1970s and have crystallized since. The South was not fertile soil for Edwards's message that black athletes needed to engage in the black cultural awakening because black athletes were only just gaining access to integrated competition.

Football and the Forces of Segregation

The complexity of the relationship between sporting culture and the forces of segregation in the South can be illustrated by looking at the events surrounding the integration of the University of Georgia, Ole Miss, and the University of Alabama. We can see that the gradual acceptance of contests against integrated teams did not lead axiomatically to sports teams themselves being desegregated. These examples and the story of how the SEC football programs were integrated help to explain why a black athletic revolt did not hit campuses across the South at the time that it was sweeping across other areas of the nation and affecting the U.S. Olympic team.

In December 1955 Governor Marvin Griffin of Georgia caused great controversy when he objected to the Georgia Tech football team playing in the Sugar Bowl against the University of Pittsburgh. Griffin did not want a team from his state to play against integrated opponents, and Pittsburgh had an African American fullback named Bobby Grier. Students at Georgia Tech protested against Griffin's attempts to stop their team going to the Sugar Bowl and rival University of Georgia (UG) students sided with them. In Athens police had to use tear gas to disperse a crowd of UG students who rallied behind a banner that read, "For Once, We're for Tech."[26] University administrators voted to let the team play in the Sugar Bowl and many viewed the incident as a victory for racial integration. In fact, when sanctioning Georgia Tech's participation in the contest, administrators passed a series of resolutions that supported the forces of segregation. Measures were put in place to try to ensure that black athletes would never be able to play in integrated contests in Georgia. College administrators placed a large emphasis on sporting victory, but it would be a decade after the Sugar Bowl controversy before Georgia Tech and the University of Georgia integrated their football teams.[27]

A year after the debate created by the game against Pittsburgh, Horace Ward's long effort to desegregate the University of Georgia was reaching a climax. Using many of the legal diversions and delaying tactics that were employed at both Ole Miss and Alabama to block the enrollment of black students, UG officials had continually rejected Ward's application. Fearing that things were going to drag on indefinitely, Ward had enrolled in Northwestern University Law School in Chicago so that he could start his studies while waiting for his application to Georgia to be approved. Realizing that this move meant that Ward would have to transfer to the UG law school in Athens, university officials claimed that he had not followed this procedure, and a court ruling in 1957 denied Ward entry.[28] UG students were moved to protest in support of their Georgia Tech rivals being allowed to play against an integrated football team the year before but in 1957 the University of Georgia maintained racial segregation on its own campus.

Civil rights activists were keen to encourage outstanding black students to apply to all-white universities in Georgia as the campaign against segregation continued. In 1959 Charlayne Hunter and Hamilton Holmes were among the brightest black high school students in the state. At first they were encouraged to apply to Georgia Tech, but they were unimpressed by the courses on offer so they tried to gain entry at UG. Lack of dormitory space was used as one of the reasons why they could not be admitted, and when they enrolled elsewhere in order to further their education officials made it very difficult for them to transfer.[29] When a trial was set for December 1960 in order to try to force their admittance, Horace Ward was delighted to join Hunter and Holmes's legal team. Finally, in January 1961 the two black students became the first to integrate UG after a judge found there was no reason other than racial prejudice for their continued exclusion.

Although their first day on campus passed without major incident, things turned ugly that evening. Following a narrow defeat by their rival Georgia Tech in a basketball game, a mob of UG students descended on the dormitory where Hunter was housed. A bedsheet was unfurled with the words "nigger go home" written on it and bricks and bottles were thrown. Hunter and Holmes were temporarily suspended from the university for their own safety after police used tear gas to break up the riot.[30] Although not as serious as events at Ole Miss a year later, the riot was a portent of that violence. Throughout their education in Athens Holmes and Hunter faced varying levels of social ostracism and racial abuse. When Holmes began his final quarter at UG he had never eaten in a university dining room, never entered the gymnasium, and never studied in the library. He had no white friends outside of the classroom and he had never visited a white friend or had them visit him.[31]

Holmes was a talented athlete, and he had held hopes of playing football for the Georgia Bulldogs while studying at the university. When he enquired about his prospects for playing shortly after enrollment he was strongly advised by the dean that it was not a good idea. It was believed that there was the serious prospect of him being killed either by his own or opposing fans.[32] The university had submitted to the integration of its campus but it was not about to submit to the integration of its football team. Despite this fact Holmes, Hunter, and the other black students who followed them still had Georgia Bulldogs bumper stickers on their cars. When asked why this was Holmes said, "Well we do go to school here. It's school spirit? No, not spirit. I'm trying to think of another word. I'll let you know."[33]

In September 1962 Mississippi governor Ross Barnett signaled his defiance in the face of federal forces of integration. Barnett told an audience, "We will not surrender to the evil and illegal forces of tyranny. . . . No school will be integrated in Mississippi while I am your governor. . . . I speak to you now in the moment of our greatest crisis since the War Between the States."[34] Heavily associated with the symbolic legacy of that conflict was the University of Mississippi, Ole Miss. The university was founded in 1848 and then closed for the duration of the Civil War, when its buildings were used as hospitals. Dead soldiers were buried on campus. In 1936 the school adopted Colonel Rebel as its mascot. During football games Ole Miss fans waved the Confederate flag and sang "Dixie." The symbols surrounding the football team were loaded with history and a sense of southern identity and defiance. As racial change swept across the nation in the 1960s, Ole Miss football games increasingly became a celebration of white supremacy.[35]

This celebration took place as the state struggled to hold back the slow-moving tide of desegregation. A 1954 law that was passed unanimously by the state legislature gave the governor the authority to close any school in Mississippi whenever he felt that this was in the interest of the majority of students. This was the law that Barnett used as the basis for his strategy of interposition in 1962. Previous attempts to integrate Ole Miss had

James Meredith. Meredith's admission to the University of Mississippi sparked violent scenes on the Ole Miss campus. *U.S. News & World Report* Magazine Photograph Collection, Library of Congress, Prints and Photographs Division.

all been rebuffed before fading away, and Governor Barnett intended to maintain this record of segregation across the state.[36] In September 1962 James Meredith tried to register at Ole Miss but was repeatedly blocked by Barnett and the university's board of trustees. The Kennedy administration put pressure on the authorities to admit Meredith. After the black student had been refused entry to the university for the third time, Bobby Kennedy telephoned Governor Barnett to try to reach a settlement. The attorney general refused the governor's request for a staged scenario in which federal marshals would draw their guns so it would appear Barnett was being forced to step aside and allow Meredith to be registered.[37]

The connection between the Ole Miss football program and the ongoing drama of the integration effort is both direct and important. At the height of Meredith's attempts to register, Ole Miss hosted Kentucky. The atmosphere at the game resembled a Nazi-style rally. Rebel flags waved as "The Star Spangled Banner" played, and a giant Confederate flag was unveiled as Barnett took to the field to give a speech. The governor's words of defiance and vows to preserve segregation whipped the crowd into a frenzy.[38] Undoubtedly affected by the atmosphere at the football game on the previous night, the next day the campus erupted into a full-scale riot as federal marshals tried to get Meredith admitted. Two people died in the violence and President Kennedy went on national television to call for calm and commit to the integration of southern universities. Again emphasizing the important role played by football in the struggle to integrate Ole Miss, Kennedy also telephoned head football coach Johnny Vaught, appealing for his help to quell the riots.[39] Once Meredith had been admitted to the university and the immediate violence had been stopped, federal authorities moved the Ole Miss homecoming game from Oxford to Jackson in an effort to avert any further trouble.[40]

In the weeks and months after Meredith was finally admitted to the university, hostility toward his presence remained and the forces of white supremacy continued to try to restrict the further integration of the university. Although Cleve McDowell became the second black student to enroll on campus in June 1963, he was later expelled for carrying a gun. In 1964 the university adopted laws that restricted the use of campus facilities to all but students, faculty, and staff. This effectively excluded blacks. Indeed, during a football game against Memphis State the law was invoked to remove the black families of visiting players from the cafeteria. Importantly, though, an integrated team had visited Ole Miss and left without major incident.[41] It was not until the early 1970s that black players would pull on the uniform for the home team in Mississippi, however.

At the University of Alabama we can see a similar connection between mass resistance to school integration and the role of the football program. As discussed above, the importance of the Alabama football team to the state's cultural identity and its engagement with the rest of the nation was significant. By 1960 the successful Crimson Tide under the direction of iconic coach Paul "Bear" Bryant was consistently ranked among the top college teams in the nation. Andrew Doyle has observed that "Bryant and his championship team had become a potent symbol of pride and cultural vitality to white southerners in the midst of a profound social transformation."[42] Football allowed Alabama to engage with the national sporting culture despite its stance on segregation. This stance had been cemented in 1956, two years before Bryant's arrival, when black student Autherine Lucy was briefly enrolled at the university. After much harassment and legal wrangling, she was forced to withdraw from Alabama.[43] This incident, combined with the success of the Crimson Tide, emboldened a defense of the southern way of life.

Bryant was a racial moderate who in fact aligned himself with members of the business community who were working for a peaceful end to segregation. Bryant was crucial in ensuring that Alabama accepted an invitation to the Liberty Bowl in 1959, where they would lose narrowly to an integrated Penn State team. Coming only three years after the Lucy affair, many saw this as a sign that the hard-line segregationist impulse was softening. Many white southerners did not view the Liberty Bowl in such terms, however. Going to play an integrated team in Pennsylvania was very different from accepting a contest against integrated opponents on home soil. Such football contests enabled white southerners to gain a sense of pride and cultural validation at the same time as they defended segregation of public schools in Alabama.[44]

The tension between maintaining segregation and gaining acceptance on the national sporting stage resulted in a significant setback for the Crimson Tide in 1961–1962, however. During the 1961 season Alabama won eleven consecutive games and was ranked the number-one team in the nation. They went on to defeat the University of Arkansas in the Sugar Bowl on New Year's Day, 1962. This victory was not, however, what Crimson Tide fans had been hoping for throughout the season. There had been speculation that they would be invited to the Rose Bowl in California, the scene of their triumph in 1926. This invitation never came, however. Student protests on campus at UCLA and a national media campaign drew attention to the segregationist practices of the University of Alabama. Bryant and his team came to be seen as an extension of the segregationists who beat freedom riders and the police chiefs who set dogs on civil rights demonstrators. The all-white Alabama team was accused of playing with the same violence and aggression that was little removed from white mobs.[45] Rather than face this criticism head on and tackle searching questions about Alabama society and the football team that represented it, university officials chose a bowl game matchup that would enable them to sidestep these issues. The all-white Crimson Tide came to represent the resolve of Alabama authorities to fight integration to the bitter end.

This fight against the forces of integration was personified by Governor George Wallace in 1963. He chose to take the doctrine of interposition to its most extreme when he physically stood in the door of the university in order to stop the court-ordered enrollment of black students Vivian Malone and James Hood. Having seen events unfold at Ole Miss, Alabama officials made the decision to suspend applications in the summer of 1962 so that any desegregation crisis would be postponed until 1963.

Paul "Bear" Bryant statue. The statue of the legendary University of Alabama coach stands outside Bryant-Denny Stadium on the university campus.
The George F. Landegger Collection of Alabama Photographs in Carol M. Highsmith's America, Library of Congress, Prints and Photographs Division.

This also allowed the Crimson Tide to enjoy their Orange Bowl invitation. The game was attended by President Kennedy and the Tide shut out Oklahoma 17–0.[46] The football team continued to project success and defend the southern way of life.

This defense was finally breached in 1963 when Hood and Malone were admitted to the university. Wallace had ensured that there would not be the same level of violence as had been witnessed in Mississippi. The Kennedy administration federalized the Alabama National Guard; Wallace made his stand before being forced to step aside. The Alabama campus was integrated, but the football team remained all white. The symbolic links between the Crimson Tide and the battle to hold back the forces of segregation that continued throughout 1963 and beyond were clear. As Birmingham became the epicenter of the civil rights struggle in the summer of 1963, notorious police chief Bull Connor erected barbed-wire cages in Legion Field to hold demonstrators. In the public imagination the connections between segregation and the Alabama football team were hard to ignore. It was not until the late 1960s that the Crimson Tide finally included black players in its ranks.

Integrating the Football Teams of the SEC

Given the struggles to integrate many of the most well-established campuses in the Deep South and the importance of football to these institutions, it is no surprise that breaking the color line in the SEC was a slow process. There was a significant time lag between the integration of the campus and the integration of the locker room. This slow process and the challenges faced by pioneering black athletes help explain why a black athletic revolt did not emerge in the South as it had in other parts of the country.

As southern colleges adopted football as an important part of their athletics programs in the early twentieth century, a large Southern Conference with over twenty teams from twelve states evolved. In 1932 thirteen members broke away and formed the SEC. By 1966 ten members remained.[47] SEC teams rejected contests against integrated northern teams on southern soil well into the 1960s, and the first black varsity player did not turn out for one of the ten members of the football conference until 1967.

Even in other parts of the South where games against integrated teams did take place there was considerable racial tension. Willie Brown, a black player for the University of Southern California, recalled problems on a trip to play Southern Methodist University of the Southwest Conference in Dallas. Brown received death threats, and when he ran back a kickoff for a touchdown he was surrounded by security on the sidelines. He and his teammates had to leave the stadium with rain capes over their heads so that he was less easily identifiable to an angry mob. "I had to put on a big cape and everything . . . so that they did not know where I was, because they did not know if the [death] threat was real."[48] Racial segregation on the sports fields of the South was a part of the region's racial mores well into the 1960s. Bill Richardson grew up in Alabama and played for the university team in the early 1960s. He remembered Little League baseball games between white and black children, but high school football was strictly segregated. Richardson and fellow Alabamian George Patton, who played for the University of Georgia in the mid-1960s, recalled watching the black high school football teams compete. The black teams used the white high school football stadium on a Saturday night after the white teams had used it for Friday evening football.[49] Despite appreciation for the skills of the players of another race, integrated sporting contests were strictly prohibited by Jim Crow customs. These customs were accepted by young athletes as a way of life. Richardson recalled, "It was nothing that we ever brought up to our coaches or anybody . . . why are we here and they [black players] over there at their training school. . . . I can't quite explain it . . . that was just the way it was."[50]

When high school teams were slowly integrated after 1965, black and white athletes faced a difficult adjustment to the new situation. Horace King, who went on to become the first African American player for the University of Georgia football team, recalled problems with his high school experience. As the schools began to integrate there were problems with the way the coaches brought the football team together. Black and white players failed to do blocking assignments for each other and the coaches failed to forge a team ethos.[51] For some black students joining a newly integrated—and so predominantly white—school there were many problems. Black students often felt isolated, and struggles to fit in at school dissuaded many black athletes from making the commitment to join a previously all-white team. Black players also faced the problem of white coaches speaking down to them, as prevailing white supremacist attitudes continued.[52] Not all black athletes faced negative experiences, however. Lester McClain, the first black varsity player at the University of Tennessee, remembered a relatively smooth transition from his all-black high school to his senior year at an integrated institution. His excellence on the football field helped him gain the respect of his fellow students.[53]

As these young men adapted to the changing racial patterns of the South and their impact on the high school sports fields of the region, the SEC remained exclusively white. The SEC was described as the "final citadel of segregation" as it held out against the changes taking place in wider society.[54] In late 1961 the president of the University of Kentucky predicted that the SEC would be desegregated within a few years. Representatives of Ole Miss, Mississippi State, Alabama, and Auburn reacted with alarm over his proposals. Worried about being isolated in the conference, Kentucky proceeded with caution.[55] A recruitment letter sent out to junior colleges around the country by the Alabama track and field coach emphasized the racial attitudes of many in the SEC. The correspondence asked for nominations of any "good white boys" who could meet the challenges of competition in the SEC.[56]

An article in the University of Tennessee student newspaper, the *Daily Beacon,* argued in October 1965 that "the forces behind the segregationist policies of the Southeastern Conference are strong and powerful." It noted that alumni of schools in the SEC threatened to withdraw funding if their alma mater integrated their athletics programs. The author of the article, Jack Topchik, drew attention to a young black sprinter, Willie Dawson, who ran the 100 yards in 9.4 seconds. Dawson expressed his desire to attend the University of Tennessee, but the athletics director argued that all the athletics scholarships were filled. Dawson was an exceptional sprinter and was snapped up by a northern university. University officials in the SEC were worried about making the first move toward integration and the subsequent drop in attendance and financial support that could follow.[57] With integration of the Atlantic Coast Conference and the Southwest Conference already apparent in the mid-1960s and with high school sports programs increasingly becoming interracial, SEC officials held out against the forces of racial change.

The forces maintaining segregation in the SEC were particularly potent. Eventually it was a border state member, Kentucky, that took the lead in integrating the football conference. This was consistent with a general pattern of less successful and established institutions taking the lead in the desegregation of playing squads. Even so, there was a large time lag between the integration of the university itself and of the athletics program. In 1954 the University of Kentucky enrolled twenty black undergraduates, and it continued to accept black students thereafter. It was not until 1967, however, that a black player made his debut for the Wildcats in a varsity game. Black players Greg Page and Nat Northington signed letters of intent in December 1965 and reported to the *Middlesboro (Ky.) Daily News* in May 1967 that they faced "no problems" in the integration process. Coach Charlie Bradshaw explained his desire to improve the football program with talented players of any race, and supporters focused mainly on the prospects of a winning team. Northington and Page reported that their focus on football was total and that they had experienced no problems. Tellingly, though, the article reported that the Wildcats' schedule for 1967 required them to visit the Deep South for only three games, at Auburn, Louisiana State, and Florida.[58]

The integration process was perhaps aided by the tragic death of Greg Page after a freak training accident in August 1967 in which he broke his neck. Page was in the hospital for thirty-three days before dying. The injury and Page's progress became a topic of conversation and focal point for the community in his hometown of Middlesborough, Kentucky, and for all connected with the university.[59] Shared sympathy for Page and his family provided a backdrop that reduced the possibility of racial tensions surrounding the integration of the team. Nat Northington overcame considerable emotional pain by competing in the Wildcats game against Ole Miss the day after Page's death. It was in this game that the SEC was integrated.[60]

Four months earlier the University of Tennessee had signed halfback Lester McClain as their first black football player.[61] McClain made his varsity debut in 1968 and had a successful four-year career with the Tennessee Vols.[62] McClain recalled that he was well received by his teammates and supporters of the team. In fact, when he took the field in his first home game, against the University of Georgia, he was given a standing ovation before he had even touched the ball.[63] Both Northington and McClain were recruited by schools with a longer tradition of enrolling black undergraduates than Deep South schools in the SEC. Furthermore, the University of Tennessee campus was located in Knoxville. Condredge Holloway, who played quarterback for the Vols in the early 1970s and in so doing became the first black to play that position in the SEC, described Knoxville as something of a racial melting pot. The university was not as heavily influenced by the forces of segregation as other SEC institutions were.[64] It is also worth noting that the Tennessee coach, Doug Dickey, had managed integrated football teams while in the military. His successor, Bill Battle, had previously coached at West Point and so too had been exposed to integrated teams.[65] Here we see racial changes in other areas of society affecting the integration of the SEC.

With integration in wider society and on campus progressing in the South, however tentatively, the SEC had only two integrated football teams by the end of the 1960s. In 1970 four more members integrated their football teams. Vanderbilt, Florida, Auburn, and Mississippi State all included black players on their varsity roster that year.[66] With the scales tipping as more SEC teams were integrated than not, the schools in the Deep South finally began to integrate in 1971. Central to this process was the University of Alabama. Their team was the dominant football force in the region and the most recognizable to the rest of the nation. Something of a myth has developed around the integration of Alabama's Crimson Tide squad. The teams of Coach Paul "Bear" Bryant had brought great sporting prestige to the University of Alabama in the 1960s. A popular image of Alabama leading the way in the integration of the SEC has perverted the actual historical record, however.

As the 1960s progressed Bryant inched closer to integrating the Crimson Tide as other SEC teams followed the lead of Kentucky and Tennessee. Folklore points to the early 1970 season defeat at the hands of the University of Southern California as prompting a radical shift in Alabama recruiting policy. Black player Sam Cunningham ran around, through, and over the Tide defense during that game. Alabama assistant coach Jerry Claiborne said that Cunningham had done more to integrate Alabama in sixty minutes on the field than Martin Luther King Jr. had done in the previous decades. In reality, however, the move toward integrating the Crimson Tide had already been taken. Wilbur Jackson watched from the stands that night as the first black player to be recruited for the freshman team.[67] At Alabama in October 1969 fifty black students staged a sit-in in the university cafeteria to draw attention to a series of issues. One of these was a call by the Black Student Union for the Alabama athletic program to recruit some black athletes.[68] It is apparent that on many southern campuses athletes were not involved in student activism and civil rights struggles in the way they were on campuses like Wyoming, Marquette, and California. There was not a black athletic revolt on the campus at Alabama because there were no black athletes.

Coach Bryant had an immensely loyal following in the state of Alabama and could have made the decision to integrate the SEC in the mid-1960s, taking a stand against the segregationist demagoguery of Governor Wallace. Nevertheless, he believed that his primary responsibility "was to win football games, not to promote social justice."[69] In this respect we again see that sport was not used to run ahead of changes in wider society in the South. By the time the Alabama football team was integrated significant moves had already been made to integrate public schools in the state and the formal elements of Jim Crow segregation had been dismantled. For Wilbur Jackson and his teammate John Mitchell, just pulling on the uniform of the University of Alabama represented significant progress.

In 1971 the University of Georgia also included a black player on its varsity team. Horace King went to play for the team after he was recruited by Coach Vince Dooley. King was impressed by the way Dooley coached the team, and once he had received assurances that he was going to be given the chance to play and was not a "token black recruit" he had no hesitations about signing. Dooley argued that the integration of public schools in Georgia a few years before King joined the team helped with the transition to interracial Bulldog rosters. Players themselves and fans in Georgia had already begun to adjust to interracial contests and integrated teams before the university team was desegregated.[70] The student newspaper reported in January 1971 that the "best move" the Bulldogs had made during the off-season was to sign some black players. The athletics department commented that they were simply interested in recruiting good players, regardless of their race.[71] A decade after undergraduate education on campus had been integrated the football team began to recruit and field black players.

Ole Miss was the last of the SEC football programs to racially integrate when Robert Williams and James Reed were recruited in December 1971. Again we see the athletics program running behind developments on the campus as a whole. In late 1969 the newly formed Black Student Union, supported by some liberal white classmates, began to articulate concerns about the school's athletics program. The lack of black players and the shouting of racial slurs and use of Confederate symbols during Rebel football games were particular problems. These calls for change were reinforced by the dismal performance of the team on the field, with a string of humiliating defeats suffered at the hands of local rivals.[72] This pressure affected a change of policy by Ole Miss administrators and so the SEC was finally fully integrated. Again, the Black Student Union could not engage with student athletes as it did elsewhere. It put pressure on administrators to recruit black athletes rather than enlisting such athletes in an attempt to press for further concessions.

Civil Rights, Sports, and the Lack of a Black Athletic Revolt

The integration of the SEC in the late 1960s and early 1970s was a large step forward, and the few black pioneers in the league carried with them a great responsibility. The first black young men to compete on previously all-white sports fields, they were charged with proving they were worthy of selection and could set an example that others would follow. Certainly in the first decade of integration the black players selected were of a high quality. As a disproportionately high number of black athletes lettered, it is fair to conclude that the quality of the black players was slightly better than that of the white players.[73]

These first black players also had to face the inevitable racial problems that accompanied the initial integration of SEC football. Horace King recalled not just racial insults on the field and from the stands but also difficulties when traveling as part of a team in certain areas of the South.[74] Haskel Stanback recalled a game in Oxford against the University of Mississippi in which the crowd howled "kill that nigger" throughout the contest.[75] Eddie Brown remembered that visiting team accommodations in places like Alabama and Mississippi were approached with caution, especially in relation to arrangements off the field. Brown recalled, "In Knoxville, pretty much that was open and friendly, but if you were on the road or out of town then you had to watch some places that you went to . . . it could get ugly."[76] Yet it would be wrong to paint a picture of blanket racial problems that greeted black players when they visited rival teams. Condredge Holloway of the University of Tennessee argued that the amount of racial tension was directly related to whether the team was winning or losing. Racial problems within a team or from fans surfaced only when that team was losing. Holloway's coach, Bill Battle, remembered, "I don't think [it] was a racial thing, it was a win and lose thing."[77] Black players who excelled were given great respect by opponents. Holloway's flamboyant style won him many plaudits. His "unreal" play was applauded by the opposition. Coach Vince Dooley explained, "I've never seen a quarterback as complete as Holloway" after an impressive performance against Dooley's Georgia Bulldogs in 1973.[78] The rivalry between different teams could also produce some bizarre racial abuse from fans. Lester McClain recalled being told that when he was tackled by a black opponent during a match one supporter was heard to shout, "You niggers get off our colored boy!"[79]

The important point is that these black pioneers in the late 1960s and early 1970s were engaging in integrated competition at the college level for the first time. They were experiencing this breakthrough many years after black athletes in other areas of the nation. This had an important impact on attitudes toward the intrusion of civil rights activism on the sporting arena. Of the thirty-seven major college campuses that Edwards claims witnessed black athletic revolts in 1968, none were SEC schools.[80] In the course of this research I have not found any documentary evidence of a black athletic revolt at any of these schools in the late 1960s and early 1970s. Unlike schools such as UTEP, which had taken a lead in recruiting black athletes, institutions in the SEC were slow to integrate their teams. As a consequence, there is not the same sort of evidence of student athletes getting involved in activism in the way they did at UTEP and other campuses around the country.

There is evidence, however, that black student activism was a feature of some of these campuses and had the potential to affect athletics programs. In 1970 when Coolidge Ball was recruited by Ole Miss to play basketball there were overtures from the Black Student Union for him to become a racial leader on campus. He was not interested in engaging with political activism, however. As Nadine Cohodas has explained, "Ball's first family on campus was his team. . . . The brotherhood of athletes was stronger than the brotherhood of skin color."[81] Horace King was approached by representatives of the Black Student Union at the University of Georgia about supporting a campaign to force concessions from the institution's administrators.[82] At the University of Tennessee black students sponsored by the Afro-American Student Liberation Force held demonstrations in 1972.[83] Haskel Stanback remembered black Olympian Ralph Boston talking to a lot of the black athletes on campus at Tennessee and offering advice to them in their role as African American athletes.[84] There was not an absence of political activity relating to the civil rights struggle on these southern campuses; however, a black athletic revolt did not manifest itself in the way it did in other parts of the country.

There was a sense that many of the black athletes, especially those born and raised in the South, were reluctant to get involved in any form of overt civil rights activism. Lester McClain argued, "We kept our mouths closed, found out that you get too much resistance when you open your mouth and say too much."[85] Horace King believed it was his role to give 100 percent as a football player, which was why he had been given a scholarship. He did not need to wear a banner or make an overt statement, as this would just distract him from his job as a football player.[86] Holloway explained that he stayed away from racial politics outside of the football arena. He asserted, "I let Martin Luther King be Martin Luther King. . . . I appreciate everything that he did but that was not my intent. My intent was to play football and get a degree."[87] White University of Alabama player Johnny Musso remembered that he did not know any African Americans who conformed to the angry black militant athlete stereotype. His black teammates just wanted to get out on the field and play. They did not want to draw attention to themselves as black but simply wanted to be treated like any other student.[88] At Ole Miss black football star Ben Williams let his football do the talking. Williams blanked out the band playing "Dixie" and the waving of the Rebel flag. The fans still cheered for him when he brought success for the team.[89] Black athletes on many southern campuses were less politically active and more conservative in their outlook than those exposed to more radical influences on the East and West Coasts.

There were, of course, some racial tensions inside the locker room between white and black players, and there were some problems between black players and their white coaches. Again, though, this did not manifest itself in boycotts and significant racial discord in the way it did on many campuses outside of the SEC. University of Georgia coach Vince Dooley recalled an incident in the early 1970s when some white players on the team became angry because a black player was pictured in the student newspaper in the middle of a Black Student Union demonstration. Dooley explained that the white players did not believe that black players on the team should be getting involved in this kind of political activism. Dooley and his staff defused the situation by bringing the team together and talking about the issue. It transpired that the black player in question had simply been watching the demonstration rather than participating in it, and the picture had misrepresented his position.[90]

As on other campuses across the country, there were racial issues surrounding facial hair on SEC football teams. Haskel Stanback recalled a situation at Tennessee in which some of the black players had discussed the possibility of boycotting the preseason Orange and White Game because they wanted to keep their facial hair. In this instance there were white players who also wanted to grow longer sideburns and mustaches.[91] Coach Battle dealt with the issue by asking the black players during a team meeting if he discriminated against them. They said no and he explained to all the players, white and black, that his rule was no facial hair. Battle recalled that this was all that was needed and that no player tried to boycott or make a serious political demonstration.[92] White University of Georgia player

Thomas Lyons recalled that his coach told all players when they arrived for spring practice that facial hair would not be accepted. It was not perceived as a racial issue but simply as a point of discipline and team rules.[93]

Condredge Holloway recalled that integrating football and other sports teams was easier than it was to integrate other areas of life. "It was all about your team winning and what was the best combination you could put out on the field. . . . So it went from not being able to play to making sure you get the best players you can from your area, so I think it [integration] was a much easier transition than in regular life."[94] This may well have been so. The key point is, however, that these other areas of life had faced the initial challenges of integration before the football teams of the SEC had to. In other parts of the country a myth had long developed that sport provided a special arena in which racial progress could be made. This was not the case in the South because long into the 1960s sport was still used as a symbol of the segregationist creed. When black and white players pulled on the colors of the Tennessee Vols or the Alabama Crimson Tide and played side by side they did so after schools, buses, and theaters had been required to integrate. The integration of the SEC was not at the forefront of the Civil Rights Movement. Football was not perceived to have blazed a trail ahead of conditions in the rest of society. As a result, a black athletic revolt did not emerge. There was not an effort to probe the discontinuity between the myth of sport as an arena that fostered racial progress and the harsher reality. Indeed, in many respects, following the integration of the SEC, sport was responsible for the development of greater racial understanding.

Vince Dooley coached the University of Georgia football team from 1964 until 1988. He saw the expansion of the number of black players in the SEC and the way in which sport could bring black and white people together. Dooley argued, "Athletics helped to integrate the South. . . . Passions run so hard with sports and when they saw white and black were playing together for a common cause then they were for that cause."[95] Clarence Pope, one of the first black players for the University of Georgia, told the student newspaper that he and his fellow black athletes had been given a "fair deal." Pope elaborated, "This is the best thing that has ever happened to me. I have received an education in and out of the classroom. I have learned that Georgia is not the school it was rumored to be in the way of treatment to blacks."[96] In the passionate atmosphere of interstate rivalry in southern football after integration, race was steadily less and less of an issue. It was about winning against old rivals and playing the game to the best of one's ability. Horace King recalled his high school days to illustrate the ability of sport to defuse racial tensions. In the first few years of integration he recalled that if the school basketball and football teams were winning then the school was unified.[97] For individual black and white southerners, integrated competition helped to break down racial barriers and to foster a shared sense of purpose and identity. Johnny Musso explained, "There is something mystically good about being a teammate; you're locked together in ways that you may not be in other walks of life."[98]

Athletes who look back on their experiences during the integration of college competition in the South maintain a belief in the positive role of sport in the development of race relations. At the University of Houston Donald Chaney, Elvin Hayes, and Warren McVea integrated the athletics department. They were featured in Olsen's 1968 *Sports Illustrated* article as men exploited by the university and subject to social ostracism. Recent interviews with the men, however, challenge Olsen's claims. The men argued that Olsen had exaggerated the problems of their position and instead praised the Houston athletics department for the experience that it gave them. The men clearly subscribe to the view that sport promoted racial progress.[99]

Among both white and black players and their coaches who were at the forefront of the integration of the SEC there also remains a deep belief that sport helped to improve race relations in the South. There is a sense of romanticism as these men look back from the early twenty-first century to those experiences in the late 1960s and early 1970s. This could provoke the assertion that their views lack veracity, but the very strong and genuine way in which they are expressed shows the endurance of the myth of sport as a positive racial force. Their commitment to the ideal that sport developed racial progress in the South is strong and real. This sentiment overlooks the way sport was used for so long to maintain segregation in the South, but in some ways it is this very fact that strengthens the ideal. Since the early 1970s, when the SEC was finally fully integrated, the number of black athletes participating in the conference has increased to the extent that in many sports they are now in the majority. The fact that blacks and whites could increasingly join together to cheer on integrated teams had an important impact on southern identity; an identity that can now be shared by blacks as they continue the process of reclaiming their southernness.

Conclusion

In March 2011 black Pittsburgh Steelers running back Rashard Mendenhall stirred controversy when he supported comments by Adrian Peterson, his Minnesota Vikings counterpart, that playing in the NFL was like modern-day slavery. Mendenhall posted on his Twitter page, "Anyone with knowledge of the slave trade and the NFL could say that these two parallel each other." What caused real outrage were posts on his official Twitter page two months later referring to the celebrations following the killing of Osama bin Laden. Mendenhall commented, "What kind of person celebrates death? It's amazing how people can HATE a man they have never even heard speak. We've only heard one side." He later posted, "For those of you who said you want to see Bin Laden burn . . . I ask how would God feel about your heart?" The running back was rebuked by his employers, who put out a statement from team president Art Rooney II. The statement read, "I have not spoken with Rashard, so it is hard to explain or even comprehend what he meant with his recent Twitter comments. The entire Steelers organization is very proud of the job our military personnel have done and we can only hope this leads to our troops coming home soon."[1]

Mendenhall later clarified his comments and insisted that he had not intended to offend anyone. This came too late for his endorsement deal with sports apparel company Champion, however. They cancelled their contract with Mendenhall, asserting, "While we respect Mr. Mendenhall's right to express sincere thoughts regarding potentially controversial topics, we no longer believe that Mr. Mendenhall can appropriately represent Champion."[2] Mendenhall's teammates also criticized his Twitter posts. Defensive captain James Farrior argued, "He made some comments that he probably shouldn't have made at the sensitive time that it was. You can voice your opinions, but you don't want to try to offend people that have strong feelings about that. You've got to think about everybody that's involved." Cornerback Ike Taylor added, "You live and you learn, and I hope everybody accepts his apology. Some mistakes are bigger than others, and I say this is a huge mistake. It's just something you can't say. He'll learn from it."[3]

Mendenhall is a professional athlete and as such he competes within a different framework from those experienced by the amateur and college athletes who have been the focus of this study. Mendenhall has signed a contract with his employers that is different from the scholarship agreements of the black fourteen, the Speed City sprinters, or basketball players at Marquette coached by Al McGuire. Indeed, this study focused on amateur rather than professional sports so as to more effectively investigate the impact of the black athletic revolt on local and national communities. Nevertheless, in the responses to Mendenhall's Twitter posts we see echoes of the problems facing athletes who wish to engage with the wider social and political agenda. As a black athlete questioning expressions of American patriotism, Mendenhall crossed a racial line and transgressed the cherished mythology of the sports world as apolitical.

The world of college sports also reacted in 2011 to the potential problems posed by Twitter. South Carolina Gamecocks football coach Steve Spurrier instated a ban on his players' use of the social media site. This ban was traced back to an incident in which one player incorrectly tweeted that his teammate had been arrested after a bar fight.[4] CNBC's sports business reporter Darren Rovell criticized the trend among college coaches to prohibit the use of Twitter. Rovell argued that the ban was evidence of players not being treated as responsible students as well as athletes.[5] There is an echo here of the frictions over team discipline during the black athletic revolts. As members of a team are players duty-bound to sacrifice certain rights of expression? What are the differences between Coach Andros insisting that Fred Milton remain clean-shaven and Coach Spurrier demanding that his players not use Twitter?

What these issues serve to illustrate is the contentious status of student athletes and their ability to express their own political views. Throughout this study we have seen how the position of athletes could work to compromise their ability to engage successfully in the black freedom struggle. When Tommie Smith and John Carlos connected with that struggle, most symbolically on the podium in Mexico City, they faced a backlash against their racial politics and the fact that their politics had infringed upon the sacred world of sport, a world dominated by the ideal that it was color-blind and provided leadership in the progress toward racial equality. At the time of writing there are fewer than one hundred days until the start of the 2012 Olympics. What would be the reaction if Tyson Gay, Justin Gatlin, or any other black member of the U.S. track and field team spoke out about racial injustice after winning a medal in London? What if they posted their comments on Twitter? The prevailing ideal that sport can and should rise above racial politics would provide the context for any discussions of any such hypothetical comments.

In the period since the black athletic revolt the role of African American athletes has been used to reinforce the myth of the sporting world as a place of uncontested racial progress. A specific black aesthetic has been used at various times to emphasize this message. Jacquelyn Dowd Hall asserts that the Old Right, on the wrong side of the quest for civil rights in the 1960s, reinvented itself by painting the Civil Rights Movement as a struggle to end institutional inequality. By the 1970s New Right "color-blind conservatives" sought to ensure that equality prevailed.[6] The skewing of the civil rights chronology and consequent efforts by the New Right to reduce the scope of the civil rights struggle are reflected in the institutional response to the black athletic revolt.

Activists such as Harry Edwards were painted as extremists with unrealistic and destructive demands, whereas the grievances of more moderate athletes were given more consideration. While continuing to defend the historical record of sport as a vehicle for racial progress, sports administrators enacted legislation to address the main complaints of black athletes. This response was often quite cosmetic, however, and was aimed at presenting an outward impression of racial progress in sports. In 1972 the NCAA set up an advisory commission that took steps to encourage the appointment of more black coaches and administrators, for example.[7] The approach of sports administrators to the problems of the black athletic revolt reflects the color-blind conservatism that Hall identifies. The legislation that was enacted was designed to prevent the most egregious individual acts of racism. Sports administrators continued, however, to resist the use of sport to protest racial injustice in wider society.

Just as the Civil Rights Movement was reduced to a distinct, narrow period and its gains minimized by the New Right, so the radicalism of the black athletic revolt was diffused by sports administrators in the 1970s and beyond. Furthermore, the black athletic revolt and the civil rights struggle from which it grew have receded into "an expanding disjuncture between African-American prosperity and poverty."[8] Sporting achievement is seen as the way out of the ghetto. Racism in sport, however, reflects the racial prejudice of society in general. A 2000 study concluded that "racial discrimination in sports continues to erode remarkable accomplishments that are being realized among African-American athletes."⁹ Disturbingly, the message of Edwards and others has been largely forgotten with the emergence of a distinctly black athletic style into the sporting mainstream.

In the years following the black athletic revolt an embrace of this black athletic style has been combined with a reassertion of the ideal that sporting competition offers an important route to racial integration and progress. Nevertheless, critics of the sporting establishment have pointed to continued examples of racial prejudice inherent in the American sports world many years after the black athletic revolt. Dave Zirin argues that NBA executives tapped into the rise of hip-hop music to craft a new and exciting image for professional basketball teams in the 1980s. The music was used to help frame a black aesthetic that glorified a new generation of exciting new players, the leaders of which were black stars like Magic Johnson and Michael Jordan. When other black players like Allen Iversen brought a more confrontational and aggressive style to the court and high-lighted the less commercially attractive elements of street culture and hip-hop, then NBA executives reacted. A new policy document and dress code were introduced with the express intention of curtailing the "negative" influence of black culture within the league.[10]

A double standard surrounding African American athletes has contin-ued years after Edwards led the black athletic revolt. When a black ath-lete such as Michael Jordan, Michael Johnson, or Tiger Woods succeeds it is presented as a story of possibility for African Americans. Neverthe-less, reaction to the problems of a Mike Tyson or Terrell Owens reveals the reality that off the field the black athlete is still, in the words of Tom-mie Smith, "just another nigger." Amy Bass has explained, "The realm of commercial endorsement working in concert with athletic excellence . . . portrays sport as one of the most democratic vehicles of social mobility."[11] The popular image of sport as the most successful force for racial prog-ress perpetuates a legend that ignores the realities of racism in the United States. The aftermath of the black athletic revolt has seen the reinvigora-tion of the very myth of sport as a universally positive racial force that the revolt tried to expose. Furthermore, many of the contradictions at the heart of African American athletes' engagement with mainstream sporting cul-ture have evolved rather than been eradicated.

This restoration of the color-blind sporting ideal displays the potency of the myth of unequivocal racial progress through sport. This myth and the history of the black sportsman's largely submissive persona help to explain the strong backlash against the black athletic revolt. The raw exposition of the racism that existed in the sporting arena and wider society confronted white athletes and administrators with a repudiation of prevailing racial stereotypes and attacked the ideal of racial liberalism in sport. In this sense we see one element of the response to the black athletic revolt as a white backlash. We can see, therefore, the reaction to the black athletic revolt as part of the wider response of the white majority to perceived liberal excess in the late 1960s. The "silent majority" sought to end the countercultural threats to American values and to combat increasingly radicalized expressions of the civil rights struggle, one of which was the use of sport to dramatize racial inequality in wider society.

Historians of race and sport in the United States must probe the relationship between these powerful influences on American life in all of their nuanced forms. It is undeniable that successful black sports stars, both now and in the 1960s, provide an inspiration to the grassroots of their community. Sport was and is used as a vehicle through which to bring greater racial understanding. It is clear that in the era after the late 1960s black southerners were able to tap into a southern identity in a way that had previously been absent because of their full participation in the sporting culture of the region. Nevertheless, this same culture had long been used to deny equality and protect white supremacy. The institutions of sport themselves, and the written and unwritten rules of conduct that dominated the environment they governed, played a crucial role in restricting the ability of black—and white—athletes to fully engage in the black freedom struggle. Those who tried faced a double backlash, both racial and sporting.

In many respects the black athletic revolt represented an incomplete revolution, and one that remains unfinished. That revolt emerged amid a period in which the Civil Rights and Black Power Movements intersected and created probably the most dramatic era of the black freedom struggle. During the aftermath of this process the vital messages of both movements were blurred and the meaning of the black freedom struggle was redefined by the New Right. In the 1980s President Ronald Reagan used both the words and legacy of Martin Luther King Jr. to reduce the civil rights struggle to a call for individual action. The federal government had delivered civil rights legislation and now it was up to black Americans to lift themselves the rest of the way to equality.[12] Radical messages about poverty and the structure of American society were lost. The radical imagery of Smith and Carlos on the podium in 1968 has been woven into a narrative that reinforces the ideal that sport unequivocally promotes racial equality.

The nuance and significance of their message and the movement that they represented have been blurred. We must focus sharply and critically on the true meanings of their stand and the problems activist athletes faced in the late 1960s if sport is to fully play its part, along with other aspects of society, in the development of the black freedom struggle.

Acknowledgments

The people who deserve the most acknowledgment for their contributions to this book are the former athletes, activists, and coaches who so generously gave of their time to speak with me about their experiences. Without their stories the wider narrative that unfolds in the pages of this book could not have been told. I thank you all sincerely.

The genesis of this work was in the PhD thesis that I completed in 2010. The first debt of gratitude is therefore owed to my supervisor, Keith Brewster, and my secondary supervisor, Susan-Mary Grant. Susan-Mary was an excellent sounding board for many of my ideas and she inspired my interest in American history as an undergraduate. Keith was the perfect supervisor. He allowed me time to develop my ideas in my own way but always provided critical and insightful advice that developed the depth and quality of the project. Without Keith and his wife, Claire, this book would not have been possible.

During the course of this project I received help from many archivists and librarians. There is a strong likelihood that there are some individuals missing from the list below, whom I have forgotten to mention. Apologies to those who have fallen through the cracks of my memory or are buried too deeply in the recesses of my e-mail inbox. Ellen Summers and Lisa Greer provided help in accessing the archives of the National Collegiate Athletic Association. Cindy Slater was very generous with her time and resources at the United States Olympic Committee library and archives. Thanks also to Shannon Bowen at the University of Wyoming; Brad Aldridge and Rich Bunnell at the University of California, Berkeley; Anne Bridges at the University of Tennessee; Michelle Sweetser at Marquette University; Barry Bunch and Becky Schulte at the University of Kansas; Jan Mazzucco at the University of Georgia; Melanie Gray at the University of Alabama; Tyra Whittaker at USA Track and Field; Linda Stahnke at the University of Illinois; Simon Elliott at UCLA; and Claudia Rivers at the University of Texas at El Paso.

Thanks to the Bulletin of Latin American Research book series and the *International Journal of the History of Sport* for permission to reproduce elements of this research published during an earlier stage of my studies.

I would like to thank Robert Mason and members of the Scottish Association for Study of the Americas for giving me the opportunity to share my ideas during an early stage of this project. Brian Ward provided many pertinent pieces of advice in the period immediately after the completion of my PhD thesis and Ben Houston pointed me in the direction of some possible publishers. A huge thanks to Anne Dean Watkins and Bailey Johnson at the University Press of Kentucky for their help, support, and encouragement during the development of this project. I could not have asked for more skillful acquisitions editors. I also owe a debt of gratitude to the anonymous readers who helped me turn a promising thesis into a readable book and to Joy Margheim for her excellent editing.

The love and support of my family continues to be an inspiration and they all deserve thanks for their interest and encouragement as I worked toward completing this book. My mother and father remain the very best teachers. To the newest members of the family, Joseph and Neve, if you are old enough to be reading this on your own then you are old enough to understand how much I love you. Finally, this book is dedicated to my lovely Laura. Thanks for everything you do, both the things you know about and the things you don't.

Notes

Preface

1. Branch, *Parting the Waters,* 922.
2. Fairclough, *Better Day Coming.*
3. P. E. Joseph, "Black Power Movement," 752.
4. Hall, "Long Civil Rights Movement."
5. Cha-Jua and Lang, "'Long Movement' as Vampire."
6. P. Joseph, *Waiting 'Til the Midnight Hour,* 9–34.
7. Bissinger, *Friday Night Lights.*
8. Hartmann, *Race, Culture, and the Revolt of the Black Athlete.*
9. Bass, *Not the Triumph.*
10. Martin, *Benching Jim Crow.*
11. Demas, *Integrating the Gridiron.*
12. Kemper, *College Football.*
13. Grundy, *Learning to Win.*
14. Rogers, "Oral History," 576.
15. Nasstrom, "Beginnings and Endings,"
16. Rogers, "Oral History," 568.

1. Locating the Black Athletic Revolt in the Black Freedom Struggle

1. Gitlin, *The Sixties,* 305.
2. Douglas Roby to Harry Parker, November 5, 1968, copy in author's possession, courtesy of Paul Hoffman.
3. Edwards, *Revolt of the Black Athlete,* 1.
4. D. Wiggins, "Leisure Time," 36–37.
5. Frederickson, *Black Image,* 241–55.
6. Wiggins, "Great Speed," 159–60.
7. Wiggins, "Prized Performers," 165–67.
8. Gems, "Blocked Shot," 140–45.
9. Shropshire, *In Black and White,* 29–31.
10. Ibid., 31.
11. For a discussion of black protest and the symbolism it exploited from the 1930s, see Sandage, "Marble House Divided." Rick Halpern draws attention to the increasingly interracial nature of unionism in the 1940s in "Organised Labour, Black Workers and the Twentieth-Century South: The Emerging Revision"; see also Korstad, *Civil Rights Unionism.* Darlene Clark Hine, in "Black Profession-

als and Race Consciousness: Origins of the Civil Rights Movement, 1890–1950," shows the ways in which the black professional class pushed for racial change during and immediately after the Second World War. All of these studies help to show that the seeds of the Civil Rights Movement of the 1960s and many of the tactics used during that decade emerged in a previous era.

12. Shropshire, *In Black and White,* 30.

13. Spivey, "End Jim Crow," 282–84, 300–302.

14. Marcello, "Integration of Intercollegiate Athletics," 316.

15. T. Smith, "Civil Rights and the Gridiron," 196–98, 204–8.

16. *New York Times,* November 25, 1967.

17. Gems, "Blocked Shot," 136.

18. Interview with Phil Shinnick, July 23, 2004.

19. Kellner, "Sports, Media, Culture, and Race," 462–65.

20. Meade, "Joe Louis," 329–34.

21. Van Deburg, *Black Camelot,* 99.

22. Marcello, "Integration of Intercollegiate Athletics," 311–12.

23. Interview with Willie Brown, October 4, 2004.

24. Moore, "Courageous Stand," 66.

25. Interview with T. J. Gaughan, October 27, 2004.

26. Interview with Larry Young, May 31, 2004.

27. Interview with David Hemery, March 25, 2004.

28. *San Jose Mercury News,* September 18, 1967.

29. Ibid.

30. Kemper, *College Football,* 42.

31. *San Jose Mercury News,* September 22, 1967.

32. Fairclough, *To Redeem the Soul of America,* 316.

33. M. L. King, "Where Do We Go From Here: Chaos or Community?," in Washington, *Testament of Hope,* 589.

34. P. Joseph, "Black Power Movement," 753.

35. Tyson, *Radio Free Dixie,* 3.

36. Ibid., 88–93.

37. Ibid., 155.

38. Umoja, "Ballot and the Bullet," 570–72.

39. Raines, *My Soul Is Rested,* 148.

40. Fairclough, *To Redeem the Soul of America,* 149.

41. Umoja, "Ballot and the Bullet," 570–73.

42. Edwards, *Revolt of the Black Athlete,* 58.

43. Van Deburg, *New Day in Babylon,* 88.

44. *New York Times,* May 12, 1968.

45. *San Jose Mercury News,* September 23, 1967.

46. *New York Times,* February 16, 1968.

47. *New York Times,* May 12, 1968.

48. Miroff, "Presidential Leverage."

49. Grundy, *Learning to Win,* 267–68.

50. Interview with Bob Abright, April 13, 2006.

51. Interview with Melvin Hamilton, April 19, 2004.

52. Roberts and Olsen, *Winning Is the Only Thing,* 166.

53. Edwards, *Revolt of the Black Athlete,* 26.

54. E. Barkley Brown, "Negotiating and Transforming the Public Sphere: African-American Political Life in the Transition from Slavery to Freedom," in Dailey, Gilmore, and Simon, *Jumpin' Jim Crow,* 52.

55. Interview with Wyomia Tyus, October 16, 2004.

56. Estes, *I Am a Man,* 98–105.

57. Kemper, *College Football,* 28–31.

58. P. Miller, "To Bring the Race along Rapidly: Sport, Student Culture, and Educational Mission at Historically Black Colleges during the Interwar Years," in Miller, *Sporting World,* 131.

59. Interview with Conrad Dobler, March 12, 2004.

60. Interview with Melvin Hamilton, April 19, 2004.

61. Interview with Harry Edwards, January 26, 2004.

62. Cleaver, *Soul on Ice,* 107.

63. Foner, *Black Panthers,* 2.

64. Van Deburg, *New Day in Babylon,* 51, 306.

65. Van Deburg, *Black Camelot,* 194.

66. Edwards, *Sociology of Sport,* 145–46, 147.

67. Van Deburg, *Black Camelot,* 194.

68. Farber, "Silent Majority," 309.

69. "The Troubled America: A Special Report on the White Majority," *Newsweek,* October 6, 1969, 20.

70. Sugrue, "Crabgrass-Roots Politics," 560–64.

71. Lewis, *Massive Resistance,* 24–25.

72. Ibid., 187.

73. Andrew, *Other Side of the Sixties,* 5.

74. McGirr, *Suburban Warriors.*

75. Andrew, *Other Side of the Sixties,* 145.

76. Schoenwald, *Time for Choosing,* 258–59.

77. Carter, *Politics of Rage,* 306–7, 349.

78. Brink and Harris, *Black and White,* 115–16, 135–36.

79. Rieder, *Canarsie,* 138, 203–5.

80. McGirr, *Suburban Warriors,* 239.

81. Klarman, "How Brown Changed Race Relations," 84.

82. Grundy, *Learning to Win,* 266.

83. R. Henderson, "Something More than the Game," 219.

84. Cobb, *Brown Decision,* 55.

85. Lewis, *Massive Resistance,* 24.

86. Interview with Vince Dooley, March 20, 2006.

87. Grundy, *Learning to Win,* 265.

88. Ibid., 269.

89. Interview with Horace King, March 31, 2006.

90. Grundy, *Learning to Win,* 280.

91. Interview with George Patton, March 24, 2006.

92. Roby to Parker, November 5, 1968, copy in author's possession, courtesy of Paul Hoffman.

2. The Olympic Project for Human Rights

1. *Chicago Daily Defender,* July 29, 1967, 15.

2. Interview with Ralph Boston, July 27, 2004.

3. New York NAACP branch to Roy Wilkins, June 12, 1961, group 3, box A3, Sports, NAACP collection.

4. Interview with Ralph Boston, July 27, 2004.

5. A. Hano, "The Black Rebel Who 'Whitelists' The Olympics," *New York Times,* May 12, 1968.

6. Van Deburg, *New Day in Babylon,* 67.

7. P. Joseph, *Waiting 'Til the Midnight Hour,* 205.

8. Hoffer, *Something in the Air,* 18.

9. Spivey, "Black Consciousness," 239–40.

10. Wilkins to Lippmann, April 15, 1964, group 3, box A3, Sports, NAACP collection.

11. A. Hano, "The Black Rebel Who 'Whitelists' The Olympics," *New York Times,* May 12, 1968.

12. *New York Times,* July 24, 1967; Hartmann, *Race, Culture, and the Revolt of the Black Athlete,* 81.

13. Edwards, *Revolt of the Black Athlete,* 52–56.

14. "OCHR Information Booklet," December 15, 1967, copy in author's possession.

15. Edwards, *Revolt of the Black Athlete,* 53.

16. "The Angry Black Athlete," *Newsweek,* July 15, 1968.

17. Hartmann, *Race, Culture, and the Revolt of the Black Athlete,* 84.

18. *Chicago Daily Defender,* February 10, 1968.

19. Moore, "Courageous Stand," 68.

20. Interview with Lee Evans, April 20, 2004.

21. *New York Times,* November 26, 1967.

22. Hartmann, *Race, Culture, and the Revolt of the Black Athlete,* 62.

23. Ibid., 62–63.

24. *New York Times,* November 26, 1967.

25. Interview with Harry Edwards, January 26, 2004.

26. Cited in Hartmann, *Race, Culture, and the Revolt of the Black Athlete,* 66.

27. *New York Times,* July 24, 1967.

28. Hartmann, *Race, Culture, and the Revolt of the Black Athlete,* 69–73.

29. *New York Times,* November 25, 1967.

30. *Chicago Daily Defender,* November 28, 1967.

31. Interview with Hal Connolly, January 13, 2004.

32. Interview with Bob Seagren, June 7, 2004; interview with Al Oerter, November 16, 2004.

33. Interview with Larry Young, May 31, 2004.

34. Interview with George Young, September 8, 2004.

35. Interview with Robert Lipsyte, June 8, 2005.

36. Interview with Larry Young, May 31, 2004.

37. Interview with Cleve Livingston, August 18, 2004.

38. Interview with Dick Fosbury, February 5, 2004.

39. Interview with Al Oerter, November 16, 2004.

40. Interview with Phil Shinnick, July 23, 2004.

41. Interview with Bruce Kidd, October 20, 2004.

42. Interview with Hal Connolly, January 13, 2004.

43. Bass, *Not the Triumph,* 145.

44. J. Robinson, "Athletic Boycott Catches on in NY," *Pittsburgh Courier,* February 17, 1967.

45. Matthews, *My Race Be Won,* 162.

46. *New York Times,* February 14, 1968.

47. Bass, *Not the Triumph,* 146–47.

48. *New York Times,* January 30, 1968.

49. *Chicago Daily Defender,* February 3, 1968.

50. Bass, *Not the Triumph,* 148.

51. *Chicago Daily Defender,* February 17, 1968.

52. Edwards, *Revolt of the Black Athlete,* 66–68.

53. *New York Times,* February 16, 1968.

54. Edwards, *Revolt of the Black Athlete,* 66.

55. Wilson to Brundage, March 13, 1968, RS 26/20/37, box 333, Important Letters 1968 file, Brundage Papers, University of Illinois.

56. Matthews, *My Race Be Won,* 164.

57. Interview with Ralph Boston, July 27, 2004; Hartmann, *Race, Culture, and the Revolt of the Black Athlete,* 124.

58. Interview with Robert Lipsyte, June 8, 2005.

59. *New York Times,* February 16, 1968.

60. *Chicago Daily Defender,* February 15, 1968.

61. *Chicago Daily Defender,* February 26, 1968.

62. Bass, *Not the Triumph,* 150–53; *Newsweek,* February 26, 1968.

63. *New York Times,* February 18, 1968.

64. Matthews, *My Race Be Won,* 162.

65. Hartmann, *Race, Culture, and the Revolt of the Black Athlete,* 122.

66. Ibid., 123.

67. Bass, *Not the Triumph,* 156–57.

68. *Chicago Daily Defender,* February 20, 1968.

69. Edwards, *Revolt of the Black Athlete,* 68; *New York Times,* February 18, 1968; *Newsweek,* February 26, 1968.

70. Edwards, *Revolt of the Black Athlete,* 69.

71. *New York Times,* May 12, 1968.

72. *New York Times,* February 10, 1968.

73. *New York Times,* May 12, 1968.

74. Interview with Robert Lipsyte, June 8, 2005.

75. Interview with Harry Edwards, January 26, 2004.

76. Ibid.

77. Moore, "Courageous Stand," 66.

78. Hoffer, *Something in the Air,* 55.

79. Interview with Robert Lipsyte, June 8, 2005.

80. Matthews, *My Race Be Won,* 168.

81. Interview with Bob Seagren, June 7, 2004.

82. Interview with George Young, September 8, 2004.

83. Interview with Hal Connolly, January 13, 2004.

84. Interview with Jane Swagerty, November 19, 2004.

85. *Newsweek,* October 6, 1969.

86. Interview with Bruce Bradley, November 22, 2004.

87. Interview with Ralph Boston, July 27, 2004.

88. Interview with Phil Shinnick, July 23, 2004.

89. Interview with Harry Edwards, January 26, 2004.

90. *New York Times,* May 12, 1968.

91. Hartmann, *Race, Culture, and the Revolt of the Black Athlete,* 128.

92. *Chicago Daily Defender,* February 29, 1968.

93. *New York Times,* February 29, 1968.

94. *New York Times,* February 1, 1968.

95. *New York Times,* March 8, 1968.

96. *New York Times,* June 9, 1968.

97. Hartmann, *Race, Culture, and the Revolt of the Black Athlete,* 128–29.

98. Edwards, *Revolt of the Black Athlete,* 71–72.

99. *New York Times,* July 23, 1968.

100. Interview with Robert Lipsyte, June 8, 2005.

101. *New York Times,* July 7, 1968.

102. *Chicago Daily Defender,* March 26, 1968.

103. *New York Times,* June 9, 1968.

104. Roby to Humphrey, telegram, March 14, 1968, White House correspondence file, Lentz Papers.

105. Guttmann, *Games Must Go On,* 233–37.

106. Braun to Brundage, April 11, 1968, RS 26/20/37, box 333, Important Letters 1968 file, Brundage Papers, University of Illinois.

107. Hartmann, *Race, Culture, and the Revolt of the Black Athlete,* 78.

108. Guttmann, *Games Must Go On,* 72.

109. Brundage to Dabrowski, February 7, 1969, box 179, Smith-Carlos Dismissal file, Brundage Papers, University of Illinois.

110. Guttmann, *Games Must Go On,* 244.

111. Edwards, *Revolt of the Black Athlete,* 93.

112. *New York Times,* May 12, 1968.

113. Statement by Brundage, April 24, 1968, reel 103, box 179, Brundage collection, IOC archives.

114. Guttmann, *Games Must Go On,* 239.

115. Edwards, *Revolt of the Black Athlete,* 92.

116. Ibid., 93–95.

117. Guttmann, *Games Must Go On,* 238.

118. Brewster and Brewster, "Mexico 1968."

119. *Chicago Daily Defender,* February 26, 1968.

120. Zolov, "Showcasing the Land of Tomorrow," 163.

121. Vazquez to Exeter, April 3, 1968, reel 103, box 179, Brundage collection, IOC archives.

122. Westerhoff to Vazquez, May 3, 1968, reel 103, box 179, Brundage collection, IOC archives.

123. Vazquez to Brundage, May 7, 1968, RS 26/20/37, box 333, Important Letters 1968 file, Brundage Papers, University of Illinois.

124. Clark to Alexander, September 5, 1968, RS 26/20/37, box 333, Important Letters 1968 file, Brundage Papers, University of Illinois.

125. Interview with Paul Hoffman, August 4, 2004.

126. Interview with Jane Swagerty, November 19, 2004.

127. Matthews, *My Race Be Won,* 167.

128. *New York Times,* April 24, 1968.

129. Cited in Bass, *Not the Triumph,* 178.

130. Roby to Brundage, August 8, 1968, RS 26/20/37, box 62, "Roby, M., Douglas F." folder, 1968 correspondence, Brundage papers, University of Illinois.

131. *New York Times,* November 24, 1967.

132. *New York Times,* August 1, 1968.

133. Ibid.; press release, July 24, 1968, Rowing file, 1968–1972, Lentz Papers. A sixth member of the crew, Andrew Larkin, signed the release but was absent from the press conference due to illness.

134. Interview with Cleve Livingston, August 18, 2004.

135. Interview with Paul Hoffman, August 4, 2004.

136. Ibid.

137. Press release, July 24, 1968, Rowing file, 1968–1972, Lentz Papers.

138. *New York Times,* August 31, 1968.

139. Edwards, *Revolt of the Black Athlete,* 100.

140. Interview with Paul Hoffman, August 4, 2004.

141. Undated questionnaire, Rowing file, 1968–1972, Lentz Papers.

142. See handwritten notes attached to undated questionnaire, Rowing file, 1968–1972, Lentz Papers.

143. *New York Times,* August 1, 1968.

144. Interview with Paul Hoffman, August 4, 2004.

145. Carlin to Barnes, September 22, 1968, Rowing file, 1968–1972, Lentz Papers.

146. Harvard crew to USOC, September 17, 1968, Rowing file, 1968–1972, Lentz Papers.

147. Interview with Paul Hoffman, August 4, 2004.

148. Ibid.

149. Ibid.; interview with Cleve Livingston, August 18, 2004.

150. *Newsweek,* October 6, 1969.

3. The Black Athletic Revolt on Campus

1. *University Daily Kansan,* May 13, 1968.

2. Interview with T. J. Gaughan, October 27, 2004.

3. Edwards, *Revolt of the Black Athlete,* 88.

4. Wiggins, "Future of College Athletics." David Zang's *Sports Wars: Athletes in the Age of Aquarius* touches on some of the events without addressing them specifically.

5. Kemper, *College Football,* 191–93.

6. Lipset, *Rebellion in the University,* 97–98.

7. Interview with Waddell Blackwell, April 18, 2006.

8. *Daily Californian* (University of California, Berkeley), January 27, 1968.

9. Wiggins, "Future of College Athletics," 307.

10. "Resolution of the Black Athletes of the University of California Regarding Discrimination and Abuse," January 23, 1968 (copy sent to author by former University of California football player Jerome Champion).

11. Ibid.

12. *Daily Californian,* January 23, 1968.

13. Edwards, *Revolt of the Black Athlete,* 80.

14. Wiggins, "Future of College Athletics," 308.

15. Interview with Robert Abright, April 13, 2006.

16. Interview with Waddell Blackwell, April 18, 2006.

17. Interview with Bob Wolfe, April 17, 2006.

18. Tom Henderson, e-mail correspondence with author, April 3, 2006.

19. *Daily Californian,* January 24, 1968.

20. *Daily Californian,* January 25, 1968.

21. Edwards, *Revolt of the Black Athlete,* 81.

22. Wiggins, "Future of College Athletics," 311; Edwards, *Revolt of the Black Athlete,* 81, 146.

23. Edwards, *Revolt of the Black Athlete,* 81.

24. Wiggins, "Future of College Athletics," 311.

25. Interview with Waddell Blackwell, April 18, 2006.

26. Interview with Robert Abright, April 13, 2006.

27. Interview with Bob Wolfe, April 17, 2006; interview with Robert Abright, April 13, 2006.

28. Interview with Waddell Blackwell, April 18, 2006.

29. Interview with Bob Wolfe, April 17, 2006; interview with Robert Abright, April 13, 2006.

30. Tom Henderson, e-mail correspondence with author, April 3, 2006.

31. Interview with Robert Abright, April 13, 2006.

32. Interview with Bob Wolfe, April 17, 2006.

33. Interview with Robert Abright, April 13, 2006.

34. Wiggins, "Future of College Athletics," 332.

35. Interview with Bob Wolfe, April 17, 2006.

36. Interview with Waddell Blackwell, April 18, 2006.

37. Wiggins, "Future of College Athletics," 330.

38. Interview with Bob Wolfe, April 17, 2006.

39. Interview with Joe Thomas, August 24, 2004.

40. Students United for Racial Equality—Correspondence, 1965–68, Marquette University Archives 8.3, series 10, box 17.

41. *Marquette (Wisc.) Tribune,* May 22, 1968.

42. "An Open Letter to Marquette," May 1, 1968, Marquette University Archives 8.5, series 3, box 4, Student Power—Respond Movement.

43. *Marquette Tribune,* May 10, 1968.

44. "Respond Bulletin," May 11, 1968, Marquette University Archives 8.5, series 3, box 4.

45. Interview with Joe Thomas, August 24, 2004.

46. "Open letter from concerned students at Marquette University," May 1968, Marquette University Archives 8.4, series 6, box 7.

47. *Marquette Tribune,* May 10, 1968.

48. Ibid.

49. *Milwaukee Journal,* May 16, 1968, Marquette University Archives 8.4, series 3, box 4.

50. *Marquette Tribune,* May 16, 1968.

51. Interview with Joe Thomas, August 24, 2004.

52. *Marquette Tribune,* May 22, 1968.

53. *New York Times,* May 18, 1968.

54. *Marquette Tribune,* May 22, 1968; interview with Joe Thomas, August 24, 2004.

55. Interview with Mike Fons, September 10, 2004.

56. Interview with Dr. James Langenkamp, September 21, 2004.

57. Interview with Joe Thomas, August 24, 2004.

58. *Marquette Tribune,* May 22, 1968.

59. Interview with Mike Fons, September 10, 2004.

60. "Account by Basketball Coaching Staff," undated, Marquette University Archives 8.5, series 3, box 1.

61. "Statement of George Thompson," May 17, 1968, Marquette University Archives 8.5, series 3, box 1.

62. Interview with Joe Thomas, August 24, 2004; "Account by Basketball Coaching Staff," undated, Marquette University Archives 8.5, series 3, box 1.

63. *Marquette Tribune,* October 18, 1968.

64. Ibid.

65. *Marquette Tribune,* May 22, 1968.

66. *Milwaukee Journal,* May 17, 1968, Marquette University Archives 8.4, series 3, box 4.

67. Interview with Joe Thomas, August 24, 2004.

68. Ibid.

69. "Letter to Alumni by President Raynor," June 1968, Marquette University Archives 8.5, series 3, box 3.

70. *University Daily Kansan,* May 10, 1968.

71. Interview with Willie Amison, October 4, 2004.

72. Interview with Bill Green, October 27, 2004.

73. Interview with Willie Amison, October 4, 2004.

74. *University Daily Kansan,* May 10, 1968.

75. *New York Times,* May 11, 1968.

76. *University Daily Kansan,* May 13, 1968.

77. Interview with Bill Green, October 27, 2004.

78. Interview with T. J. Gaughan, October 27, 2004.

79. Interview with Willie Amison, October 4, 2004.

80. Interview with Bill Bell, August 30, 2004.

81. Interview with Willie Amison, October 4, 2004.

82. Interview with T. J. Gaughan, October 27, 2004.

83. Interview with Willie Amison, October 4, 2004.

84. Bradley, *Harlem vs. Columbia University,* 64–65; Rojas, *From Black Power to Black Studies,* 28–29.

85. Rojas, *From Black Power to Black Studies,* 55–56.

86. Bradley, *Harlem vs. Columbia University,* 74–75, 188–89.

87. This was later published as a full-length book, Olsen, *The Black Athlete: A Shameful Story; The Myth of Integrated Sport.*

88. Plant to Hansen, August 2, 1968, Racial Matters file, Byers Papers.

89. Hansen to Plant, August 13, 1968, Racial Matters file, Byers Papers.

90. Hansen to Owens, August 21, 1968, Racial Matters file, Byers Papers.

91. NCAA Executive Council Minutes, 1968, Council, NCAA file, Byers Papers.

92. Plant to Hansen, August 22, 1968, Racial Matters file, Byers Papers.

93. Hartmann, *Race, Culture, and the Revolt of the Black Athlete*, 216–18.

94. NCAA Executive Council Minutes, August 15, 1968, 13, Council, NCAA file, Byers Papers.

95. NCAA Executive Council Minutes, August 20, 1969, 3, Council, NCAA file, Byers Papers.

96. Hansen to Plant, August 13, 1968, Racial Matters file, Byers Papers.

97. Hartmann, *Race, Culture, and the Revolt of the Black Athlete*, 222.

98. Ibid.; Hansen to Plant, August 13, 1968, Racial Matters file, Byers Papers; my emphasis.

4. Black Gloves and Gold Medals

1. Hoffer, *Something in the Air*, 183–88.

2. Interview with Ralph Boston, July 27, 2004.

3. Interview with Harry Edwards, January 26, 2004.

4. Matthews, *My Race Be Won*, 189; Moore, "Courageous Stand," 71.

5. Interview with Ralph Boston, July 27, 2004.

6. Interview with Paul Hoffman, August 4, 2004.

7. Miroff, "Presidential Leverage."

8. Hartmann, *Race, Culture, and the Revolt of the Black Athlete*, 143; Edwards, *Revolt of the Black Athlete*, 99.

9. Brundage to Roby, August 5, 1968, RS 26/20/37, box 62, "Roby, Douglas F., correspondence 1968, Illinois" folder, Brundage papers, University of Illinois.

10. Roby to Brundage, August 8, 1968, RS 26/20/37, box 62, "Roby, Douglas F., correspondence 1968, Illinois" folder, Brundage papers, University of Illinois.

11. E. Barnes, Notice to USOC Board of Directors, September 18, 1968, Rowing file, 1968–1972, Lentz Papers.

12. Rodda, "Prensa, Prensa."

13. Interview with Harry Edwards, January 26, 2004.

14. Interview with Paul Hoffman, August 4, 2004.

15. *International Herald Tribune*, October 17, 1968.

16. Ibid.; Hartmann, *Race, Culture, and the Revolt of the Black Athlete*, 152.

17. Interview with Ralph Boston, July 27, 2004.

18. Interview with Robert Lipsyte, June 8, 2005.

19. Interview with Paul Hoffman, August 4, 2004.

20. Guttman, *Games Must Go On*, 244.

21. Brundage to Belles, November 18, 1968, box 179, Smith-Carlos Dismissal file, Brundage papers, University of Illinois.

22. Roberts and Olson, *Winning Is the Only Thing,* 210.

23. Interview with Hal Connolly, January 13, 2004.

24. Pope, *Patriotic Games,* 160.

25. Skrentny, "Effect of the Cold," 262.

26. Moore, "Courageous Stand," 72.

27. Hartmann, *Race, Culture, and the Revolt of the Black Athlete,* 153.

28. Carlos made this claim during a talk to college students on June 16, 2007; see http://www.youtube.com/watch?v=7Wh169BA4Dk&NR=1, accessed July 28, 2011.

29. Carlos with Zirin, *John Carlos Story,* 110.

30. Matthews, *My Race Be Won,* 196.

31. Interview with Lee Evans, April 20, 2004.

32. Carlos with Zirin, *John Carlos Story,* 80–83.

33. Moore, "Courageous Stand," 73.

34. Interview with Peter Norman, April 14, 2004.

35. R. Paul, "Setting the 1968 Record Straight," 15.

36. Interview with Neil Amdur, November 16, 2005.

37. Hartmann, *Race, Culture, and the Revolt of the Black Athlete,* 23.

38. Carlos with Zirin, *John Carlos Story,* 121.

39. Interview with Peter Norman, April 14, 2004; interview with Paul Hoffman, August 4, 2004.

40. *New York Times,* October 19, 1968.

41. Bass, *Not the Triumph,* 240.

42. Carlos with Zirin, *John Carlos Story,* 121.

43. Interview with Paul Hoffman, August 4, 2004.

44. Interview with George Young, September 8, 2004.

45. Edwards, *Revolt of the Black Athlete,* 104.

46. R. Paul, "Setting the 1968 Record Straight," 15.

47. Roby to Brundage, August 8, 1968, RS 26/20/37, box 62, "Roby, M., Douglas F." folder, 1968 correspondence, Brundage papers, University of Illinois.

48. Guttmann, *Games Must Go On,* 243.

49. R. Paul, "Setting the 1968 Record Straight," 15.

50. Brundage to Pratt, November 13, 1968, box 179, Smith-Carlos Dismissal file, Brundage papers, University of Illinois.

51. Statement of U.S. Olympic Committee, October 17, 1968, box 179, Smith-Carlos Dismissal file, Brundage papers, University of Illinois.

52. Brundage to Rudnetsky, November 18, 1968, box 179, Smith-Carlos Dismissal file, Brundage papers, University of Illinois.

53. Brundage to Pratt, November 13, 1968, box 179, Smith-Carlos Dismissal file, Brundage papers, University of Illinois.

54. Brundage to Dunne, November 13, 1968, box 179, Smith-Carlos Dismissal file, Brundage papers, University of Illinois.

55. Quoted in Bass, *Not the Triumph,* 274–78.

56. *Pittsburgh Courier,* October 26, 1968.

57. *Newsweek,* October 28, 1968.

58. *Chicago Daily Defender,* October 23, 1968.

59. *Chicago Daily Defender,* November 6, 1968.

60. *Pittsburgh Courier,* October 26, 1968.

61. Moore, "Courageous Stand," 73.

62. Shaw, "Two Warring Ideals," 33.

63. Bass, *Not the Triumph,* 245.

64. Proceedings of the Meeting of the Executive Committee of the United States Olympic Committee, December 1, 1968, Mexico City incident file, 1968–69, Lentz Papers.

65. *Chicago Daily News,* March 28, 1968.

66. Moore, "Courageous Stand," 68.

67. Matthews, *My Race Be Won,* 191.

68. Interview with Lee Evans, April 20, 2004.

69. Carlos with Zirin, *John Carlos Story,* 114.

70. Edwards, *Revolt of the Black Athlete,* 78.

71. Matthews, *My Race Be Won,* 191.

72. Interview with Hal Connolly, January 13, 2004. In the course of writing this work I spoke briefly with Ed Burke, but he did not want to comment on the events of that meeting or the 1968 Olympics in general, arguing that he had made his stand then and that was all he had to say on the matter.

73. Ibid.

74. *New York Times,* October 19, 1968.

75. Roby to Parker, November 5, 1968, copy in author's possession.

76. Waddell and Schapp, *Gay Olympian,* 107.

77. Interview with Paul Hoffman, August 4, 2004.

78. Interview with Harry Edwards, January 26, 2004.

79. Group 3, box A3, Sports, NAACP collection.

80. Interview with Robert Lipsyte, June 8, 2005.

81. Bass, *Not the Triumph,* 245.

82. Van Deburg, *New Day in Babylon,* 28.

83. M. A. Rutter to Brundage, October 18, 1968, box 179, Smith-Carlos Dismissal file, Brundage Papers, University of Illinois.

84. Zirin, "Interview with John Carlos."

85. Interview with Robert Lipsyte, June 8, 2005.

86. Harding, "Beyond Amnesia," 476.

87. Hartmann, *Race, Culture, and the Revolt of the Black Athlete,* 267–69.

88. Ibid., 269.

89. M. M. Smith, "Frozen Fists," 394, 405–6.
90. S. Henderson, "Nasty Demonstration."
91. Scott, *Athletic Revolution*, 87–88.
92. *New York Times*, October 19, 1968.
93. *International Herald Tribune*, October 18, 1968.
94. Matthews, *My Race Be Won*, 197.
95. Murphy, *Last Protest*, 276–77.
96. Moore, "Eye of the Storm," 64.
97. Interview with Lee Evans, April 20, 2004.
98. Ibid.
99. *New York Times*, October 19, 1968.
100. Interview with Lee Evans, April 20, 2004.
101. Matthews, *My Race Be Won*, 205.
102. Moore, "Eye of the Storm," 64.
103. Edwards, *Revolt of the Black Athlete*, 105.
104. Matthews, *My Race Be Won*, 205.
105. Interview with Lee Evans, April 20, 2004.
106. Moore, "Eye of the Storm," 64.
107. Interview with Paul Hoffman, August 4, 2004.
108. *New York Times*, October 19, 1968.
109. Interview with Cleve Livingston, August 18, 2004.
110. Bass, *Not the Triumph*, 252.
111. *New York Times*, October 19, 1968.
112. Interview with Bruce Bradley, November 22, 2004.
113. Bass, *Not the Triumph*, 252.
114. Interview with Lee Evans, April 20, 2004.
115. Interview with Bob Seagren, June 7, 2004.
116. Bass, *Not the Triumph*, 306–9.
117. *New York Times*, October 19, 1968.
118. Interview with George Young, September 8, 2004.
119. Ibid.
120. Interview with Jane Swagerty, November 19, 2004.
121. Ibid.
122. Interview with Dick Fosbury, February 5, 2004.
123. Interview with Ralph Boston, July 27, 2004.
124. Interview with Larry Young, May 31, 2004.
125. Ibid.

5. Beyond Mexico City

1. Interview with Alan Zerfoss, September 12, 2004.
2. Interview with Melvin Hamilton, April 19, 2004.
3. Demas, *Integrating the Gridiron*, 131.

4. Cited in Scott, *Athletic Revolution,* 16. The full speech to the 1969 California State Conference of Athletics Directors is reprinted in Scott, *Athletic Revolution,* 14–22.

5. Zang, *SportsWars,* xviii–xix.

6. Ibid., xii.

7. Oriard, *Sporting with the Gods,* 456.

8. Underwood, "Desperate Coach," 66.

9. Ibid., 73.

10. A. Ripley, "Irate Black Athletes Stir Campus Tension," *New York Times,* November 16, 1969.

11. Underwood, "Desperate Coach," 68.

12. Ibid., 68.

13. Lipset, *Rebellion in the University,* 10–11.

14. Peterson, *Black Students on White Campuses,* 207.

15. Underwood, "Desperate Coach," 68.

16. Edwards, *Sociology of Sport,* 150.

17. Bradley, *Harlem vs. Columbia University,* 168.

18. Rojas, *From Black Power to Black Studies,* 34.

19. P. Joseph, *Waiting 'Til the Midnight Hour,* 151.

20. Ibid., 257.

21. Estes, *I Am a Man,* 136.

22. Van Deburg. *Black Camelot,* 70.

23. X, *Autobiography of Malcolm X,* 138–39.

24. Wiggins, "Future of College Athletics," 316.

25. Underwood, "Shave Off That Thing," 22.

26. Wiggins, "Future of College Athletics," 317–18.

27. Interview with Dick Fosbury, February 5, 2004.

28. Underwood. "Shave Off That Thing," 23.

29. Interview with Dick Fosbury, February 5, 2004.

30. Edwards, *Sociology of Sport,* 145–46.

31. Ibid., 147.

32. Interview with Dick Fosbury, February 5, 2004.

33. Wiggins, "Future of College Athletics," 325.

34. Underwood, "Concessions and Lies," 37.

35. Ibid., 32.

36. Hartmann, *Race, Culture, and the Revolt of the Black Athlete,* 184–85.

37. Interview with John Dobroth, October 29, 2004.

38. UAA—Report to Athletes, November 2, 1971, copy in author's possession, courtesy of John Dobroth.

39. Interview with John Dobroth, October 29, 2004.

40. Cassell to Dobroth, November 29, 1971, copy in author's possession.

41. "Report of Olympic Games, Mexico City, 1968—Recommendations

for Future Games," Proceedings—Meeting of the Executive Committee of the USOC, December 1, 1968, USOC Archives.

42. "Report from the Board of Consultants to the United States Olympic Committee Board of Directors," Proceedings—Meeting of the Executive Committee of the USOC, December 1, 1968, USOC Archives.

43. "Investigation of Black Athlete Problem," November 10, 1969, Racial Matters file, Byers Papers.

44. Ibid.

45. Scott, *Athletic Revolution,* 110.

46. *Congressional Record,* July 22, 1969, McClellan Collection.

47. "Investigation of Black Athlete Problem," November 10, 1969, Racial Matters file, Byers Papers.

48. Minutes of the NCAA Council, October 20–22, 1969, NCAA Archives.

49. Hartmann, *Race, Culture, and the Revolt of the Black Athlete,* 247.

50. See Racial Matters file, Byers Papers.

51. Demas, *Integrating the Gridiron,* 110.

52. Interview with Joe Williams, November 7, 2004.

53. Edwards, *Revolt of the Black Athlete,* 85–86. The racial situation in general at the University of Texas, El Paso, was highlighted by Jack Olsen in *The Black Athlete.*

54. *New York Times,* November 8, 1969.

55. Interview with Melvin Hamilton, April 19, 2004.

56. *New York Times,* November 1, 1969.

57. Demas, *Integrating the Gridiron,* 115.

58. "Athletes proposed statement of facts," undated, Schubert Papers, box 1, folder 7.

59. Ibid.

60. Putnam, "No Defeats," 27.

61. Interview with Joe Williams, November 7, 2004.

62. *New York Times,* November 8, 1969.

63. Demas, *Integrating the Gridiron,* 117–18.

64. Interview with Melvin Hamilton, April 19, 2004.

65. Ibid.

66. Ibid.

67. Michener, *Sports in America,* 161. It is unclear whether the player Michener refers to was in fact Hamilton, although it is worth noting that Hamilton did not mention such an incident in his interview with this author.

68. *New York Times,* November 1, 1969.

69. Interview with Melvin Hamilton, April 19, 2004.

70. *New York Times,* November 1, 1969.

71. Interview with Alan Zerfoss, September 12, 2004.

72. Interview with Dr. Michael Newton, August 16, 2004; interview with Conrad Dobler, March 12, 2004; interview with Joe Williams, November 7, 2004.

73. Hartmann, *Race, Culture, and the Revolt of the Black Athlete,* 224.

74. *New York Times,* November 1, 1969.

75. Putnam, "No Defeats," 27.

76. "Student Senate, Executive Committee," October 18, 1969, Schubert Papers, box 1, folder 12.

77. "Student-faculty Committee Resolution," October 22, 1969, Schubert Papers, box 1, folder 12.

78. "Faculty Senate," October 28, 1969, Schubert Papers, box 1, folder 12.

79. "Testimony of William Carlson, 1969," Schubert Papers, box 2, folder 12.

80. *New York Times,* November 1, 1969.

81. Interview with Joe Williams, November 7, 2004; interview with Melvin Hamilton, April 19, 2004.

82. Interview with Melvin Hamilton, April 19, 2004.

83. "Black Student Alliance Statement," October 28, 1969, Schubert Papers, box 1, folder 8.

84. *International Herald Tribune,* October 23, 1969.

85. *International Herald Tribune,* October 27, 1969.

86. *New York Times,* November 8, 1969.

87. "Black Student Alliance Statement," October 28, 1969, Schubert Papers, box 1, folder 8.

88. Demas, *Integrating the Gridiron,* 126–27.

89. Interview with Melvin Hamilton, April 19, 2004.

90. Interview with Alan Zerfoss, September 12, 2004.

91. Interview with Gary Fox, August 22, 2004.

92. Interview with Alan Zerfoss, September 12, 2004.

93. Interview with Ken Hustad, March 21, 2004.

94. Interview with Alan Zerfoss, September 12, 2004.

95. Interview with Gary Fox, August 22, 2004.

96. Ibid.; interview with Ken Hustad, March 21, 2004; interview with Alan Zerfoss, September 12, 2004; interview with Dr. Michael Newton, August 16, 2004.

97. Interview with Dr. Michael Newton, August 16, 2004.

98. Interview with Ken Hustad, March 21, 2004.

99. Interview with Conrad Dobler, March 12, 2004.

100. Lipsitz, *Possessive Investment in Whiteness,* 21.

101. *New York Times,* November 1, 1969.

102. *New York Times,* November 10, 1969.

103. Demas, *Integrating the Gridiron,* 130.

6. Dixie and the Absence of a Black Athletic Revolt

1. Interview with Eddie Brown, October 23, 2006; interview with Haskel Stanback, October 17, 2006.

2. Pope, *Patriotic Games,* 65–67, 103–4.

3. R. Gudmestad, "Baseball, the Lost Cause, and the New South in Richmond, Virginia," in Miller, *Sporting World,* 52–80.

4. Pope, *Patriotic Games,* 91–93.

5. A. Doyle, "Turning the Tide: College Football and Southern Progressivism," in Miller, *Sporting World,* 114–15.

6. Borucki, "You're Dixie's Football Pride," 481.

7. Doyle, "Turning the Tide," in Miller, *Sporting World,* 122.

8. Kemper, *College Football,* 89.

9. Miller, "To Bring the Race along Rapidly: Sport, Student Culture, and Educational Mission at Historically Black Colleges during the Interwar Years," in Miller, *Sporting World,* 129.

10. Cobb, *Redefining Southern Culture,* 127.

11. Kemper, *College Football,* 137.

12. T. Ownby, "Manhood, Memory, and White Men's Sports in the American South," in Miller, *Sporting World,* 336–39.

13. The SEC was made up of the Universities of Alabama, Auburn, Florida, Georgia, Louisiana State, Mississippi State, Ole Miss (University of Mississippi), Kentucky, Tennessee, and Vanderbilt.

14. Klarman, "How Brown Changed Race Relations," 84.

15. Martin, *Benching Jim Crow,* 57–87.

16. Wallenstein, "Black Southerners and Nonblack Universities," 33–35.

17. Ibid., 21.

18. Martin, *Benching Jim Crow,* 92, 117, 125.

19. Ibid., 204.

20. Jeffries, "Fields of Play," 269–70.

21. Interview with Steve Sloan, November 19, 2006.

22. J. E. Davis, "Baseball's Reluctant Challenge: Desegregating Major League Spring Training Sites, 1961–64," in Miller, *Sporting World,* 200–218.

23. New York NAACP branch to Wilkins, June 12, 1961, group 3, box A3, Sports, NAACP collection.

24. Martin, "Integrating New Year's Day," 194.

25. R. Henderson, "Something More than the Game," 235.

26. Demas, *Integrating the Gridiron,* 72–74.

27. Ibid., 88–93; Pratt, *We Shall Not Be Moved,* 46.

28. Pratt, *We Shall Not Be Moved,* 61–63.

29. Ibid., 71–75.

30. Ibid., 93–97.

31. Trillin, *Education in Georgia,* 83.

32. Pratt, *We Shall Not Be Moved,* 121.

33. Trillin, *Education in Georgia,* 90.

34. Cohodas, *Band Played Dixie,* 74.

35. Thornton, "Symbolism at Ole Miss," 255–65.

36. Catsam, "Sic 'Em White Folks!," 88.

37. Cohodas, *Band Played Dixie*, 78–82.

38. Catsam, "Sic 'Em White Folks!," 93–94.

39. Clark, *Schoolhouse Door*, 164–65.

40. Cohodas, *Band Played Dixie*, 89.

41. Ibid., 104–15.

42. A. Doyle, "An Atheist in Alabama Is Someone Who Doesn't Believe in Bear Bryant: A Symbol for an Embattled South," in Miller, *Sporting World*, 248.

43. Clark, *Schoolhouse Door*, 140–43.

44. Doyle, "Atheist in Alabama," in Miller, *Sporting World*, 253–55; Kemper, *College Football*, 135–37.

45. Doyle, "Atheist in Alabama," in Miller, *Sporting World*, 254–57; Kemper, *College Football*, 140–41.

46. Clark, *Schoolhouse Door*, 164–66.

47. Martin, "Hold That (Color) Line!," 168.

48. Interview with Willie Brown, October 4, 2004.

49. Interview with Bill Richardson, January 22, 2008; interview with George Patton, March 24, 2006.

50. Interview with Bill Richardson, January 22, 2008.

51. Interview with Horace King, March 31, 2006.

52. Grundy, *Learning to Win*, 270.

53. Lester McClain oral history, 1992, University of Tennessee Special Collections.

54. Martin, "Hold That (Color) Line!," 166.

55. Ibid., 171.

56. Borucki, "You're Dixie's Football Pride," 486.

57. Topchik, "First Move Awaits UT in Getting Negro Athletes," *Daily Beacon* (University of Tennessee), October 8, 1965.

58. "Integration? No Problem," *Middlesboro (Ky.) Daily News*, May 2, 1967.

59. *Middlesboro (Ky.) Daily News*, October 3, 1967.

60. Martin, "Hold That (Color) Line!," 175.

61. "Nashville Negro Ace to Sign with Vols," *Knoxville (Tenn.) Journal*, May 9, 1967.

62. Martin, "Hold That (Color) Line!," 178.

63. McClain oral history, 1992, University of Tennessee Special Collections.

64. Interview with Condredge Holloway, October 4, 2006.

65. Interview with Bill Battle, November 20, 2006.

66. Martin, "Hold That (Color) Line!," 179.

67. Borucki, "You're Dixie's Football Pride," 487.

68. Martin, *Benching Jim Crow*, 276.

69. Doyle, "Atheist in Alabama," in Miller, *Sporting World*, 271.

70. Interview with Horace King, March 31, 2006; interview with Vince Dooley, March 20, 1968.

71. *Red and Black* (University of Georgia), January 12, 1971.

72. Martin, "Hold That (Color) Line!," 189–90.

73. J. Paul, McGhee, and Fant, "Arrival and Ascendance of Black Athletes," 288.

74. Interview with Horace King, March 31, 2006.

75. Interview with Haskel Stanback, October 17, 2006.

76. Interview with Eddie Brown, October 23, 2006.

77. Interview with Condredge Holloway, October 4, 2006; interview with Bill Battle, November 20, 2006.

78. *Red and Black,* November 2, 1973.

79. McClain oral history, 1992, University of Tennessee Special Collections.

80. Edwards, *Revolt of the Black Athlete,* 88.

81. Cohodas, *Band Played Dixie,* 165.

82. Interview with Horace King, March 31, 2006.

83. *Daily Beacon,* October 16, 1972.

84. Interview with Haskel Stanback, October 17, 2006.

85. McClain oral history, 1990, p. 13, University of Tennessee Special Collections.

86. Interview with Horace King, March 31, 2006.

87. Interview with Condredge Holloway, October 4, 2006.

88. Interview with Johnny Musso, November 27, 2006.

89. Cohodas, *Band Played Dixie,* 171–72.

90. Interview with Vince Dooley, March 20, 2006.

91. Interview with Haskel Stanback, October 17, 2006.

92. Interview with Bill Battle, November 20, 2006.

93. Interview with Thomas Lyons, March 21, 2006.

94. Interview with Condredge Holloway, October 4, 2006.

95. Interview with Vince Dooley, March 20, 2006.

96. *Red and Black,* November 4, 1971.

97. Interview with Horace King, March 31, 2006.

98. Interview with Johnny Musso, November 27, 2006.

99. Lopez, *Cougars of Any Color,* 160–66.

Conclusion

1. "Mendenhall Creates Stir with Bin Laden Tweets," *Lincoln (Ill.) Courier,* May 4, 2011, accessed August 5, 2011, http://www.lincolncourier.com/sports/pro/x449047096/Mendenhall-creates-stir-with-bin-Laden-tweets.

2. Scott Brown, "Twitter Comments Cost Mendenhall Endorsement Deal," *Tribune-Review* (Pittsburgh), May 6, 2011, accessed August 5, 2011, http://www.pittsburghlive.com/x/pittsburghtrib/sports/steelers/s_735693.html.

3. Scott Brown, "Steeler Veterans Address Mendenhall Flap," *Tribune-Review* (Pittsburgh), May 14, 2011, accessed August 5, 2011, http://www.pittsburghlive.com/x/pittsburghtrib/sports/steelers/s_737055.html.

4. "Steve Spurrier Bans His Team from Using Twitter," SportingNews.com, NCAAF, August 4, 2011, accessed November 15, 2011, http://aol.sportingnews.com/ncaa-football/story/2011–08–04/steve-spurrier-bans-south-carolina-gamecocks-from-using-twitter.

5. Darren Rovell, "Coaches Ban of Twitter Proves College Sports Isn't about Education," CNBC, August 8, 2011, accessed November 15, 2011, http://www.cnbc.com/id/44058540/Coaches_Ban_Of_Twitter_Proves_College_Sports_Isn_t_About_Education.

6. Hall, "Long Civil Rights Movement," 1237–38.

7. Hartmann, *Race, Culture, and the Revolt of the Black Athlete*, 245–47.

8. Bass, *Not the Triumph*, 345.

9. Brooks and Althouse, "Fifty Years After Jackie Robinson," 318.

10. Zirin, *Welcome to the Terrordome.*

11. Bass, *Not the Triumph*, 346.

12. Bostdorff and Goldzwig, "History, Collective Memory," 682.

Bibliography

Oral History Interviews

Abright, Robert. April 13, 2006.
Amdur, Neil. November 16, 2005.
Amison, Willie. October 4, 2004.
Battle, Bill. November 20, 2006.
Bell, Bill. August 30, 2004.
Blackwell, Waddell. April 18, 2006.
Boston, Ralph. July 27, 2004.
Bradley, Bruce. November 22, 2004.
Brown, Eddie. October 23, 2006.
Brown, Willie. October 4, 2004.
Connolly, Hal. January 13, 2004.
Dobler, Conrad. March 12, 2004.
Dobroth, John. October 29, 2004.
Dooley, Vince. March 20, 2006.
Edwards, Harry. January 26, 2004.
Evans, Lee. April 20, 2004.
Fons, Mike. September 10, 2004.
Fosbury, Dick. February 5, 2004.
Fox, Gary. August 22, 2004.
Gaughan, T. J. October 27, 2004.
Green, Bill. October 27, 2004.
Hamilton, Melvin. April 19, 2004.
Hemery, David. March 25, 2004.
Hoffman, Paul. August 4, 2004.
Holloway, Condredge. October 4, 2006.
Hustad, Ken. March 21, 2004.
Kidd, Bruce. October 20, 2004.
King, Horace. March 31, 2006.
Langenkamp, Dr. James. September 21, 2004.
Lipsyte, Robert. June 8, 2005.
Livingston, Cleve. August 18, 2004.
Lyons, Thomas. March 21, 2006.
Musso, Johnny. November 27, 2006.

Newton, Dr. Michael. August 16, 2004.
Norman, Peter. April 14, 2004.
Oerter, Al. November 16, 2004.
Patton, George. March 24, 2006.
Richardson, Bill. January 22, 2008.
Seagren, Bob. June 7, 2004.
Shinnick, Phil. July 23, 2004.
Sloan, Steve. November 19, 2006.
Stanback, Haskel. October 17, 2006.
Swagerty, Jane. November 19, 2004.
Thomas, Joe. August 24, 2004.
Tyus, Wyomia. October 16, 2004.
Williams, Joe. November 7, 2004.
Wolfe, Bob. April 17, 2006.
Young, George. September 8, 2004.
Young, Larry. May 31, 2004.
Zerfoss, Alan. September 12, 2004.

Archival Material

Brundage, Avery, Collection. International Olympic Committee archives, Lausanne, Switzerland.
Brundage, Avery, Papers. University of Illinois, Urbana-Champaign.
Byers, Walter, Papers. National Collegiate Athletic Association, NCAA Library and Archives, Indianapolis.
Lentz A., Papers. U.S. Olympic Committee archives. Colorado Springs, Colorado.
Marquette University Archives, Milwaukee, Wisconsin.
McClellan, Senator John L., Collection. Special Collections, Riley-Hickingbotham Library, Ouachita Baptist University, Arkadelphia, Arkansas.
National Collegiate Athletic Association (NCAA) Archives, NCAA Library and Archives, Indianapolis.
National Association for the Advancement of Colored People (NAACP) collection. Sports files. Library of Congress, Washington, D.C.
Schubert, Irene Kettunen, Papers, American Heritage Center, University of Wyoming, Laramie.
University of Tennessee Special Collections and University Archives, Knoxville, Tennessee.
U.S. Olympic Committee (USOC) archives, Colorado Springs, Colorado.

Newspapers and Periodicals

Chicago Daily Defender
Daily Beacon (University of Tennessee)
Daily Californian (University of California, Berkeley)

International Herald Tribune
Knoxville (Tenn.) Journal
Marquette (Wisc.) Tribune
Middlesboro (Ky.) Daily News
Newsweek
New York Times
Pittsburgh Courier
Red and Black (University of Georgia)
San Jose Mercury News
Sports Illustrated
University Daily Kansan

Secondary Source Material

Andrew, J. A. *The Other Side of the Sixties: Young Americans for Freedom and the Rise of Conservative Politics.* New Brunswick, N.J.: Rutgers University Press, 1997.

Badger, A. *The New Deal.* Chicago: Ivan R. Dee, 2002.

Bass, A. *Not the Triumph but the Struggle: The 1968 Olympics and the Making of the Black Athlete.* Minneapolis: University of Minnesota Press, 2002.

Bissinger, H. *Friday Night Lights.* London: Yellow Jersey Press, 2000.

Borucki, W. "You're Dixie's Football Pride: American College Football and the Resurgence of Southern Identity." *Identities: Global Studies in Culture and Power* 10 (2003): 477–94.

Bostdorff, D. M., and S. R. Goldzwig. "History, Collective Memory, and the Appropriation of Martin Luther King, Jr.: Reagan's Rhetorical Legacy." *Presidential Studies Quarterly* 35 (2005): 661–90.

Bradley, S. M. *Harlem vs. Columbia University: Black Student Power in the Late 1960s.* Urbana: University of Illinois Press, 2009.

Branch, T. *Parting the Waters: America in the King Years, 1954–63.* New York: Simon and Schuster, 1988.

Brewster, C., and K. Brewster. "Mexico 1968—Sombreros and Skyscrapers." In *National Identity and Global Sports Events: Culture, Politics, and Spectacle in the Olympics and Football World Cup,* edited by A. Tomlinson and C. Young, 99–116. Albany: State University of New York Press, 2005.

Brink, W., and L. Harris. *Black and White: A Study of U.S. Racial Attitudes Today.* New York: Simon and Schuster, 1967.

Brooks, D., and R. Althouse. "Fifty Years after Jackie Robinson: Equal Access but Unequal Outcome." In *Racism in College Athletics,* edited by D. Brooks and R. Althouse, 301–10. Morgantown, W.Va.: Fitness Information Technology, 2000.

Brundage, W. F., ed. *Under Sentence of Death: Lynching in the South.* Chapel Hill: University of North Carolina Press, 1997.

Bryant, N. *The Bystander: John F. Kennedy and the Struggle for Black Equality.* New York: Basic Books, 2006.

Carlos, J., with D. Zirin. *The John Carlos Story.* Chicago: Haymarket Books, 2011.

Carter, D. T. *The Politics of Rage: George Wallace, the Origins of New Conservatism, and the Transformation of American Politics.* New York: Simon and Schuster, 1995.

Catsam, D. "Sic 'Em, White Folks!: Football, Massive Resistance, and the Integration of Ole Miss." *Sport History Review* 40 (2009): 82–98.

Cha-Jua, S. K., and C. Lang. "The 'Long Movement' as Vampire: Temporal and Spatial Fallacies in Recent Black Freedom Studies." *Journal of African-American History* 92, no. 2 (2007): 265–88.

Clark, E. Culpepper. *The Schoolhouse Door: Segregation's Last Stand at the University of Alabama.* New York: Oxford University Press, 1993.

Cleaver, E. *Soul on Ice.* New York: Delta, 1968.

Cobb, J. *The Brown Decision, Jim Crow, and Southern Identity.* Athens: University of Georgia Press, 2005.

———. *Redefining Southern Culture: Mind and Identity in the Modern South.* Athens: University of Georgia Press, 1999.

Cohodas, N. *The Band Played Dixie: Race and the Liberal Conscience at Ole Miss.* New York: Free Press, 1997.

Dailey, J., G. E. Gilmore, and B. Simon, eds. *Jumpin' Jim Crow: Southern Politics From Civil War to Civil Rights.* Princeton, N.J.: Princeton University Press, 2000.

Demas, L. *Integrating the Gridiron: Black Civil Rights and American College Football.* New Brunswick, N.J.: Rutgers University Press, 2010.

Eagles, C. W. "Toward New Histories of the Civil Rights Era." *Journal of Southern History* 66, no. 4 (2000): 815–48.

Edwards, H. *The Revolt of the Black Athlete.* New York: Free Press, 1969.

———. *The Sociology of Sport.* Homewood, Ill.: Dorey Press, 1973.

Estes, S. *I Am a Man: Race, Manhood, and the Civil Rights Movement.* Chapel Hill: University of North Carolina Press, 2005.

Fairclough, A. *Better Day Coming: Blacks and Equality, 1890–2000.* New York: Penguin, 2002.

———. *To Redeem the Soul of America: The Southern Christian Leadership Conference and Martin Luther King, Jr.* Athens: University of Georgia Press, 2001.

Farber, D. "The Silent Majority and Talk about Revolution." In *The Sixties: From History to Memory,* edited by D. Farber, 291–316. Chapel Hill: University of North Carolina Press, 1994.

Foner, P., ed. *The Black Panthers Speak.* Cambridge, Mass.: Da Capo Press, 2002.

Frederickson, G. *The Black Image in the White Mind.* New York: Harper and Row, 1971.

Gems, G. "Blocked Shot: The Development of Basketball in the African-American Community of Chicago." *Journal of Sport History* 22, no. 2 (1995): 135–48.

Gerstle, G. *American Crucible: Race and Nation in the Twentieth Century.* Princeton, N.J.: Princeton University Press, 2001.

Gilmore, A. "The Black Southern Response to the Southern System of Race Relations." In *The Age of Segregation,* edited by R. Haws, 67–88. Jackson: University Press of Mississippi, 1978.

Gilmore, G. *Gender and Jim Crow: Women and the Politics of White Supremacy in North Carolina.* Chapel Hill: University of North Carolina Press, 1996.

Gitlin, T. *The Sixties: Years of Hope, Days of Rage.* New York: Bantam Books, 1987.

Grundy, P. *Learning to Win: Sports, Education, and Social Change in Twentieth-Century North Carolina.* Chapel Hill: University of North Carolina Press, 2001.

Guttmann, A. *The Games Must Go On: Avery Brundage and the Olympic Movement.* New York: Columbia University Press, 1984.

Hall, J. Dowd. "The Long Civil Rights Movement and the Political Uses of the Past." *Journal of American History* 91, no. 4 (2005): 1233–63.

Halpern, R. "Organised Labour, Black Workers, and the Twentieth-Century South: The Emerging Revision." In *Race and Class in the American South since 1890,* edited by M. Stokes and R. Halpern. Providence, R.I.: Berg, 1994.

Harding, V. G. "Beyond Amnesia: Martin Luther King and the Future of America." *Journal of American History* 74, no. 2 (1987): 468–76.

Hartmann, D. *Race, Culture, and the Revolt of the Black Athlete.* Chicago: University of Chicago Press, 2003.

———. "Rethinking the Relationships between Sport and Race in American Culture: Golden Ghettos and Contested Terrain." *Journal of Sociology of Sport* 17 (2000): 229–53.

Henderson, R. "'Something More Than the Game Will Be Lost': The 1963 Mississippi State Basketball Controversy and the Repeal of the Unwritten Law." In Miller, *Sporting World of the Modern South,* 219–43.

Henderson, S. "Crossing the Line: Sport and the Limits of Civil Rights Protest." *International Journal of the History of Sport* 26, no. 1 (January 2009): 101–21.

———. "'Nasty Demonstration by Negroes': The Place of the Smith-Carlos Podium Salute in the Civil Rights Movement." In *Reflections on Mexico '68,* edited by K. Brewster, 78–92. Oxford: Wiley-Blackwell, 2010.

Hine, D. Clark. "Black Professionals and Race Consciousness: Origins of the Civil Rights Movement, 1890–1950." *Journal of American History* 89, no. 4 (2003): 1279–94.

Hoberman, J. *Darwin's Athletes: How Sport Has Damaged Black America and Preserved the Myth of Race.* New York: Houghton Mifflin, 1997.

Hoffer, R. *Something in the Air: American Passion and Defiance in the 1968 Mexico City Olympics.* New York: Free Press, 2009.

Hylton, K. *"Race" and Sport: Critical Race Theory.* London: Routledge, 2009.

Jeffries, H. K. "Fields of Play: The Mediums through which Black Athletes Engaged in Sports in Jim Crow Georgia." *Journal of Negro History* 86, no. 3 (2001): 264–75.

Joseph, G., and D. Nugent. "Popular Culture and State Formation." In *Everyday Forms of State Formation: Revolution and the Negotiation of Rule in Modern Mexico,* edited by G. Joseph and D. Nugent, 367–78. Durham, N.C.: Duke University Press, 2000.

Joseph, P. E. "The Black Power Movement: A State of the Field." *Journal of American History* 95, no. 4 (2009): 751–76.

———. *Waiting 'Til the Midnight Hour: A Narrative History of Black Power in America.* New York: Holt, 2006.

Kellner, D. "Sports, Media, Culture, and Race: Some Reflections on Michael Jordan." *Journal of Sociology of Sport* 13 (1996): 458–67.

Kemper, K. *College Football and American Culture in the Cold War Era.* Urbana: University of Illinois Press, 2009.

Klarman, M. J. "How Brown Changed Race Relations: The Backlash Thesis." *Journal of American History* 81, no. 1 (1994): 81–118.

Korstad, R. *Civil Rights Unionism: Tobacco Workers and the Struggle for Democracy in the Mid-Twentieth-Century South.* Chapel Hill: University of North Carolina Press, 2003.

Levine, L. *Black Culture and Black Consciousness: African-American Folk Thought from Slavery to Freedom.* Oxford: Oxford University Press, 1977.

Lewis, G. *Massive Resistance: The White Response to the Civil Rights Movement.* New York: Oxford University Press, 2006.

Lipset, S. M. *Rebellion in the University.* Chicago: University of Chicago Press, 1976.

Lipsitz, G. *The Possessive Investment in Whiteness.* Philadelphia: Temple University Press, 1998.

Lopez, K. *Cougars of Any Color: The Integration of University of Houston Athletics, 1964–1968.* Jefferson, N.C.: McFarland, 2008.

Marable, M. *Race, Reform, and Rebellion: The Second Reconstruction in Black America, 1945–1982.* London: MacMillan, 1984.

Marcello, R. "The Integration of Intercollegiate Athletics in Texas: North Texas State College as a Test Case, 1956." *Journal of Sport History* 14, no. 3 (1987): 286–315.

Martin, C. H. *Benching Jim Crow: The Rise and Fall of the Color Line in Southern College Sports, 1890–1980.* Urbana: University of Illinois Press, 2010.

———. "Hold That (Color) Line!: Black Exclusion and Southeastern Conference Football." In *Higher Education and the Civil Rights Movement: White*

Supremacy, Black Southerners, and College Campuses, edited by P. Wallenstein, 166–98. Gainesville: University Press of Florida, 2008.

———. "Integrating New Year's Day: The Racial Politics of College Bowl Games in the American South." In Miller, *Sporting World of the Modern South,* 175–99.

Matthews, V. *My Race Be Won.* New York: Charterhouse, 1974.

Matusow, A. *The Unraveling of America: A History of Liberalism in the 1960s.* New York: Harper and Row, 1984.

McGirr, L. *Suburban Warriors: The Origins of the New American Right.* Princeton, N.J.: Princeton University Press, 2001.

McRae, D. *In Black and White: The Untold Story of Joe Louis and Jesse Owens.* London: Scribner, 2003.

Meade, C. "Joe Louis as Emerging Race Hero in the 1930s." In *Major Problems in American Sport History,* edited by S. Riess, 329–36. Boston: Houghton Mifflin, 1997.

Michener, J. *Sports in America.* Random House: New York, 1976.

Miller, P. B., ed. *The Sporting World of the Modern South.* Urbana: University of Illinois Press, 2002.

Miroff, B. "Presidential Leverage over Social Movements: The Johnson White House and Civil Rights." *Journal of Politics* 43, no. 1 (1981): 2–23.

Moore, K. "A Courageous Stand." *Sports Illustrated,* August 5, 1991.

———. "The Eye of the Storm." *Sports Illustrated,* August 12, 1991.

Morgan, W. "Hegemony Theory, Social Domination, and Sport: The MacAloon and Hargreaves-Tomlinson Debate Revisited." *Journal of Sociology of Sport* 11 (1994): 309–29.

Murphy, F. *The Last Protest: Lee Evans in Mexico City.* Kansas City: Windsprint Press, 2006.

Nasstrom, K. L. "Beginnings and Endings: Life Stories and the Periodization of the Civil Rights Movement." *Journal of American History* 86, no. 2 (1999): 700–711.

Olsen, J. *The Black Athlete: A Shameful Story; The Myth of Integrated Sport.* New York: Time-Life, 1968.

O'Neill, W. *Coming Apart: The History of America in the 1960s.* New York: Random House, 1971.

Oriard, M. *Sporting with the Gods: The Rhetoric of Play and Game in American Culture.* Cambridge: Cambridge University Press, 1991.

Owens, J., with P. Neimark. *Blackthink: My Life as a Black Man and a White Man.* New York: Morrow, 1970.

Paul, J., R. V. McGhee, and H. Fant. "The Arrival and Ascendance of Black Athletes in the Southeastern Conference, 1966–1980." *Phylon* 45, no. 4 (1984): 284–97.

Paul, R. "Setting the 1968 Record Straight." *Journal of Olympic History* 5 (1997): 15–16.

Peterson, M. *Black Students on White Campuses: The Impacts of Increased Black Enrollments.* Ann Arbor: University of Michigan Press, 1978.

Pope, S. *Patriotic Games: Sporting Traditions in the American Tradition, 1876–1926.* Oxford: Oxford University Press, 1997.

Pratt, R. *We Shall Not Be Moved: The Triumphant Story of Horace Ward, Charlayne Hunter, and Hamilton Holmes.* Athens: University of Georgia Press, 2002.

Putnam, P. "No Defeats, Loads of Trouble." *Sports Illustrated,* November 3, 1969.

Raines, H., ed. *My Soul Is Rested: Movement Days in the Deep South Remembered.* New York: Penguin Books, 1983.

Rieder, J. *Canarsie: The Jews and Italians of Brooklyn against Liberalism.* Cambridge, Mass.: Harvard University Press, 1985.

Roberts, R. *Papa Jack: Jack Johnson and the Era of White Hopes.* New York: Free Press, 1985.

Roberts, R., and J. Olson. *Winning Is the Only Thing: Sports in America since 1945.* Baltimore: John Hopkins University Press, 1989.

Rodda, J. "Prensa, Prensa: A Journalist's Reflections on Mexico '68." In *Reflections on Mexico '68,* edited by K. Brewster, 11–22. Oxford: Wiley-Blackwell, 2010.

Rogers, K. L. "Oral History and the History of the Civil Rights Movement." *Journal of American History* 75, no. 2 (1988): 567–76.

Rojas, F. *From Black Power to Black Studies: How a Radical Social Movement Became an Academic Discipline.* Baltimore: John Hopkins University Press, 2007.

Roseberry, W. "Hegemony and the Language of Contention." In *Everyday Forms of State Formation; Revolution and the Negotiation of Rule in Modern Mexico,* edited by G. Joseph and D. Nugent, 355–66. Durham, N.C.: Duke University Press, 2000.

Ross, C. K., ed. *Race and Sport: The Struggle for Equality on and off the Field.* Jackson: University Press of Mississippi, 2004.

Runstedtler, T. E. "In Sports the Best Man Wins: How Joe Louis Whupped Jim Crow." In *In the Game: Race, Identity, and Sports in the Twentieth Century,* edited by A. Bass, 47–92. New York: MacMillan, 2005.

Sammons, J. *Beyond the Ring: The Role of Boxing in American Society.* Urbana: University of Illinois Press, 1990.

Sandage, S. "A Marble House Divided: The Lincoln Memorial, the Civil Rights Movement, and the Politics of Memory, 1939–1963." *Journal of American History* 80, no. 1 (1993): 135–67.

Scott, J. *The Athletic Revolution.* New York: Free Press, 1971.

Schoenwald, J. M. *A Time for Choosing: The Rise of Modern American Conservatism.* Oxford: Oxford University Press, 2001.

Shaw, T. C. "'Two Warring Ideals': Double Consciousness, Dialogue, and African American Patriotism Post-9/11." In *Free at Last?: Black America in the*

Twenty-First Century, edited by J. Battle, M. Bennett, and A. Lemelle, 33–50. New Brunswick, N.J.: Transaction Publishers, 2006.

Shropshire, K. *In Black and White: Race and Sports in America.* New York: New York University Press, 1996.

Sitkoff, H. *The Struggle for Black Equality, 1954–1992.* New York: Hill and Wang, 1993.

Skrentny, J. "The Effect of the Cold War on African-American Civil Rights: America and the World Audience, 1945–1968." *Theory and Society* 27, no. 2 (1998): 237–85.

Smith, E. "The African-American Student-Athlete." In *Race and Sport: The Struggle for Equality on and off the Field,* edited by C. K. Ross, 121–45. Jackson: University Press of Mississippi, 2004.

Smith, M. M. "Frozen Fists in Speed City: The Statue as Twenty-First-Century Reparations." *Journal of Sport History* 36, no. 3 (2009): 393–414.

Smith, T. "Civil Rights and the Gridiron: The Kennedy Administration and the Desegregation of the Washington Redskins." *Journal of Sports History* 15, no. 3 (1987): 189–208.

Spivey, D. "Black Consciousness and Olympic Protest Movement, 1964–1980." In *Sport in America: New Historical Perspectives,* edited by D. Spivey, 239–62. Westport, Conn.: Greenwood Press, 1985.

———. "End Jim Crow in Sports: The Protest at New York University, 1940–41." *Journal of Sport History* 15, no. 3 (1988): 282–303.

Sugrue, T. J. "Crabgrass-Roots Politics: Race, Rights, and the Reaction against Liberalism in the Urban North, 1940–1964." *Journal of American History* 82, no. 2 (1995): 551–78.

Thornton, K. "Symbolism at Ole Miss and the Crisis of Southern Identity." *South Atlantic Quarterly* 86, no. 3, 1987: 254–68.

Trillin, C. *An Education in Georgia: Charlayne Hunter, Hamilton Holmes, and the Integration of the University of Georgia.* Athens: University of Georgia Press, 1991.

Tygiel, J. *Baseball's Great Experiment: Jackie Robinson and His Legacy.* New York: Vintage Books, 1983.

Tyson, T. *Radio Free Dixie: Robert F. Williams and the Roots of Black Power.* Chapel Hill: University of North Carolina Press, 1999.

Umoja, A. "The Ballot and the Bullet: A Comparative Analysis of Armed Resistance in the Civil Rights Movement." *Journal of Black Studies* 29, no. 4 (1999): 558–78.

Underwood, J. "Concessions and Lies." *Sports Illustrated,* September 8, 1969.

———. "The Desperate Coach." *Sports Illustrated,* August 25, 1969.

———. "Shave Off That Thing." *Sports Illustrated,* September 1, 1969.

Van Deburg, W. *Black Camelot: African-American Culture Heroes in Their Times, 1960–1980.* Chicago: University of Chicago Press, 1997.

————. *New Day in Babylon.* Chicago: University of Chicago Press, 1992.

Waddell, T., and T. Schapp. *Gay Olympian.* New York: Alfred Knopf, 1996.

Wallenstein, P. "Black Southerners and Nonblack Universities: The Process of Desegregating Southern Higher Education, 1935–1965." In *Higher Education and the Civil Rights Movement: White Supremacy, Black Southerners, and College Campuses,* edited by P. Wallenstein, 17–59. Gainesville: University Press of Florida, 2008.

Washington, J., ed. *A Testament of Hope: The Essential Writings and Speeches of Martin Luther King, Jr.* San Francisco: Harper, 1986.

Wiggins, D. "Critical Events Affecting Racism in Athletics." In *Racism in College Athletics,* edited by D. Brooks and R. Althouse, 15–36. Morgantown, W.Va.: Fitness Information Technology, 2002.

————. "The Future of College Athletics Is at Stake: Black Athletes and Racial Turmoil on Three Predominantly White University Campuses, 1968–1972." *Journal of Sport History* 15, no. 3 (1988): 304–33.

————. "Great Speed but Little Stamina: The Historical Debate over Black Athletic Superiority." *Journal of Sport History* 16, no. 2 (1989): 158–85.

————. "Leisure Time on the Southern Plantation: The Slaves' Respite from Constant Toil, 1810–1860." In *Sport in America: New Historical Perspectives,* edited by D. Spivey, 25–50. Westport, Conn.: Greenwood Press, 1985.

————. "Prized Performers, but Frequently Overlooked Students: The Involvement of Black Athletes in Intercollegiate Sports on Predominantly White University Campuses, 1890–1972." *Research Quarterly for Exercise and Sport* 62, no. 2 (1991): 164–77.

X, M. *The Autobiography of Malcolm X.* London: Penguin Classics, 2001.

Zang, D. *Sports Wars: Athletes in the Age of Aquarius.* Fayetteville: University of Arkansas Press, 2001.

Zirin, D. "An Interview with John Carlos." *Counterpunch,* October 31–November 2, 2003. http://www.counterpunch.org/2003/11/01/an-interview-with-john-carlos/.

————. *Welcome to the Terrordome: The Pain, Politics, and Promise of Sports.* Chicago: Haymarket Books, 2007.

Zolov, E. "Showcasing the Land of Tomorrow: Mexico and the 1968 Olympics," *The Americas* 61, no. 2 (2004): 159–88.

Index

Page numbers in *italics* refer to photographs.

219

CIVIL RIGHTS AND THE STRUGGLE FOR BLACK EQUALITY
IN THE TWENTIETH CENTURY

SERIES EDITORS
Steven F. Lawson, Rutgers University
Cynthia Griggs Fleming, University of Tennessee

Freedom's Main Line: The Journey of Reconciliation and the Freedom Rides
Derek Charles Catsam

*Subversive Southerner: Anne Braden and the Struggle for Racial Justice
in the Cold War South*
Catherine Fosl

*Constructing Affirmative Action: The Struggle for Equal Employment
Opportunity*
David Hamilton Golland

Sidelined: How American Sports Challenged the Black Freedom Struggle
Simon Henderson

Becoming King: Martin Luther King Jr. and the Making of a National Leader
Troy Jackson

Civil Rights in the Gateway to the South: Louisville, Kentucky, 1945–1980
Tracy E. K'Meyer

*Democracy Rising: South Carolina and the Fight for Black Equality
since 1865*
Peter F. Lau

Civil Rights Crossroads: Nation, Community, and the Black Freedom Struggle
Steven F. Lawson

Freedom Rights: New Perspectives on the Civil Rights Movement
edited by Danielle L. McGuire and John Dittmer

This Little Light of Mine: The Life of Fannie Lou Hamer
Kay Mills

After the Dream: Black and White Southerners since 1965
Timothy J. Minchin and John A. Salmond

Fighting Jim Crow in the County of Kings: The Congress of Racial Equality in Brooklyn
Brian Purnell

Thunder of Freedom: Black Leadership and the Transformation of 1960s Mississippi
Sue [Lorenzi] Sojourner with Cheryl Reitan

For Jobs and Freedom: Race and Labor in America since 1865
Robert H. Zieger

CPSIA information can be obtained at www.ICGtesting.com
Printed in the USA
BVOW030321220313

316160BV00002B/4/P